The Development of
Modern Stillwater
Fishing

*To my Hostess and Dear Friend
Valerie Lady Bowden, in grateful
acknowledgment of the many happy
days spent with her at Marsh Court.*

David Jacques

The Development of Modern Stillwater Fishing

Adam & Charles Black
London

© 1974 DAVID JACQUES

First published 1974 by
A. & C. BLACK LTD
4, 5 & 6 Soho Square
London W1V 6AD

ISBN 0 7136 1470 6

PRINTED IN GREAT BRITAIN AT
THE PITMAN PRESS, BATH

Contents

Illustrations

7

Alder larva (*Sialis lutaria*)
Discarded Alder shuck

FIGURES IN THE TEXT

Foreword & Acknowledgments

The traditional face of angling has been so radically changed in the last few years by the increase of reservoir construction and their adaptation to fly-fishing as a secondary role, that I thought it best to alter my original intention of recording the history of Two Lakes in isolation, and to relate it in the context of a wider arena. Nevertheless, Two Lakes and its remarkable creator, Mr Alex Behrendt, who transformed an overgrown waste into one of Europe's foremost trout fisheries, dominate the narrative and remain the focal points to which all else is subsidiary; and although I have relied with advantage on other sources, the bulk of the mechanical and structural data was supplied by Mr Behrendt over a period of four years and was based on his successful format at Two Lakes.

To him therefore my gratitude must first be extended, not only for his patience in the face of my unending questioning, but also for his perusal of the text at all stages of its preparation. I freely admit that he could justifiably be described as co-author of a substantial portion of this book. And I think it would be fitting for me to add another tribute, not only from myself, but, I sincerely hope, from anglers everywhere in Britain, for his inauguration in this country of an annual three day convention held at Two Lakes, where a select company of about 150 fishery managers, fish farmers, zoologists and scientists of allied disciplines meet and listen to contemporary papers being read, and later discussed, by some of the most distinguished pisciculturists in the world. This non-profit-making venture, now on a firm footing, establishes Mr Behrendt as an authentic and much needed benefactor of British angling.

I also gratefully acknowledge my indebtedness to Mr Struan Malcolm-Brown, an outstanding angler and a most agreeable companion, for the valuable assistance he gave me on so many occasions.

9

In retrospect, I shudder with horror when I think of the blunders that, but for his scrutiny of the text, might have sneaked into the commentary in spite of the care I had taken.

Once again I have to thank John Goddard, a comrade of numerous fishing expeditions, for the superb photographs he so kindly supplied and for which he is justly renowned. They enhance and grace any book in which they appear.

Thanks are due as usual to my dear friend Eric Horsfall Turner for putting his encyclopaedic knowledge of angling so frequently at my disposal, and for his chapter on tackle; and to Mr George Moody for keeping a watchful eye on my trigonometry and for making the long trip to Two Lakes to sketch the Spillway.

Thanks also to Lt Col A ("Rags") Locke for reading part of the typescript and for his very valid criticisms and suggestions. Nor must I fail to acknowledge the practical assistance of Lt Col Terence Arnold and Henny, Lt Col Ronnie Cross, Alan Dalton, John Elliott, Jim Frazier, Phil Gregory and all those members of Two Lakes who so kindly completed the questionnaire.

In particular, I must express my admiration and appreciation of the fortitude of Doreen Thompson in bearing the strain, so capably and cheerfully, of typing page after page of the text, from early draft to revisions and to finality, for a period of four years, and in doing so, straightening out many distortions of syntax, construction and spelling.

Finally, my apologetic thanks to Elizabeth for listening without demur to the sound of my voice interminably spouting long passages from the script.

London S W 1. March 1973   David Jacques

[1]
Antiquities

He leadeth me beside the still waters. He restoreth my soul.

PSALM XXIII

This is the story of a fishery, a trout fishery. It is a man-made fishery, built on a marshy waste that had lain stale and barren for countless centuries. The story tells of its transformation, in spite of the most discouraging advice, into one of the foremost angling stillwaters of our time, providing excellent recreation and producing from a hitherto unproductive source upward of seven tons of highly-prized food per year.

The fishery is known as Two Lakes, although paradoxically it consists of a group of lakes, eight in all. Of the man—and his wife— who built the fishery I shall say little; the fishery itself already serves as a lasting monument to their vision and enterprise.

In probing the origin of the fishery and its creators, I found myself going back to the flooded sandpits of Continental Europe and to the early years of the twentieth century. The more I probed the more I receded in terms of time, until I became enmeshed in the pisci-cultural literature of the Middle Ages and drawn into that of ancient China, Greece and Rome. My peace of mind demanded that I go the whole hog and begin my story at the very frontiers of angling, as far as they are known. In doing so, I discovered why my fingers itch to grasp a rod, and why the thought of a fishing outing hovers over me joyfully like a sonnet over a poet in Springtime.

At what stage in the history of man he first became a fish eater is unknown and will, in all probability, remain unknown. It may well be that his partiality for fish was a heritage from some anthropoid ancestor, for even today there are terrestial creatures of a lower order than the higher apes which live successfully on an exclusive fish diet. Perhaps he or his simian forbears acquired the taste after

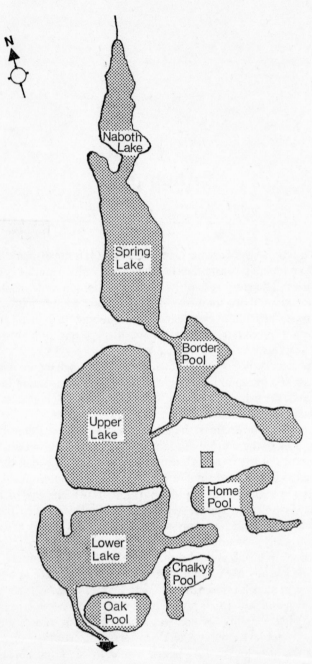

Sketch map of Two Lakes (not to scale).

eating the thousands of fish left stranded by the receding flood waters of the great rivers. There is no lack of evidence, circumstantial though it may be, to justify the widely-held belief that fish has been a major, and at times a sole source of food for mankind in all corners of the globe from the earliest days.

One of the difficulties facing us as our story unfolds is the unreality to our minds of the vast expanses of time involved, but their enormity may be realised if we bear in mind that history's oldest recorded dates go back only a matter of 5,000 years or so. Using this figure as a yardstick, admittedly a poor one, we might be able to grasp these great lapses of time with some degree of comprehension. And as we follow the tracks backwards into the mists of antiquity, we shall find ourselves relying to some extent on legend, myth and primitive theology for the scraps of evidence that hook up like a jigsaw puzzle into an articulate picture of events, as well as on the more complicated deductions based on systematic comparisons, sequences and other indirect testimonies. Because much of it is vague and open to conflicting constructions, our conclusions tend to be imprecise, but they nevertheless act as signposts to the truth, even if they are unable to pinpoint it.

Contrary to a proclamation in 1897 by the then Bishop of Durham that the universe was created in 4004 B C, on October 23rd, at 9 a m precisely, it is believed that the earth on which we live is at least 4,000,000,000 (four thousand million) years old. Pausing for a moment to allow the immensity of this figure to be digested, I continue with the information that for the first 3,500,000,000 years, that is for the first seven-eighths of its existence, no life appeared except perhaps for some algae. The first fossil records in our possession, except for some vague ones of algae, date back to about 500,000,000 years ago, At this time, the invertebrates began to appear, to be followed about 100,000,000 years later by the vertebrates. A little later, at a time estimated to be about 350,000,000 years ago, the fishes began to attain their known characteristics. They emerged from the evolutionary chaos before the insects, the reptiles, the higher plants, the birds and the mammals. However approximate this estimate may be, it is certain that fish had become stabilised into their modern form no later than 100,000,000 years ago.

What about man? What was his position in the progression of species? The answer is, near the tail-end. In contrast to fish he is a newcomer, an upstart, for the latest research seems to indicate that he branched off an extinct species of anthropoid ape about 50,000 years ago. Until recently, it was generally accepted that Homo sapiens was about 1,000,000 years old. But re-examination by the newest methods of the relics of those primitive men thought by palaeontologists to have been the first human beings possessing, more or less, the intelligence of modern man suggested that the lesser figure was the more likely, and this is now regarded by researchers as very close to the truth.

The preceding premise illustrates quite clearly that the waters of the world we live in, fresh and marine, running and still, were densely populated with fish by the time the first humans arrived, irrespective of whether it was 50,000 or 1,000,000 years ago. Within these milieux, early man found an inexhaustible supply of food, savoury and nutritious, if only he could secure it.

Indeed, there are strong grounds for the assumption that our great rivers and lakes offering, as they did, a dependable source of food, were responsible for man's first settlements rather than the discovery of the agricultural arts. We do not know, however, when man first learned how to catch these evasive, shadowy creatures whose lives were spent in a medium into which he could not pursue them. It is thought that spearing was one of the earliest methods, but at the best this could achieve only limited success. Netting, essentially an operation requiring organisation and technique, was probably beyond the capacity of the emerging humans. But there is ample evidence to show that at an early date they learned to offer the fish a morsel of food in which was concealed a stone or flint with a groove cut in it to which the tendril of a plant was tied. If the fish took the food, and was unable to eject the "gorge", as these stones or flints are called, its capture was assured.

When did all this first happen? According to the Chinese, it happened about 8,000 years ago, in the days of the great Sui Yan, the first Emperor of China, during the great flood. He is said to have introduced the custom of marriage, and to have taught the people how to make fire and how to fish, although the methods were not revealed until 2,000 years later by the Emperor Fuk Hei, who, in his turn, taught the art of net making. It is doubtful if any greater credence can be attached to this than to Izaak Walton's repetition of an old belief that Seth the son of Adam taught angling to his sons; or to the Polynesian belief that angling was the pastime of the

Creator of the world, and that it was while fishing in the mighty primeval waters that he hooked the earth and set it above the waters.

In countless ancient religions, stories abound testifying the importance of fish in the eyes of the primitive world, an importance that can hardly be overstated. Either in their living form, or symbolically, they occupied a place in man's hopes, desires, fears and in his secret mysteries that were as real to their undeveloped minds as sunrise and sunset are to us. The deification of fish was common, and superstitions regarding them and the problems of catching them dominated the lives of the people. In Chinese Buddhism, the goddess of mercy and salvation, Kwanyim, is depicted riding on a fish. The first Avatar of Vishnu is a fish, and at the feast held in the first month of the year, the god is depicted as a golden fish. From one of the oldest writings, the Rig Veda, containing over 1,000 poems, hymns and prayers, we learn that the paramount concern of the people was to obtain from their gods the things necessary for their survival; in particular, fertility and plenty of water. This, in a tropical country, is easy to understand, but their god Indra, who controlled the waters, was the recipient of the overwhelming majority of the supplications. According to their tradition, the great rivers had been imprisoned by an evil giant, which Indra slew, causing the waters to flow once more.

Those of us who remember the Old Testament will recollect the powerful god of the Philistines, Dagon, who was described as half man, half fish. The word "dag" both in Biblical and modern Hebrew means fish. His followers were numerous in many lands, even among the Israelites. According to Phoenician legend, his father was the Sun and his mother the Earth, a most exalted parentage. He is identified with Oannes the Wise, the ancient fish god of the Chaldees, and with Enki, who was worshipped in Babylon before the flood.

In Peru, the fish-eating natives actually worshipped fish and ate them as a sort of holy sacrament. Some distributed money to the fish in the water by way of compensation for the loss of members of their families which had been caught and eaten. In Canada, the ancient tribes sent their most eloquent preachers to persuade the salmon to come and be caught. It was believed that the dead fish rose from the dead in the salmon Paradise, and it was forbidden to dispose of their bones by any other means than by returning them to the water, so that the resurrected fish could re-animate them.

In New Zealand, the Maoris returned the first batches of fish they caught unharmed to the water, so that they could inform the other fish that there was no danger in being captured.

According to an ancient Hebrew legend, the Almighty killed the female Leviathan as it lay coiled round the world, as he feared that its progeny would destroy the universe. He then salted the flesh and stored it until the arrival of the Messiah, when the righteous will be summoned to participate in a Heavenly repast.

Early Christianity did not hesitate to graft pagan and non-Christian conventions on to orthodox custom and ritual. The early Church Sacramental fish-meal, borrowed from the Jews who took it from the Babylonians during the captivity, gave rise to the routine eating of fish on Friday, for this was the day held sacred in Babylon to Ishtar (Astarte, Ashtoreth, Atargartis) the goddess of fertility, whose symbol was a fish.

To anglers, one of the most engrossing examples of religious plagiarism is to be found in the ancient stories of the quest for the mysterious object known as the Holy Grail. It was long believed that the original text was a Christian ecclesiastical one, and throughout the centuries its many occult references have been interpreted on that basis alone. It has now been shown that it is closely akin to a much older theme, folk-lore in origin, pre-dating Christianity considerably. I do not intend to delve into the argument, but only to isolate what is relevant to angling.

In the different versions, whether the hero is Galahad, Gawain or Perceval, we are struck by a common and distinctive characteristic, even though it bears the scars of variations, which, indeed, stamp it with a hallmark of authoritive antiquity. This characteristic relates to the recurring theme of the Ruler of the Waste Land, known as the Fisher King, Le Roi Pescheur. In spite of the variations, it describes how the king sickened and the country became desolate. "This land whose streams no water fed, its fountains dry." The task of the hero was to restore the King to health, or to take his place, or to find a successor. But it was vital that whoever occupied the throne was to be no mere titular King, but one endowed with the knowledge and the ability to bring back the waters and to make them fertile. Only this would bring back prosperity to the Waste Land.

As the early Christians studied the Greek Testament, they soon discovered that the reverence with which fish were held throughout the millenia was vindicated by the affinity between the Greek word for fish and the Founder of their religion, expressed in its anagram Jesus Christ Son of God Saviour. We also have the delightful, if lengthy, sermon preached at Padua by St Anthony to the fishes of the world, which congregated miraculously from all the oceans to listen to him. The text of the sermon was that fish should be grateful that they were divinely privileged to fill the bellies of devout Christians.

The above examples have been selected from thousands of stories, all in similar vein, and all pointing to the obsession of our earliest ancestors with thoughts of fish. It may be supposed that the stories are nothing more than the normal imageries of undeveloped minds, and that any attempt to magnify their importance is specious. But it is well known that the imaginations of all peoples tend to focus on the vital issues of their existence, and the very constancy of the fish content of the legends is important evidence of its urgency. The critical dependance on fish, this thin thread upon which human life hung, is clearly apparent no matter from what angle we view the primitive scene. It is even possible that the first gods were fish gods, and that it was only later as national cultures replaced the tribal, and as the practices of agriculture and animal husbandry reduced the exclusive dependance on fish, that they were merged into fertility gods, or replaced by others closer associated with man's growing activities. The veneration of fish, and their close association with the gods which were believed to be especially responsible for the preservation of life shows with certainty that they were Life symbols of the utmost importance and of immemorial antiquity.

We must remember that the ancient gods were not regarded by the people as remote or vague abstractions, but rather as closely related guardians of communal welfare. Failure by the deities to respond favourably to the demands of the community might result in the transfer of loyalty to a rival god. Even in later times, the Emperor Augustus punished Neptune for raising a storm at sea, which wrecked some Roman ships, by removing his image from the Imperial procession which marked the opening of the Games.

Recorded history amply corroborates our assumptions founded on the intangibles of pre-history. Fish hooks, which were comparative late comers in the advance of fishing techniques, were mentioned in the book of Amos written nearly 3,000 years ago. Even earlier, Homer wrote of fishing rods, hooks, and of casting. A literary gentleman named Athenaeus, writing nearly 2,000 years ago, cites

Fisherman using an inflated bladder for support. Seventh century BC.

Lead weights from Tel-Alagul, south of Gaza.

Fish drawings on pottery. Tel-Alagul, sixteenth century BC.

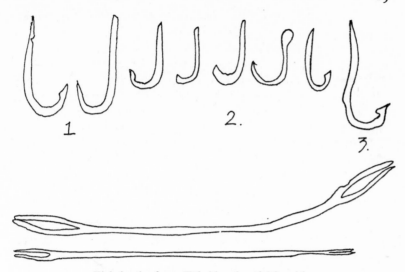

Fish hooks from Tel-Alagul and Meggido.

Preparing and preserving fish-balls in Ancient Egypt.

about 1,200 written works and 800 authors, a very large proportion of which mention fish and fishing. Only a handful remain known to us, but the very abundance bears witness to the hold that fishing had on the mass of the population long before his time.

At about this period, and for the next few centuries, books which tell us a great deal about fishing began to appear in increasing numbers. I do not intend to weary the reader with information published many time:, except to say that among the ancient writers are to be found Plutarch, Martial, Aelianus, Oppian, Arrian, Pollux, Herodotus, Aristotle, Theocritus, Virgil, Ovid and Pliny.

We must now make a brief excursion from the world of legend and literature to the twentieth century world of science. In America, Dr Willard Libby developed the Carbon-14 method of dating. Because of its radio-active properties, and its known half-life, it became possible to calculate the age of any material that contained carbon, with an upper limitation of 25,000 years. It showed that a wooden platform built by pre-historic man around the marshy edge of a lake near Starr Carr was 9,488 years old. We can only guess the function of the platform, but it is generally accepted that it was connected wth fishing. Dr Libby also examined the wood of a primitive fish trap found near Boston, U S A, and found it to be nearly 5,000 years old.

[2]
Pisciculture, Old and New

And the parched land shall become a pool, and the thirsty land springs of water. ISAIAH. CHAPTER 35:7

As man grew in mental stature, it was inevitable that his thoughts should turn to the possibilities of rearing fish in controlled enclosures where their capture at will could be assured. If, as we are logically at liberty to assume, the pursuit of fish constituted the first form of hunting, we may also assume that fish farming preceded animal farming or soil cultivation. There is evidence that cattle were being raised for food in Anatolia more than 8,000 years ago, and if our assumptions are correct, we must set our sights for the beginnings of fish culture much further back than has previously been done. This is more than speculation, though the evidence to support it is not particularly conclusive. But let us examine the known facts, and draw whatever conjectures we can from them.

The ancient city of Babylon, one of the great cities of the world, was at the peak of its power and influence about 6,000 years ago. Its origin and earliest settlements have not been traced, but they may well stretch back to the days of man's first emergence from the animal stage, or from the twilight age of *Homo erectus or Homo habilis*. Indeed, the conditions here existed for just such an event. Situated on a narrow strip of fertile land between the great rivers Euphrates and Tigris, it was ideally located for the first men to exploit the rich waters for the food they contained and upon which their lives depended. It therefore comes as no surprise to learn that one of the earliest gods of the region was Enki, or Ea, the Water-god. He was the father of Nina, the Queen of the Waters, and associated with Ningirsu, the god of Irrigation. But with the spread of civilisation over the thousands of years, and with the diversification of people's activities to agriculture, animal rearing, travelling, making war and

21

so on, a new element began to dominate the religious sentiment. The hitherto neglected cult of Marduk, the son of Enki, gradually overshadowed that of any other god, and eventually Marduk himself attained the uppermost position as Creator of the world. It is interesting to note that many have seen in the ascendency of Marduk the beginning of monotheism, and it may well be that it played a positive role in the emergence of the later Hebrew concept. Whether or not this is so, the history of Babylon is in line with the progressive growth of an exclusive fish eating community to one of more varied outlook and activities.

In Babylon we find early allusions to fish rearing. In the cult of Ishtar, the goddess of fertility, whose symbol was a fish, the connection of fish with the renewal and sustenance of life was undeniable. Her influence extended over a wide area, and in Ashkelon, now a desolate site a little to the north of Gaza, fish were reared and preserved in ponds within the confines of her Temples. Any unauthorised interference with the fish constituted the grave offence of sacrilege, but at mystic banquets held on certain Fridays the priests of the cult ate liberally of this food, in the belief that they thus partook of the flesh of the goddess. This is held to have been the origin of the Christian Friday fish meal, Friday being the day dedicated to Ishtar.

From an ancient Sumerian document, believed to be about 7,000 years old, we known that a fish-pond was leased for a substantial annual payment. We also know that at that period fish was being exported on a large scale to foreign countries. Certainly the Babylonian Hebrews, long before the birth of Christ, had incorporated in their oral law, later to be formulated in their complex Talmudic thesaurus, the litigable principles regarding fish-ponds acquired as dowry.

According to the Japanese, fish culture originated in China about 4,000 years ago, and spread from there to Japan and to Europe. Unfortunately, the difficulties of getting information on the subject are enormous, and although what has been obtained has been checked and rechecked, inaccuracies and misinterpretations may have crept in. Very rarely do scholars agree entirely with translations of old Chinese writings; indeed, even Chinese experts themselves find the older Chinese literature difficult to read. A further cause of confusion lies in the use of the Mandarin and Cantonese forms of names and places, scholars sometimes separating them when in fact they refer to one and the same thing. Dr Joseph Needham, Master of Caius and Gonville, in a recent letter to me, mentions the fragmentary remains of a treatise on the subject of pisciculture, the Yang Tu Ching, written about 2,000 years ago. Unfortunately, no translation is available, although Dr Needham hopes to remedy this at some time in the future.

Fortunately, however, a paper published in English some years ago by the University of Lingnang was photostated and passed to me by a friend at the British Museum. It deals primarily with fish culture in the Kwantung Province, although there are references to conditions elsewhere. According to the paper, over 4,000 years ago the Chinese Emperors, themselves keen fishermen, appointed officials to improve the numerous fisheries in the Province. A fish tax was levied more than 3,000 years ago, and the Emperors themselves personally visited and inspected the artificial fisheries. The first description of fish rearing methods was given by Faan Lai about 2,500 years ago in a book entitled "Classic of Fish Culture", and as it is the first I have been able to find, I give an extract from a translation in full.

"Construct a pond of six mow and plant many water grasses there. Get twenty female carp three feet long and four males of the same length, and place them quietly into the pond in the second month. In the fourth month put one turtle into the pond, in the sixth month put two, and in the eighth month three. Then in the second month of the next year you will get 15,000 one-foot carp, 10,000 two-foot carp, and 45,000 three-foot carp, and these can be sold for 1,250,000 cash. In the third year you get 100,000 one-foot carp, 50,000 two-foot carp and the rest may be sold for 5,150,000. The carp will not harm each other and can easily be reared."

The bit about the turtles is most interesting. In Europe, as far as my inquiries tell, it would be unthinkable to introduce a turtle into a fish rearing pond, but in Israel, where fish farming is conducted on an extensive scale, they are quite common. The turtles possess the imposing name of Rivulated Caspian Water Turtles, and they eat fish, frogs, etc., but are beneficial to fish ponds rather than harmful, as they eat all dead, sick or injured fish. They are not fast enough to catch a healthy, vigorous fish, nor do they eat fish spawn.

For the next 1,000 years, little appears to have been written, except a book giving recipes for cooking fish, and an agricultural

Fish pond in Mesopotamia, from an Assyrian
tablet of the seventh century BC.

Assyrian fisherman fishing a canal near the
king's palace, Ninevah. Seventh century BC.

Egyptian nobleman, with wife, fishing his fish pond.

Egyptian nobleman, with wife, at his fish pond, *c.* 2000 BC. He has two rods, each with double lines. One of them has caught two fish and is being handed back to the wife for de-hooking. The pond is symmetrical and has a deeper channel in the centre for drainage. It is well stocked with water plants. The fish can be recognised as Tilapia from the gold markings on the tails. From a drawing on a grave.

treatise by Ka Sz Hip which repeats much of Faan Lai's earlier advice on fish farming. Then about 1585 A D a book by Ch'ui Kwong K'ai goes deeply into many aspects of pisciculture. The reader is told that fish ponds should be constructed with a curve so that the fish may grow more rapidly, that sheep should be allowed to graze on the banks, that grape vines extending over the water will prevent the excrement of birds getting into the water and that the tree *Hibiscus mutabilis* (Rose mallow) keeps otters away. Recommended food are the shells of preserved eggs, hemp leaves, and straw soaked in urine. The main disease appears to have been known as "floating", and this could be controlled by feeding the fish with human excrement, and with macerated banana leaves. Another disease, known as "white spotted disease", caused by sudden rain, was cured by putting pine needles into the pond.

One of the earliest mentions of an artificial fish-pond, the Moeris, was by Herodotus nearly 3,000 years ago. It was connected by a canal to the R Nile, which when in flood, filled it with fish, and when receding, left them behind to be collected at leisure. The project was a Royal monopoly, and the profit, estimated by Radcliffe to be equivalent to £45,000 per annum (Fishing from the Earliest Times. Page 333) was all spent on cosmetics for the Queen.

The only positive mention in the Old Testament of fish-ponds is in Isaiah 19:10, but in a homiletic interpretation of the Scriptures, called the Midrash, written nearly 2,000 years ago, the phrase "I made me pools of water" in Ecclesiastes 2:6 attracted the commentary "I made me pools of water, Piscinae", the latter being the Latin name for fish-ponds. However, an English translation of the Midrash (Soncino Press) substitutes "reservoirs" for "piscinae".

A drawing on a grave about 4,000 years old shows an Egyptian noble sitting in an armchair, his wife beside him, fishing an artificial fish-pond. He is using two rods, each with double lines, and is passing one of the rods, with a captured fish on each line, to his wife, obviously for de-hooking. The pond itself is constructed with a deep centre channel for drainage, and water plants grow freely. The fish can be recognised as belonging to the genus *Tilapia*, probably *Tilapia nilotica*, of the sub-order Peroidei, among which are included perch, bass, ruff and pope.

Works on Pisciculture are numerous, many of them dating back to the middle ages and even to classical times. Of the latter, the best known are those by Marcus Terentius Varro (116-27 B C) and by Lucius Junius Moderatus Collumnella (circa A D 60). They were followed by Rutilius Taurus Palladius in the 4th century, a gentleman whose writing was somewhat monotonous but who frequently interspersed his instruction on the rearing of fish by proclaiming his expertise, an example widely followed at the present time.

Collumnella is worth reading. He writes that his ancestors were such enthusiastic fish farmers that they kept sea fish in fresh water, bringing the spawn from the sea into lakes they constructed. Then an age followed when people enclosed the very sea itself, an event remembered "by their own grandfathers". Fish ponds were sold for fantastic sums; the species of fish cultivated were, among others, red mullet, wrasse, sole, turbot, sea-pike, bass, flounders, and, above all, lampreys. They were fed on decaying pilchards and sardines, on salted herrings, and the entrails and refuse of mackerel, dog-fish, and spindle-fish. Also recommended were green figs, sorb-apples, milk curds, bits of bread and fruits in season cut into small pieces.

From other sources we learn that wealthy Roman patricians would willingly pay between £100 and £1,000 for a dish of fish, and that eels were fed with the flesh of slaves. It is amusing to read that connoisseurs claimed they could tell the difference in the taste of fish that had been caught at one bank of a river as opposed to the other bank, even though they were invariably smothered in the most pungent sauces.

It is fairly safe to assume that even in the days when these ancient books were written, fish cultivation was an ancient art.

In the succeeding years, books and papers on fish culture followed each other in rapid succession. In addition, many angling books devoted some space to the subject, and a number of them may well be studied with considerable profit. The fish concerned were mostly carp, but many other fish were reared, and extensive schemes for rearing sea fish in isolated channels achieved some success. As far as can be ascertained, trout entered into the picture only recently.

Until the middle of the 18th century, the rearing of fish from the egg stage had been accomplished from eggs that had been naturally spawned. In the year 1763, a German naturalist named Jacobi extracted some ova from a dead trout, and successfully raised live fish from them after mixing them with fresh milt. It is thought that he was anticipated by five years by another German naturalist,

Count von Golstein. However, the credit was given to Jacobi, and as a result he was awarded a Government pension. The process became known in other countries, but remained an academic curiosity practised by scientists without any regard for its practical applications.

Here the matter rested for nearly 100 years until, in the year 1840, two humble French peasants, who had never heard of Jacobi or his work and who knew nothing of Natural History, began to explore the way trout produced their young. They were stimulated to the task by the alarming reduction of the trout supply in the rivers surrounding the obscure village of La Bresse in which they lived. With crude methods and apparatus, the two men, Remy and Gehin, succeeded in hatching their first trout eggs and continued doing so for the next three years. Before long, news of their enterprise reached the most distinguished quarters, and eventually the Paris Academy of Sciences brought it to the attention of the appropriate Government Department which established the world's first trout hatchery at Hunige in the year 1854.

In the next few years other trout hatcheries were built in many European countries. In England curiosity in the new development was aroused by a book, "Fish Hatching", written by Frank Buckland in the year 1863. Five years later the first hatchery in the country was constructed in Cumberland by J. J. Armistead.

One of the first reservoirs to make use of the new process was Lake Vyrnwy in North Wales, but from an angling point of view errors were made in the construction that later reservoirs were able to avoid. Nevertheless, this beautiful lake, so well served by the hotel standing on its banks, has given enormous pleasure to many thousands of fishermen.

Until close to the end of the 19th century, the impregnation of the ova was performed in recepticles in the presence of water. The female spawn was ejected into the water and the male sperm introduced. But as the effective life of the sperm in water is only about 45 seconds, it was found that a considerable number of the sperm were unable to effect penetration into ova before they perished. In practice, successful insemination of 75 per cent of the ova was considered very good. But a Russian, M Vrasski, soon discovered that the dry life of the milt was far greater than its wet life, and he introduced what is now known as the "Dry" method. Mixing is done in a dry sieve, the ova and the milt being thoroughly mixed with a feather, and allowed to stand awhile before being immersed in water. This gives almost 100 per cent fertility.

In Great Britain, the opening of Blagdon reservoir in 1904 began a new era in stillwater fishing. The growing angling population and the shortage of natural trout fishing coincided with the construction of huge reservoirs up and down the country built, not for fishing, but to supply water to the increasing populations and industries of the twentieth century. With no little foresight, planners have realised the economic and social advantages such inland waters could provide in the way of trout fishing, sailing, and other popular diversions. That their calculations were correct is evidenced by the profusion of similar enterprises in all parts of the country. Although few of them live up to the prodigality of their opening years and, in some cases, suffer serious setbacks they eventually settle down to provide fly-fishing of a high standard for thousands of anglers to whom these waters are the only ones conveniently available.

What the future holds for man-made trout fishing none can say but, if we look across the Atlantic to the United States of America, we find the emergence on a large scale of a type of fishing known as "Catch and Release", As the term implies, no fish are killed but all are returned to the water, much as our coarse fish are returned. The flies, with barbless hooks, are provided by the fishery, and they are often tied to imitate the food pellets with which the fish are fed. Whether this type of fishing will survive remains to be seen; it is thought that the constant handling of the fish by anglers might introduce infection into the fishery, or that the instinct of the fish to rise to the surface food will be destroyed. If however it spreads, angling will perhaps evolve into a sport as academic as hunting game with a camera. Whether it will have the same compensations is doubtful.

The glimpses we have had into the antiquities and origins of fishing leave us with the suspicion that it is one of the oldest activities of mankind. It is as much a part of our physical and mental make-up as the marrow in our bones, and possibly within the spirals of the chromosomes in every human being there now exists a fishing gene that frequently becomes dominant in the character of an individual, even though it might lie dormant for generations. The individual so subjected finds absolute composure only in the feel of a rod in his hand and the sharp scents of the waterside in his nostrils.

Between the lines of the following chapters such a one will sense the long stillnesses of summer days that end with the rise of trout against a sunset of saffron and scarlet. He will see in the printed page the tone variations of massed blooms reflected from the still waters and will hear, in the distance, bird songs borne on light breezes softened by the surrounding woodlands. As he reads he will recall with quickening pulse the battles between fighting fish and his quivering rod as it strains into changing parabolas. These and other memories are the confections each reader must provide from his own experiences to flavour the pragmatic history of the Two Lakes Fishery.

[3]

Basic Principles

Whate'er its mission, the soft breeze can come
To none more grateful than to me; escaped
From the vast city, where I long had pined
A discontented sojourner.   WORDSWORTH

In its simplest terms a lake is merely a hole in the ground filled with water. The hole may have been formed by primitive earth convulsions, or by the slow erosion of ice and glacier movements, by the subsidence of the land surface, by volcanic eruption, or it may have been excavated by man for his profit or pleasure. A further type, which has been humorously described as "a hole sticking up" is one where a suitable site is enclosed by an artificial dam and flooded. The latter, a comparatively recent development, is becoming more and more commonplace.

Although it is not my purpose in these pages to wax academic, on a number of occasions I have been asked to define the difference between lakes, ponds and reservoirs. Alas, even those specialised scientists known as Limnologists (students of aquatic fauna) have been unable to ascribe to lakes and ponds descriptions which will satisfactorily designate the individual characteristics of each and I hesitate to step in where my betters have failed. Perhaps the easiest way is to rely on size and on the passivity of the water. Thus a lake may be described as a fairly large expanse of stillwater with an inflow and an outlet, even though the latter may be due entirely to evaporation; whereas a pond is a small body of water dependent for its supply mainly on rain or morning dew. An irritating drawback to this compromise is the unlikelihood of any two human beings agreeing on the dividing line between large and small.

A reservoir is a large lake artificially constructed by damming an appropriate site primarily for use as a place for storing water.

31

The fact that the Water Authority, under whose mandate a reservoir is built, goes to a great deal of trouble to render it suitable for fishing should not blind us to the fact that fishing is not its main function. At best it is only a secondary consideration, the prime purpose being to store water for communal use, and this function must take precedence over all others, certainly at the expense, if necessary, of the fishing. Herein lies a serious handicap to the status of a reservoir as a fly-fishery, but more of this later.

All lakes—natural, artificial and reservoirs—are now generally referred to by anglers everywhere as stillwaters and, except on those occasions when it is necessary to differentiate between the various types, I shall do the same. Also, when discussing trout, I shall be referring to both the native brown trout (*Salmo trutta*) and its American cousin the rainbow trout (*Salmo gairdneri*) except, again, when it is necessary to discuss their individual traits.

It is axiomatic that if we are to understand trout fishing, we must understand trout. We must understand what they thrive on and what injures them, what food they prefer and which they decline. We must know their enemies and something of the creatures in the water around them. We must delve deeply, not only into their lives and their customs, but also into the lives and behaviour patterns of the vast multitudes of aquatic fauna among which they live. As our continued enjoyment of trout, both as instruments of sporting angling and as valuable additions to our diet, is subject to the creation of conditions where they may flourish in comfort and in safety, a study of the subject matter is obligatory.

In fly-fishing for trout, as in all forms of angling, we achieve our aim by pandering to the appetites of our quarry. We must, therefore, assume that the artificial flies to which the fish rise and which they accept appear to them, if not to us, as authentic food, recognisable by their appearance, their behaviour and by the absence of any suspicious circumstances associated with their presence. Fortunately for the fly-fisher, the range of aquatic creatures upon which stillwater trout will readily feed at one time or another is so wide in species, size, colour and behaviour, that our task, if not exactly simple, is within our capacity if we are prepared to trouble ourselves to acquire the rudimentary facts of aquatic activity. It is a paradox that in so troubling ourselves, we find that we are indulging in a pastime that gives us considerable pleasure.

It might reasonably be supposed that because stillwaters have supported life continuously for millions of years that they are viable entities, but this is not so. Life, however lowly, requires a continuous supply of basic materials to build up its tissues and, although death and decay eventually return these materials to the water, this depends on the death actually occuring within its confines. The extraction of fish, in addition to other losses, is in reality an extraction of the vital substances upon which the whole complex of life under water relies for its very existence. This depletion, if continued, will in time impoverish the water to such an extent that life within it will become extremely tenuous unless the substances can be replenished from outside sources. What are these substances, and whence do they come?

The first and foremost is sunlight, of which the supply is fortunately perpetual and without which all life would cease. It has been calculated that barely 1 per cent of the solar energy falling on stillwaters is made use of, but in any event, it is a commodity that we mortals are unable to modify except in a very small way. Secondly, there are the various compounds of basic organic and inorganic materials which are washed in by feeder streams or springs, or which drain into the water from the surrounding countryside. Thirdly, there is the oxygen content obtained from the air in contact with the water surface and from the release by water plants during the hours of daylight. Finally, there is a small bonus in the physical composition of odd terrestrial creatures that accidentally find a watery grave, though this source of accretion is of limited value however welcome it may be at the time to the permanent inhabitants.

Exactly how the build-up of living cells occurs is largely unknown. It all starts, in waters everywhere, fresh and marine, with the appearance in spring of astronomical quantities of simple microscopic growths known as algae. These are primitive chlorophyll-containing plants, without true leaves, stems or roots, and mostly with single cell reproductive organs. There are roughly 18,000 types, each exclusive either to fresh or salt water. Their extent is of such magnitude that they often make the water turgid and colour it green, blue-green, red or brown. The materials used in the construction of their tissues, apart from solar energy, are the elementary components of minerals, salts, gases and other nutrients that are present in the water. Carbon dioxide, water and sunlight can, through the agency of chlorophyll, be synthesised into sugar and starches, while oxygen is released in the process. Silica is essential for the construction of the outer case of one of the most prolific organisms, the tiny single-cell Diatom, with more than 5,500 different species, of which about 1,200 are native to the United Kingdom. Nitrates and phosphates play important roles in the manufacture of proteins, and calcium compounds assist the efficient breakdown of organic matter into its constituent parts for use by succeeding generations of aquatic fauna. Oxygen must be breathed by all the water animals and utilized by the bacteria present in the water as they work on the decomposition of the decaying animal and vegetable tissue. Other combinations of magnesium, sulphur, chlorine, sodium and iron are also present in stillwaters and furnish the requirements of the various algaeic growths. It is interesting to note that frogs prefer to spawn in the region of waters rich in potassium, probably because the algae which utilize it are suitable for tadpoles.

Some algae become attached to vegetation, to stones or to other fixed objects, and some are free-floating. The former provide pasture for nymphs, snails and other small herbivorous animals. The latter are known as plankton or, to be more precise, phytoplankton, meaning "plant wanderers", to distinguish them from the later arriving animal plankton, or zooplankton. Some of the latter, known as the nannoplankton, are so incredibly small, measuring barely one ten-thousandth of an inch ($\cdot$002 mm), that they cannot be filtered out of the water, but are separated out for research purposes by means of centrifuges.

We must conceive the algaeic mass, and the sunshine, and the basic substances from which they are derived, as the foundation on which the ladder of stillwater life stands and on which it is supported. If it should fail through lack of materials or for any other reason, the whole of the stillwater life would fail, and fish could only survive if they were hand-fed like goldfish in a glass bowl, a dismal and expensive prospect indeed. The importance of the algae and of the materials which sustain them cannot be over-emphasised, for on them all else depends.

By an extraordinary—or miraculous—indulgence, Mother Nature permits the algae to attain maximum growth and expansion before the first spring appearance of the zooplankton. This host of minute animals, lacking the synthesising ability of chlorophyll-containing plants, begins to browse voraciously on the phytoplankton for the carbohydrates and the proteins they need. It has been estimated that the proportion of zooplankton to phytoplankton is 7 to 93 by weight, thus permitting a conversion ratio of about thirteen to one from plant tissue to animal tissue. This seems a little high compared with the conversion ratio in cattle, where it is reckoned that about 6 lb (or Kilogrammes) of grazing provides 1 lb (or Kilogramme) of meat, but it is possible that this is accounted for by the greater water content of the aquatic algae. The total mass of both phyto-plankton and zooplankton is thought to be between 25 and 62 tonnes per hectare (10 and 25 tons per acre) of water surface, but it is well to bear in mind that so little is known of the subject that these figures, though well within the bounds of credibility, must be regarded with some caution.

The zooplankton feed not only on the phytoplankton but on each other. The variety of species is enormous. Among them may be found the Protozoa, the lowest form of living animal, of which about 20,000 species have been classified; Rotifers, those most attractive animalculae with vibrating bristles which appear to be spinning wheels; Crustaceans, the most prolific of all, including Copepods and Daphnia (Water fleas) in their ranks; and hosts of others whose names will convey little or nothing to the lay reader, but which certainly include the very young of insects, worms and other fauna.

The zooplankton, following hard on the heels of the phyto-plankton which promote and sustain them, constitute the first animal links in the complex chain of life in stillwaters. Some are carnivorous, some herbivorous, some saprophytic, and some are scavengers. But to a large extent this is unexplored territory. What is important is that as the inhabitants grow so must the size and quan-tity of the food intake, and, in particular, predators must hunt and devour the largest prey they are capable of overcoming. In a trout fishery, the trout, almost entirely carnivorous, when adult seek their food as near the apex of the food chain as possible. It is obvious that they will not long survive in the absence of the intermediate links between themselves and the algaeic plants, however rich and abundant the latter may be. And it is with these intermediate links that we are deeply concerned, for if they are unsuitable for the trout's diet, or if they compete with it, the fishery will suffer.

It is doubtful if a comprehensive list of all the living creatures that any single stillwater supports can ever be made. Beyond the plankton, however, are the snails (*Mollusca*), the worms (*Annelidae*), the shrimps, the water lice and the water fleas (*Crustacea*), the water mites and the spiders (*Arachnidae*), the pond skaters and the water boatmen (*Hemiptera*), the phantom larvae and the midges (*Diptera*), the duns (*Ephemeroptera*), the sedges (*Trichoptera*), the alders (*Megaloptera*), the dragon flies (*Odonata*), the beetles (*Coleoptera*), and a host of others. Many of these contribute directly to the diet of trout but some, particularly certain surface dwellers, appear to be virtually immune. Most of the above are insects, which dominate numerically many or even most of the stillwaters, as they do the world we live in.

The information to be gleaned from all this is of no little importance. The basic substances so vital to the health of a stillwater lie for the most part within the physical make-up of its fauna and flora. If they die within the confines of the water, they eventually decompose and return these substances to the water to be used again by succeeding generations. But as the purpose of trout fishing it to capture trout and to remove them from the fishery, a constant depletion of the resources of the water is taking place and, unless this depletion is made good from natural sources, the result will be an impoverishment of the organic treasury and an eventual deterioration of the fishing. How can this be avoided? Certainly not by putting in more fish, for this would be as sensible as sitting down a dozen people to dinner where there was food only for two or three. The answer lies in maintaining a balance between the fish crop and the fundamental nutrients that, through the planktonic growths, animate every link in the food chain. This can be done in a number of ways.

Firstly, the fishing can be restricted until the balance is restored and the optimum fish crop is determined, and not exceeded; unfortunately, this will not carry much appeal.

Secondly, ruthless methods must be adopted to curb the depredations of competing fish, birds and animals.

Thirdly, we can resort to manuring the water in order to reinforce the lost substances that are not naturally replaced in full.

In a trout fishery, coarse fish are undesirable. Unfortunately, they are almost impossible to eliminate entirely. Frequent netting will reduce their numbers, but inevitably many will escape. On the larger lakes of Westmorland, or on the lochs of Scotland and the loughs of Ireland and, indeed, on the large reservoirs, netting would be unthinkable because of the magnitude of the task. Where stillwaters are intended exclusively for trout, fishing for coarse fish may be permitted in the close season, but this is of doubtful value as a great deal of damage can be done to the trout as well as to the coarse fish. The answer lies in emptying the stillwater, removing the coarse fish and treating the exposed bed with quicklime. After a few weeks, the effect of the quicklime wears off, the water can be restored and the trout stock returned minus the coarse fish. This remedy, however, is not possible on a reservoir, as any such operation would be on too large a scale, would take too long and would cause communal disturbances that could not be contemplated.

Coarse fish can be efficiently destroyed by the use of Rotenone, a poison which is manufactured from derris root or synthetically. Unfortunately it is lethal to trout too and therefore its value in an established trout fishery might be limited. However, there may be occasions when the loss of a few trout is a small price to pay for the complete elimination of predatory or competing fish from a still-water, as is possible with Rotenone. If a trout population exists in water to be treated, some of them can be saved by netting them when they appear on the surface in a distressed condition and immersing them immediately in prepared tanks of clean water. Great care must be exercised when applying the poison not to contaminate neighbouring waters. Although the cost of Rotenone is reasonable, the task of administering it effectively can be difficult and expensive.

Apart from coarse fish, the rich life of stillwaters attracts the attention of birds and terrestrial animals. Aquatic insects suffer heavily from swallows, swifts and martins and, to a lesser extent, from warblers and wagtails. The dabchick, or little grebe, picturesque though it may be, should be persuaded by all means to perform its acrobatics elsewhere, for it feeds on small fish and most invertebrates. The coot and the moorhen, both almost vegetarian, do little harm even if at times their noisy bickerings disturb the summer quiet. But cormorants and, to a lesser degree, heron should be rigorously excluded if the trout stock is to be protected. The kingfisher, if present, earns its fish as a small fee for the glorious explosion of colour that illuminates the rustic scene.

Of the animals, the otter is a menace, particularly when it is teaching its cubs to hunt. At such times it can do enormous damage. It is not easy to discourage as it sleeps during the day, often at some distance from the water, and hunts at night. At Two Lakes, dog patrols are mounted after dark and the kennel bedding suspended from branches at selected spots around the banks. The scent acts as an efficient deterrent to these elusive marauders. The vole, being largely vegetarian does little harm except perhaps to a dam by burrowing. It is often mistaken for a rat and persecuted, but it is easily recognised by its blunt snout and by the fact that its ears are almost hidden in its fur. The shrews, of which there are several, are about the size of mice, with long tapering muzzles. They are usually dark grey or brownish and, being generally nocturnal, are not easily spotted. They feed on insects, snails, worms and small mammals. They may be tolerated without anxiety. Minks, if present, must be ruthlessly destroyed.

No mention has been made of eels, which should be discouraged, but more of this later.

It will be agreed that on the smaller fisheries, one man with a gun and a dog can exercise a measure of control over outside predators, including poachers who, incidentally, should not be underrated. It would require any army of assistants to do so effectively on a large reservoir.

When the basic minerals are deficient, either naturally or because of excessive fish cropping, manures can be added to the water to restore them. The type of manure will depend largely on the nature of the water under consideration. Acid waters with a low pH value will benefit from the addition of chalk or some other calcelarious substance. Stillwaters with clay or sandy infrastructures should be treated with either stable manure or sewage sludge. Restoration of resources to waters where they have been expended too rapidly may be accomplished with commercial artificial manures containing nitrogen, phosphoric acid, potash and sodium, applied in doses of about 1 cwt per acre at intervals. The proportions of the mixture can be varied in consultation with the fertiliser producer to suit the fishery. It must be stressed, however, that the practice is in its infancy and it may well be many years before water manuring can be elevated to a science.

Reservoir fishing for trout has brought fly-fishing within the reach of thousands of anglers to whom it had previously been denied. As more reservoirs are built to satisfy the needs of the growing population of our cities, stillwater fishing will come to dominate the world of trout. Blagdon, which was opened in 1904, first showed that the demand existed; it was followed more than fifty years later by Chew Valley, which was the first of the many post-war reservoirs which catered for the trout fly-fisher. The greatest credit must be

SEASON 1972

Place	Water Area	Number of Fish Caught	Average Weight	Fishing Yield	
				per acre	per hectare
Grafham	1,570 acres (635 hectares)	16,668	2 lb 1 oz (0·94 kg)	21¾ lb	25 kg
Chew	1,200 acres (485 hectares)	15,700	2 lb 7 oz (1·10 kg)	32 lb	36 kg
Blagdon	430 acres (174 hectares)	6,575	2 lb 3 oz (1·00 kg)	33½ lb	38 kg
Two Lakes	14 acres (5·7 hectares)	6,915	2 lb 5 oz (1·05 kg)	1,142 lb	1,280 kg

given to those responsible; they have bestowed a monumental boon on the angling community. But it must again be stressed that their use as civic water storage reserves precludes them from adopting the measures we have outlined to attain the optimum trout production. This must be the business of the smaller fisheries oriented exclusively in the direction of trout fishing. This can be shown by the data in the Table on page 39.

[4]
Construction

In the year 1948, the countries of Europe were still grappling with the pressing problems of the post-war years. Food, clothing and fuel were all rationed; housing was desperately short and labour insufficient to provide the elementary requirements of populations which for so long had been deprived of their basic needs. Above all, people whose lives had been shattered by the ravages of war were seeking ways and means of re-establishing themselves on better and more stable foundations than previously.

Among the many whose past lives had been disrupted by the tragic events of the last few years were Katharine Armstrong and Alex Behrendt, who, drawn together from widely divergent backgrounds by the unpredictable proddings of Armageddon, had recently married. The common realisation that each envisaged an ideal future within a rural encompassment, adequately wooded, with a stretch of stillwater where fish would flourish and where tufted duck and mallard would make their home, instilled in them a determination to turn their ideal into reality. They began to search for a suitable site for their experiment, for experiment it was to be, but disappointment dogged their footsteps, and hope of finding one began to fade until....

On a perfect day in June they had their first glimpse of a tract of land on the outskirts of Romsey in the County of Hampshire. Here they saw rhododendrons in full bloom surging in masses around the banks of a secluded lake, partly hidden behind the billowing purple flowers. Overhead soared Spruce and Beech, dark Scots Pine, Larch and pale Silver Birch, their translucent filigrees of green leaves half screening the mottled white trunks. The surrounding land, barren only from a human point of view, was prolific with a fascinating amalgam of contrasting vegetation. Feathery Cocksfoot, coarse Rye and Timothy grasses contended with bracken in a scramble for the precious soil and sunshine; together they had existed in elemental strife with the thistles, the stately yellow flags, the oval leafed brooklime and the numerous herbs of the field for countless centuries, and now they combined to resist the passage of the human interlopers as though they knew that the days of their archaic and anarchic occupation were about to end.

In the undergrowth a wren scolded the intruders, and from a high branch a blackbird joined the melody of a nearby song thrush in an avian duet. A robin and a hedge sparrow trilled faintly from the thick bush, and a newly-arrived chiff-chaff echoed the motif of the willow warbler as it cascaded down to the ears of the hushed Behrendts. The swarms of insects emerging from the lake were welcomed by the excited screams of high-flying swifts and the twitterings of swooping sand martins. And when a solitary owl hoo-oo-ed them derisively, they knew with a happy unanimity that this was the land of their dreams.

But it was all in a sad state of neglect. The lake, choked with chaotic growth and barely half full of water, was disfigured by rusted tins of all sizes, empty bottles, a wide variety of floating and stationery rubble, and a small perilous raft that testified to the presence, past and future, of adventurous boys. A broken dam separated the lake, which covered an area of about four acres, from a small, shallow pond, even more delapidated than its larger neighbour.

The owner of the site, located after much search and inquiry, was reluctant to sell, but eventually, impressed by the enthusiasm of the would-be purchasers, he consented, but not without conditions, the severest of which stipulated that the land be enclosed within three months by a cattle-proof fence. This, in the years of shortage, was a formidable task but, like all other difficulties, it was overcome, and eventually the Behrendts took possession of the site and named it Two Lakes. The making of a fishery was about to begin.

Man's creative ability is by no means a monadic endowment. On the contrary, it is a compound of many ingredients, among which are toil, determination and patience. That these ingredients are possessed by the Behrendts cannot be doubted. From the moment the owner agreed to sell, before the legal formalities were concluded or even started, the work of clearing the land and the lake, and repairing the broken dam, was well on the way. Posts for the fence had been bought and construction put in hand. The inimical nature of the ground made access to the lake possible only by an intrepid assault on the riotous overgrowth and a defiance of the boggy subsoil. All this time, by statutory requirements, Behrendt was employed full time as a labourer at a nearby farm, and the back-breaking work at Two Lakes was done in his "leisure" hours, supplemented by hired daily labour at a wage considerably more than the one he was receiving from his employment at the farm.

His determination was bolstered by the spirit of adventure that dominated the project. No disappointment or failure, and there were many, was allowed to persist beyond a momentary depression or a mildly blasphemous explosion. Setbacks became stimuli for fresh efforts and new methods, and successes were regarded as nothing more than milestones on a craggy road. Night after night, with dogged resolution, the Behrendts tooks turns in patrolling the grounds to ward off nocturnal predators, leaving the comparative comfort of their leaky caravan every two hours from dusk until dawn. The complete loss of their initial stock of 250 yearling trout to the native perch, a severe blow, was an object lesson out of which was learned much that was profitable. The comparative failure of their first attempt at netting persuaded them that fallibility and inexperience went hand in hand. The collapse of a dam and the reluctance of an exhaust hatch to open in response to their frantic efforts to reduce the water pressure on the remaining portion were responsible for improvements to the design of both dam and hatch.

Viability was not around the corner, or even a short distance away. Their eyes were firmly focused on the future and on the realisation of their dream however long it took. With philosophic patience they awaited the slow growth of beech and oak trees from beech nuts and acorns they had themselves collected and planted in a newly cleared tree nursery. Here too they raised from seed Scots Pine, Sitka and Norway Spruce. And five long years passed before the first trout, a $1\frac{1}{4}$ lb (570 grms) brownie, was taken on a fly, a dry Alder. Speed was repudiated and thoroughness embraced; neither weariness nor disappointment was allowed to deflect them from their objective.

In the meantime, Behrendt, thoroughly trained in pisciculture from boyhood, read every book on fly-fishing he could lay his hands on with the perseverence of a zealot. Scientific publications from countries more advanced in this field than Great Britain were secured and studied. Journals devoted to the art of fly-fishing were subscribed to and fly fishers closely questioned at every opportunity. But still the heavy work continued without respite.

At about this time, it was decided that an expert should be consulted to assess the suitability of the lake for trout fishing. After the assessment had been made, the report that was submitted was wholly depressing. It drew attention to the unfavourable effect of rhododendron and other leaves on aquatic fauna, and commented adversely on the acidity of the water, although some reservation was made in this respect owing to the presence of milfoil, celery and water cress, plants which thrive usually in an alkaline environment. The scarcity of shrimp and the absence of snail were held to confirm the negative diagnosis. The report concluded by depicting the lake as a typical coarse fish one. The fact that the expert in later years courageously admitted that his assessment was wrong is greatly to his credit, but I am not sure that his original conclusion was far off the mark. Perhaps his greatest failure was in not recognising the Behrendt syndrome, but of course his expertise lay in trout culture and not in human psychology.

The acidity or alkalinity of water is expressed in terms of a pH value followed by a number, which, in theory, can be anywhere between one and fourteen. There is nothing mysterious about these numbers, and anybody with a slight knowledge of logarithms can understand why. Water contains positively charged hydrogen ions and negatively charged hydroxyl ions. An ion is one of the components that result from the decomposition of a chemical compound by an electric charge. A hydroxyl is a radical, or root, consisting of an atom of hydrogen joined to an atom of oxygen. In a litre of pure water at a temperature at $18°C$ ($64°F$), there are equal quantities of hydrogen ions and hydroxyl ions, the amount in each case being $1/10^7$ ($1/10,000,000$) of a gramme. This is easier denoted as pH7, using the index of the reciprocal power of the hydrogen ion content as a simple figure.

As the quantity of hydrogen ions increases, the index of the reciprocal power reduces (It will be seen quite clearly that $1/10^2$ ($1/100$) is greater than $1/10^3$ ($1/1000$)). If therefore the pH number is reduced, we are indicating that the number of hydrogen ions is increased, and if the pH number is increased, we are indicating that the number of hydrogen ions is reduced. It must be remembered that a reduction in the number of hydrogen ions means an increase in the number of hydroxyl ions, and vice versa.

In practice, when the hydrogen and hydroxyl ions are equal, that is when the pH value is 7, the water is said to be neutral. When the former are in excess, it is said to be acid, and when the latter are in excess, it is said to be alkaline. Thus any pH value below 7 is acid, and any above 7 is alkaline.

The acidity or alkalinity of water can be reliably tested with colour indicators. But the reliability is only momentary, and not absolute, owing to different readings being obtained at different times. As a typical example, readings I have taken between 9 am and 3 pm at one of the lakes at Two Lakes have varied between 6 and 8·5, the higher figures occuring later in the day. This is due to the reduction in the carbon dioxide content, (which tends to form carbonic acid when dissolved in water) as it is converted to oxygen and carbohydrates by photosynthesis as the day waxes. The water becomes more acid during the night when the vegetation gives off carbon dioxide, and absorbs oxygen.

Water chemists nowadays prefer describing water as "hard" or "soft", the designation depending on the parts per million of calcium carbonate in solution. In small or medium bodies of water, any deficiency can be remedied without much difficulty by applications of chalk, either in powdered form for quick action, or in solid form for more durable action.

The expert's report that snails were absent was not correct. A number were found when the lake was emptied in 1951. The final conclusion, however, that the lake was suitable only for coarse fish, appeared superficially to be true, but it was decided to test it.

In May 1949, 250 five inch (12 cms) rainbow trout were introduced into the lake. They were observed throughout the summer, and were seen to be active and presumably in good health. By the end of the summer, however, they had all vanished without a trace, and it was presumed that they were eaten by the native perch, of which there was a large population. The following spring, in 1950, the lake was stocked with 75 eleven inch (28 cms) brown trout, and these, too large to become perch fodder, survived and prospered.

Meanwhile, an attempt to net out the coarse fish had not been a great success. A new attempt, this time with professional assistance, was more successful, and over 4,000 coarse fish were taken out. But it was soon apparent that the problem of the coarse fish had by no means been solved, and the following year, in 1951, both the lake and the adjacent pond were emptied. From the pond, 345 tench were removed and, from the lake, the following:

Carp	328
Tench	1,304
Perch	991
Bream	727
Roach	5,091
Trout	72
Eels	uncounted, but many hundreds.

The carp were up to 7 lb (3·2 kgs), and the perch up to 3 lb (1·3 kgs). It is significant that only three trout were lost between April 1950 and November 1951. The beds of the lake and the pond were heavily quicklimed, and the former refilled.

At this point, with the indulgence of the reader, I propose to move eight years ahead of my story, for in the year 1959 the lake, now named the Upper Lake, was again emptied. On this occasion, the only coarse fish found were tench, and there were no less than 17,895 of them. It is believed that they were the original fish which, when the lake was previously emptied in 1951, were small and hardy enough to survive by burying themselves deep in the bottom mud, and their descendants. This is borne out by the following record of the sizes and quantities of the captured fish.

Size	Quantity
10″ to 13″ (25–33 cms)	105
8″ to 10″ (20–25 cms)	520
6″ to 8″ (15–20 cms)	1,470
4″ to 6″ (10–15 cms)	3,200
3″ to 4″ (7–10 cms)	12,600

Reverting to our chronological order, in 1952 the lake was stocked with 100 five inch (12 cms) brown trout, in addition to the 72 larger trout previously netted out. Also, many thousands of shrimps (*Gammarus pulex*) and snails (*Limnaea peregra*) were deposited in the littoral regions. In September of the same year, the five inch trout varied between 14 ozs (·4 kgs) and 1 lb (·454 kgs).

The temperature of the water, even in the hottest summer seldom exceeded 21°C (70°F), well within the range of trout toleration. A close examination of the lake population revealed prolific quantities of Water Fleas (*Daphnia*), Sedge larvae, Phantom larvae, Midge larvae, Alder larvae, Blackfly larvae, Dayfly and Dragonfly nymphs, Water Slaters (*Asellus*), Water Boatmen, and many other aquatic creatures. The high fecundity of the coarse fish testified to the abundance of natural food produced by the lake. The decision to proceed with raising trout commended itself, and plans were made accordingly.

Precedence was given to the enlargement of the small pond to a size approximately that of its larger neighbour, and in anticipation of its completion, it was named the Lower Lake, in contrast to the former, now named the Upper Lake. This was fed by a small stream called the Ganger, which rose from natural springs a short distance away. Its outspill was to be utilised to feed the Lower Lake, whose outspill would, in turn be directed into the lower course of the original Ganger stream, later to join the Tadburn stream, one of the tributaries of the middle Test.

Unless the topography is particularly favourable, construction must start with the excavation of the lake site. The displaced earth is then used for building the dam. A spillway, not less than 24" (60 cms) from the top of the dam, must be provided, so that even in the worst spate conditions, no water is likely to run over the dam. A drainage system for emptying the lake must be built-in at the deepest point, unless water pumps are to be used for this purpose. The optimum depth must be determined before excavating begins, but, as will be seen later, this is not entirely a matter of choice.

Earth shifting is a highly developed mechanical art where bulldozers, with their enormous implanted power, make light work of the heavy task. Fortunately, they can be hired, together with their crews, and usually by a choice of method. One can arrange either a fixed sum of money for the job to be done, or they can be hired on a time basis at so much per hour for machine and crew. The Behrendts chose the latter, and by cultivating good relations with the driver and his assistant, and by pandering to their perpetual passion for cups of tea, they ensured that the hours they paid for produced the maximum output. The saving in cost was considerable.

In determining depth, account must be taken of its effect on the vital ingredients of the water. As we have seen, sunlight is the essential substance that kindles and renews the fundamental living tissues. Water, however, resists the passage of sunlight, and the denser the organic constituents in the water, the more it resists. In waters rich with organic constitutents, it may penetrate to a depth of about 20 ft (6 m), whereas in less rich water, it may penetrate to a depth of about 30 ft (9 m). Below this sunlit zone, the temperature falls very rapidly, and all is dark and cold. Here vegetation is absent and conditions are too inhospitable for the bulk of living organisms, the only exceptions being a few specialised creatures that have adapted themselves to an existence in a low oxygen environment. Active creation is confined almost entirely to the upper layer through which the sun's light permeates. The cold layer below and the warm layer above do not mix throughout the summer, but they do so in winter when both layers are reduced to the same temperature.

At Two Lakes, the maximum depth is not more than 15 ft. (4·6 m), thus ensuring that creative activity is total over the lake. The fall in temperature during the summer is fairly constant at about 1° C for every 60 cms (2 ft) of depth, so that the difference between the top and extreme bottom of the lake is no more than 6° or 7° C. This results in a wealth of animal and plant life with its consequential benefit to fish production. There are certain drawbacks however. In the first place, the intensive creative activity can result in excessive growth of water plants which restrict the amount of fishing space and hamper free trout movement. Secondly, the water tends to overheat in summer, losing much of its oxygen, particularly if the season is dry and the water level falls. At such times, masses of algae aggregate and cover the surface, irritating the anglers and perhaps giving off noxious smells. The combined action of the algae and the excessive plant growth can be lethal to trout during the hours of darkness when the vegetation absorbs much of the already low oxygen content.

Fortunately, the problem of excessive algaeic growth is not as severe in Great Britain as in many other countries, although it can be a nuisance to fishermen and to water engineers. Some species of algae can be poisonous to man, animals and fish, and where these and non-toxic types exist, it has been found that they can be controlled by applications of copper sulphate, which is not only effective and easily applied, but also fairly cheap. The sensitivity of fish to it depends on the type of fish, the density of organic matter in the water, its hardness, temperature and other conditions. One of the simplest ways of administering it is by spraying a 10 per cent solution of $CuSO_4 \, 5H_2O$ onto the surface from a boat. Nowadays, in Europe and America it is used more as a prophylactic than a cure; in fact, all researchers agree that, properly used, no damage is caused to the fish and algaeic blooms are retarded or destroyed according to the dosage. In Israel, a recent spectacular bloom, which was so heavy that attempts to remove it with pitchforks failed, began to fade two days after applying 5 kgs per acre (12 kgs per Hectacre), and completely disappeared after five days without any deleterious effect on the fish. It must be remarked that the fish were carp, which can withstand about twice as great a concentration of the sulphate as trout before being affected. It is interesting to note that experiments over a period of years in a series of lakes at Fairmont show that where copper sulphate was used as a prophylactic, the fish crop increased by 9 per cent.

[5]

The Dam

I heard (alas! 'twas only in a dream)
Strains—which, as sage Antiquity believed,
By waking ears have sometimes been received
Wafted adown the wind from lake or stream;
A most melodious requiem, a supreme
And perfect harmony of notes.   WORDSWORTH

All rivers, large and small, run downhill, the gradient varying from river to river and from place to place. One of the easiest ways to construct an artificial lake is to dig a hole in the path of a river, stream or brook, and to wait for it to fill with water. Within the limits of the available land, the size of the lake is a matter of choice, as are its depth and contours. The more gradual the gradient, the easier the task. This uncomplicated prescription is probably justified when ornament or landscaping is the objective, but for a fishery, particularly a trout fishery, its inadequacy lies in the protracted task of getting rid of the water when emptying the lake is necessary. This can be done only with the aid of water-pumps, a tedious and perhaps costly business.

Another simple method, but with the advantage that a practical gravity drainage system can be incorporated without difficulty and at moderate expense, is to erect a dam across the narrowest part of a valley which is intersected by a stream. Where the gradient and the steepness of the banks are favourable, it is possible to dispense with excavating, but locations of this type are not easy to find.

In most cases, both excavating and the erection of a dam will be necessary, but whether excavating is necessary or not, providing a gravity drainage system is to be included in the structure, we find ourselves subject to a set of rules or principles, that must be observed irrespective of topographical features, if the lake is to survive.

Our main concern is with the dam, which is the buttress and the

50

backbone of an artificial lake. From time immemorial dams have been constructed of earth, stones, timber and of masonry, but in recent years the materials have been concrete, and even steel, in addition to earth and masonry. Here we are concerned only with earthen dams, and only where the lake concerned is constructed with an integral gravity drainage system that can be operated simply at will. It should at once be stressed that, providing the rules are observed, earthen dams are permanent, convenient to build if material is readily at hand, and very cheap to install and maintain.

The function of a dam is twofold; first, to withstand the pressure of the water it supports, even when the pressure is reinforced by gales, and secondly, to resist the more insidious ravages of unseen seepage. It must be watertight, for any water passing through the dam, or over the top, will form ruts which constant scouring will enlarge and develop into breaches. This can be prevented by the design of the dam, and by the provision of a spillway, or outfall, cut into the dam, preferably adjacent to it in the virgin soil, formed in concrete or masonry, so that the level of the lake surface is always below the top of the dam even in times of spate. It is an added advantage to form the core of the dam out of clay or fine impermeable silt, but this is not essential.

Irrespective of any other consideration, the dam must key itself to the virgin soil upon which it is built. Any failure of the bond between the two will open up a fissure through which the water will leak and eventually cause considerable mischief. To obviate this, a trench not less than 1 metre wide, but more if possible, should be cut for the whole length of the dam site at its central position before building is started. The depth of the trench should be sufficient to reach an impermeable stratum. In addition, all vegetation must be removed from the soil on which the dam is to sit; if not, it will rot and leave a gap through which the water will escape. Nor must any timber, or wood of any kind, fresh or seasoned, be built into the dam, for as it decays, it will leave cavities through which seepage will occur.

The spillway should be provided at about 1 metre below the top of the dam, but on no account should it be less than 60 cms (24 in). It must be wide enough to deal effectively with all flood water likely to enter the lake under the most extreme conditions. Many dams have been severely damaged by the failure of the builder to recognise that a small placid feeder stream can change to a raging torrent after many consecutive days of heavy rain, a phenomenon not unknown in this country. At Two Lakes, the spillway is about 4 metres (13 ft) wide. It is obvious that the position of the spillway will govern the surface level of the lake, and as this is exactly at the same level of the point where the feeder stream enters the lake, it follows that the top of the dam will be about 1 m above the level of the latter. Care must be taken to avoid constructing a spillway above the height of the point of stream entry into the lake, for unless this is done, the lake water will flow up the feeder stream and perhaps cause difficulties with the owners of the neighbouring land.

For emptying the lake, a pipe of adequate diameter is laid at the bottom of the lake at the deepest part sloping gently down through the dam to its outer foot or thereabouts, so that when the lake is drained, the water will be discharged close to the lower course of the feeder stream. The opening of the pipe is controlled by a sluice, but more of this later.

As the pipe is to slope downwards from the deepest part of the lake to a point near the outer foot of the dam, it follows that there is a close association between the two locations in terms of height level. Obviously, no part of the lake can be deeper than the point of discharge if complete water evacuation is wanted by a gravity fall. Therefore, the depth of the lake is dependent on the contour of the land, or the gradient of the stream. This is a factor of great importance, and I propose to set it out in clear terms as follows: the maximum depth of the lake depends on the position where the external wall of the dam meets the stream and, as this depends on the gradient, the maximum depth of the lake depends on the gradient.

For the purposes of my calculations and illustrations, I have adopted as my datum line the actual course of the stream. Gradients given are those of the stream, and distances are between points on the stream. Moreover, I have reduced gradients to straight lines although in most cases they will be varied, at some places being steeper than at others. Neither this nor my assumptions that the course of the stream is a straight line will affect the issue, unless the curvature of the stream is very complex. My concentration on the course of the stream does not imply that the contour of the banks is unimportant; indeed, it is very important, for the extremities of the dam must join the banks within the land available, and if the latter do not rise sufficiently to meet the top of the dam, it must be continued along the flanks of the lake. Providing, however, that the main principles are observed, this should present no difficulty, apart from the extra cost involved.

The main principles are few in number. They are:—

(1) The gradient of the inner wall of the dam must not be steeper than 1 in in 4. (Angle 14° approx.)

(2) The gradient of the outer wall of the dam must not be steeper than 1 in 3. (Angle 18° 30 mins approx.)

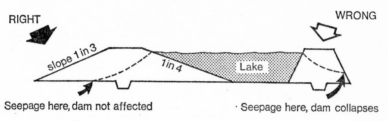

Cross section of a dam.

(3) The width of the dam at the top (to which we will refer as "the plateau") shall not be less than the height of the dam at the centre of the plateau.

A dam built on these precepts will withstand the pressures generated by the water, and will not be susceptible to seepage. The diagram above illustrates the dangers of the latter, and how it is overcome by correct design.

I propose to describe the practical operations of building the dam on the principles enunciated in the previous pages. Before doing so I must explain that the need for clarity both of calculation and of descriptive illustrations has persuaded me to adopt theoretical dimensions and gradients for the lake site, that are untypical and uneconomic. As, however, no two sites are alike, each lake must be tailored individually and it is only the method that matters; the form of structure can be calculated to suit the site. The calculations require simple trigonometry, but it can be done almost as simply by scale drawings on ordinary graph paper.

The first thing to determine is the point in the feeder stream at which the lake is to begin. The next is to determine the point of "the pivot", which is the position on the stream directly below the centre of the plateau. This will depend upon the amount of land available, but it must be borne in mind that the steeper the gradient of the stream, the more the space that will be wanted for the outer wall of the dam. It is as well, therefore, to make no positive commitment until the whole of the dam dimensions have been calculated and shown to be containable within the site.

When the two positions, the stream entry and the pivot, have been marked on the site, the difference in height levels must be obtained. This can be done precisely by a Surveyor engaged for the purpose, or fairly closely by a handyman with a couple of straight poles, a ball of string, a builder's tape measure, and a decent spirit level. The difference in height levels, or the landfall, governs the height of the dam, which will be equal to the landfall plus 1 metre. The gradient can now be calculated by dividing the distance between the two points by the landfall. Thus, if the distance is 120 units and the landfall 12 units, the gradient is 1 in 10. (A unit can be a metre, a foot, a yard, or any dimension.) This ignores compound and varying gradients within the distance. It will be recognised that the steeper the gradient, the taller will be the dam, and as the width of the plateau must be equal to the height of the dam, the wider the plateau.

The next important position to find is the foot of the outer wall of the dam. This is a problem rather like that of the chicken and the egg, for in order to find this position, we must first know the gradient, and to find the gradient we must first know the position. In practice, however, one can get a good idea of the gradient by checking at two or three different positions. The outer wall, when plotted, will determine the amount of land wanted, but it is vital to verify the gradient once this position is found, and if necessary, to plot the wall again, and to verify again. The Table on page 57 will be useful in estimating the distance involved for various gradients. From it can be seen that the steeper the gradient, the more the land that will be wanted to complete the dam. The site therefore must be apportioned correctly if one does not wish to encroach on neighbouring land, or alternatively, to accept the risk of disregarding an essential principle.

It must be stressed once again that the spillway and the point of entry of the stream into the lake are to be at the same level, which will be the surface level of the lake. The height of the spillway from the pivot will therefore be equal to the landfall between the point

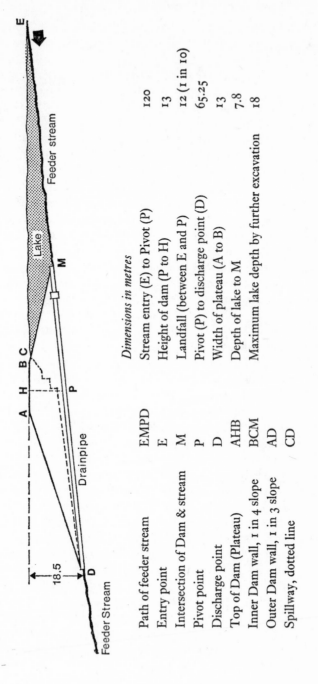

Landfall 1 in 10

Feeder stream

Lake

Drainpipe

18.5

Feeder Stream

Path of feeder stream	EMPD
Entry point	E
Intersection of Dam & stream	M
Pivot point	P
Discharge point	D
Top of Dam (Plateau)	AHB
Inner Dam wall, 1 in 4 slope	BCM
Outer Dam wall, 1 in 3 slope	AD
Spillway, dotted line	CD

Dimensions in metres

Stream entry (E) to Pivot (P)	120
Height of dam (P to H)	13
Landfall (between E and P)	12 (1 in 10)
Pivot (P) to discharge point (D)	65.25
Width of plateau (A to B)	13
Depth of lake to M	7.8
Maximum lake depth by further excavation	18

of stream entry and the pivot. The top of the dam will be about 1 metre above the spillway, but on no account must it be less than 65 cms, (24 ins).

Let us now suppose that we have a site which is 220 m (721 ft) long. The width is unimportant at this stage. We start our lake at a point in the feeder stream 20 metres (65 ft) from the top boundary, leaving 200 metres (656 ft) at our disposal for the lake and dam. We mark out our pivot at 120 metres (393 ft) from the entry of the stream, and we find the landfall between them to be 12 metres (39 ft), a gradient of 1 in 10. Our dam will now be 13 metres (43 ft) high and the plateau will be the same width. The spillway will be constructed 1 metre (3 ft) below the top of the dam, if possible in virgin soil. We plot all this on drawing or graph paper, as shown on page 55.

The inner wall can be plotted at a gradient of 1 in 4. It will meet the stream at a point we mark M. The outer wall can also be plotted, and assuming that the gradient beyond the pivot is still 1 in 10, the wall will meet the stream approximately 65 metres (213 ft) from the pivot. The outer wall will thus end about 15 metres (45 ft) from our lower boundary, and about 18·5 metres (62 ft) below the surface level of the lake. The depth of the lake to point M will be 7·8 metres (25½ ft), and although excavation deeper than this is possible, it is best avoided owing to complications that may arise. In any case the maximum depth possible is less than 18·5 metres (62 ft).

It will be seen from the Table on page 57 that the length of the dam, its height, the maximum depth of water and the length of the lake depend on the gradient of the land, or on the landfall between the salient features. However, although gradients of 1 in 5 and 1 in 10 are included in the Table, neither are practical or economic. They have been included to illustrate the importance of the gradients. The gradient 1 in 20 is suitable for small lakes of the order of about 120 metres (393 ft) long. Gradients less steep than 1 in 40 are suitable for larger lakes, but factors such as the height of the dam and its length must be first calculated and taken into account. It must not be taken for granted that the gradient from the point of stream entry to the pivot will be the same as from the pivot to the foot of the outer wall. Indeed, if the land should fall away rapidly beyond the pivot, difficulty may be encountered in constructing the outer wall at all. The smaller the landfall beyond the pivot, the better.

We will now assume that the main features of the lake have been plotted and marked on the site. The maximum depth will have been

The Spillway under construction

Alex Behrendt (left) and the author

Sedge fly (*Rhyacophila dorsalis*) Ronald's sand fly

A quiet corner of Border Lake

Brown Trout, 9 lb 11 oz. caught at Two Lakes,
September 1968 by Barrie Welham

decided and located, and we know where the foot of the outer wall of the dam will meet the lower course of the stream, which we will now refer to as the discharge point. At this stage, a trench must be dug along the bank of the stream from the proposed deepest point of the lake to the discharge point. The trench, which should be cut as near as possible to the stream without actually penetrating the

P PIVOT, i.e. Centre of Dam at Stream level.
E Entry of Feeder Stream into Lake.
D Discharge Point at Outer Foot of Dam.
H Height of Dam from PIVOT.
M Point where inner wall meets stream.

LENGTH FROM STREAM ENTRY TO PIVOT (E–P) = 120 METRES (394 Ft.)

Gradient	Pivot to discharge P–D	Height of dam P–H	Max. possible lake depth	Length of lake	Depth at point M
1 in 5	224 m (735 ft)	25 m (82 ft)	69 m (226 ft)	103 m (340 ft)	10·5 m (34 ft)
1 in 10	65 m (213 ft)	13 m (43 ft)	18 m (60 ft)	109·5 m (359 ft)	7·8 m (25 ft)
1 in 20	28·8 m (95 ft)	7 m (23 ft)	7·4 m (24 ft)	112·5 m (369 ft)	4·6 m (15 ft)
1 in 40	15·1 m (49 ft)	4 m (13 ft)	4·4 m (14 ft)	114 m (374 ft)	2·5 m (8 ft)
1 in 10 to Pivot 1–5 from Pivot to Discharge	116 m (380 ft)	13 m (43 ft)	34·9 m (115 ft)	109·5 m (359 ft)	7·8 m (25 ft)

water table or causing a break of the bank, should start at the discharge end, so that all seepage water runs away without becoming a nuisance. At the lake end, the depth of the trench should reach as far as the proposed maximum depth of the finished lake, which, it must be remembered, cannot be lower than the point of discharge. In fact, it must be a little higher, so that the pipe housed in the trench will slope down from the lake to the discharge point. At Two Lakes, the pipe is concrete, 30 cms (12 in) in diameter, and is laid in sections, each fitting into its neighbour. The last three or four sections are cemented at the joints and are embedded in a concrete block to prevent shifting due to water pressure. One or two large concrete collars built around the pipe below the lake end of the dam would prevent leakage of water on the outside of the pipe, but this would not be essential if the core of the dam is impermeable to water.

At the lake end, the pipe rests on a large concrete foundation, the dimensions of which depend on the nature of the subsoil and the depth of the lake. If the subsoil is soft and likely to turn into mud, the area of the block must be sufficient to prevent it subsiding. This foundation will be required to support the substantial concrete walls of the sluice that will rise from it. The height of the walls will be something more than the proposed depth of the water, probably to the extent of about 30 cms (1 ft). At Two Lakes, the foundation is about 3 metres, × 3 metres, × 1 metre (9 ft × 9 ft × 3 ft), and the depth of the water above its top face about 4 metres (13 ft). The walls of the sluice are high enough to protrude above the water surface 30 cms (1 ft). The walls themselves are 20 cms (8 ins) thick.

The pipe, securely resting on its foundation, does not extend beyond it into the lake. The rear wall of the sluice will be built around the pipe and cemented to it so that there are no gaps between them. The two side walls will also be erected, and the front wall. The latter, however, which faces the lake, will have a gap of about 30 cms (1 ft) wide, like an open doorway, running from top to bottom, with grooves about 4 cms (1½ ins) wide incorporated in the two sides of the open gap into which a board or shutter can be introduced to slide up or down. At Two Lakes, the grooves are formed by inserting channel-iron lengths into the sluice walls while the concrete is still wet. The board or shutter must be watertight and well greased with silicon or water-pump grease to facilitate movement up or down. The material used should be non-warping, and if of timber, probably cedar or elm are as good as any. Oak should not be used in iron grooves, for when immersed in water it exudes a substance which corrodes the metal. Needless to say, the concrete walls of the sluices must be sufficiently strong to withstand the pounding of the water under flood conditions.

The sluice is closed when the shutter is down, resting on the concrete foundation, and open when the shutter is raised. Care in the construction is essential in order to ensure a smooth action in the shutter movement, and frequent inspection is advisable to test the action so that no jamming will occur if for any reason a speedy water evacuation is necessary.

The shutter, or hatch as it is usually called, is operated in most cases mechanically, either by rack and pinion, or by some similar method. The hatch is raised when draining commences, and the water filters out from the bottom. The method used at Two Lakes is different. Here the hatch is not a single shutter, but consists of 5 loose boards, made of elm wood, each sitting on top of a lower one, with the bottom one sitting on the foundation block. When the lake is to be emptied, the top board is removed, and the water spills out from the top. As soon as the surface level is down to the next board, it too is lifted out, and so on, each board being lifted out in turn until the lake is drained. This method has the advantage of being so simple that no mechanism nor any device for holding the hatch suspended in an elevated position is required. In addition, short boards are less likely to distort and jam in raising and lowering than long ones.

Prevention of leakage through the hatch may be something of a problem, but this can be overcome by the liberal use of water-pump grease at joints, and by throwing hot ashes from a fire into the water immediately in front of the sluice. The ashes must be hot to ensure that they are perfectly dry, for when they are carried by the water onto the sluice, they clog the grease, and as they become saturated, swell and fill the tiny crevices.

In practice, it may be found that if the fit of the boards is good enough to render the hatch water-tight, removing them will prove to be a laborious task, and this could be serious during an emergency. On the other hand, if they are to remain a good easy slide fit, the hatch will probably leak a little. This will be of no concern where the inflow of water is plentiful, but is undesirable if the feeder stream dries up in summer. At Two Lakes, the more important hatches are tightly sealed, and in the event of an emergency, the boards are chopped out with an axe. The cost of replacing them on the few occasions when it is necessary, is quite small, and is amply compensated by the conservation of the water.

Our next step will be to divert the stream into the drainage pipe, thus providing a dry base for constructing the dam. The pipe is now in its permanent position and the sluices constructed, but the hatch boards not yet fitted.

Excavating can now begin, either with a bulldozer, or, if the site is soft and muddy, with a mechanical excavator that runs on tracks. As the soil is removed, it is immediately transferred to the dam site, where it becomes consolidated by the frequent passage of the bull-dozer. It is vital that the dam should be well rolled and compacted, each layer of fresh soil being treated individually.

Unlike the dam, the slope at the edges of the lake or at the base of the inner dam wall, where excavating into virgin soil commences, can be at any angle, but it is as well to keep it gentle at the edges in case an angler loses his balance and falls into the water, a circumstance not entirely unknown.

When excavating, one must remember that if the banks of the proposed lake are thickly wooded, or too steep for comfortable walking, anglers will be unable to cast their flies for lack of a clear background. Therefore a number of land spurs must be left intact, extending about 10 metres (30 ft) into the lake onto which the angler can walk, and, if he feels like it, bring a stool to sit on. On a steep bank, a path must be cut wide enough for walking in comfort.

Finally, the bed of the lake should contain no hollows where water will lie when the lake is drained. Such hollows will form pockets where undesirable fish will lie concealed and so defeat the object of draining.

[6]

The Spillway and Eel Trap

Est in aqua dulci non invidiosa voluptas.
(There is a delight in sweet waters that none will grudge.)
                    OVID. Epistulae ex Ponto. BK 2, 7, 73

The depth of the dam, which is at its maximum at the point where it meets the feeder stream, gradually reduces as it stretches out along the rising banks, until it merges with the virgin soil. At this position, or close to it, the Spillway should be situated.

Its function, as has already been explained, is to prevent the level of the lake rising above it, and thus it must be capable of quickly exhausting the maximum amount of water likely to enter the lake even under exceptional conditions. It may be many years, if ever, before it will be called upon to cope with such conditions, but in a matter of such importance, it is better to be safe than sorry.

Even under ordinary conditions, the force of water flow concentrated against the Spillway and its adjacent soil can be very strong; in spate conditions, it can become an angry torrent, tearing and raging at the flanks of the Spillway as though determined to enlarge it and release itself from the confinement of the dam. The construction therefore demands that Spillway flanks, where it meets the dam or the embankment, should be protected by stout shields of concrete or masonry.

The Spillway is formed by removing a section of the soil at the top of the dam adjacent to the natural bank to a depth of about 2 metres (7 ft), and about 3 or 4 metres (10–13 ft) wide. This should remove all the built-up earth and leave us on virgin soil. The bottom of the cut-out, or trench, thus formed, should be parallel to the plateau and in line with it for a distance equal to half its width. It should then slope down, preferably in a series of deep wide steps, until it reaches the outer foot of the dam close to the lower course of the feeder stream. The trench itself can narrow down from the lake end to about half its width at the outer dam foot.

A front wall, with a strong foundation, must now be built of brick or cement partially to close the cut-out, immediately below the edge of the plateau, to a height of about 1 metre (3 ft) below the top of the dam; the wall should be continued along either side of the dam beyond the cut-out for a distance of about 60 cms (2 ft), and upwards to the top of the dam, or even a little higher, to protect the flanks of the Spillway from erosion of the water flow. Inside the cut-out, the brick or cement front wall must be buttressed for the whole of its height by a solid block of concrete formed at an angle of 45°. The floor of the cut-out must be cemented, and the sides lined with substantial concrete or brick walls to the full height of the dam. The soil which was removed from the dam or embankment on the lake side of the front wall can be replaced, so that the bank immediately in front of the Spillway front wall slopes gently down instead of being precipitous.

For the time being, we shall leave the Spillway, and turn our attention to eels, a species of fish of great interest to biologists because of their unique life history. Born in incalculable numbers in the depths of the Sargasso Sea, where it is presumed their parents perish, they begin their journey to Europe borne on the ocean currents. At this stage they are translucent blobs of protoplasm, incapable of controlling their movements; but as they approach the shores of Europe about 3 years later they develop into young eels known as elvers. They head for the estuaries and ascend the rivers, making their homes in any running or stillwater that will sustain them, sometimes travelling overland to reach their objective. About 8–12 years later, fully matured, they leave their freshwater homes and return to their birth-place where they spawn and die.

They eat any animal food, alive or dead, and although there is some doubt concerning their danger to trout, they undoubtedly consume a significant proportion of the available food of the lakes they inhabit. This diminution of the biomass is permanent as their victims are lost forever to the economy of the lake when the eels eventually leave for their spawning grounds.

For this reason it is thought desirable to exclude them from the lakes, on the principle that keeping them out is far better than trying to get them out once they are in.

In the normal way the path of the eels into the lakes would take

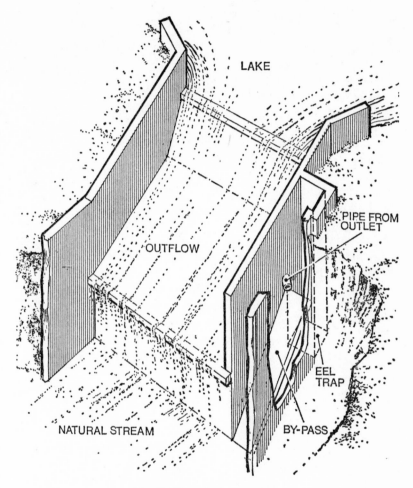

LAKE

PIPE FROM
OUTLET

OUTFLOW

EEL
TRAP

NATURAL STREAM

BY-PASS

The Spillway and Eel Trap.

them up the feeder stream and through the Spillway. Should the design of the latter prevent their progress they would leave the stream and wriggle their way over the dam. To prevent this the dam and the embankment in the vicinity of the Spillway should be planted liberally with Scots Pine and/or Larch, both of which regularly shed their needles onto the soil below. These sharp needles prevent the passage of the eels very effectively.

The Spillway itself prevents them passing through by the bottom steps having overhanging edges or lips, the overhang being about 15 cms (6 in). Although the eels could possibly climb the steps they cannot negotiate the overhanging lips.

A further safeguard is provided by a small, false Spillway, about 30 cms (12 in) wide, and about 2 metres (6 ft) long, cut at the side on the genuine Spillway at the outer foot of the dam, which terminates into a deep pit into which the eels fall and out of which they cannot climb. The false Spillway is fed with water through a pipe which communicates with it through the genuine Spillway floor. It must be remembered, however, that the pipe must be suspended above the floor of the false Spillway by about 30 cms (12 in), so that the eels cannot reach it and swim through it.

[7]

The Offset Lake

I also love a quiet place
That's green, away from all mankind;
A lonely pool, and let a tree
Sigh with her bosom over me.

                                                  W. H. DAVIES

In the previous chapters, the methods described are those adopted and developed at Two Lakes, and are eminently suitable for sites of similar conditions and geography. Now, however, we must consider an alternative lay-out where the characteristics of the feeder stream or the land either do not permit replication or, if adopted, might in time seriously impair the project and its economy.

First and foremost the nature of the stream and its constituents must be examined. If because of a rapid current or because of the type of country it traverses it carries a substantial or even moderate suspension of sand, gravel, mud or similar sedimentation, there is a fair probability that any lake it flows through will silt up and become unsuitable for trout unless it is occasionally dredged. The latter would be costly.

This inconvenience could be obviated by constructing an offset lake which the stream would fill but which it would permanently by-pass; topping up would be comparatively easy when necessary. The diagram on page 67 illustrates the simplicity of the design.

Indeed, when planning an artificial lake, the benefits of an offset design over that of the orthodox type already described must be seriously considered. It certainly could have many advantages to compensate the added cost, which might not necessarily accrue in any case. The doctrine that an offset lake, lacking a continuous oxygenated flow of water through it, would be deleterious to the trout is demonstrably incorrect. They could be quite happy in flowless stillwaters providing other conditions are suitable. Of

65

course it can be argued, and indeed it is, that even flowless waters do in fact experience a current of sorts due to wind action, to seepage from the surrounding countryside, and to thermal factors; but these add little, if anything, to the oxygen content.

What, then, in addition to freedom from silting, are the benefits of an offset lake, and what are the criteria that influence the planning decision?

In the first place, an offset lake avoids the risk borne by an orthodox lake of overflowing its dam because the spillway cannot exhaust flood water quickly enough. Unfortunately, it is impossible to forecast accurately whether an apparently gentle stream flowing through a lake is so potentially dangerous that it could cause damage in exceptional spate conditions. The best yardstick is probably the width of the stream; if it is normally expressed in centimetres or inches, it is fairly safe to run it through a lake, but if it is normally expressed in feet or metres an offset lake would be safer.

The second important criterion is the presence of coarse fish in the stream. These can be excluded comparatively easily from an offset lake, but not from one that engulfs the stream. Even fine screening which will impede the passage of the smallest fish will eventually become blocked with debris, and although it can be kept clear for the short period of filling and of topping up an offset lake, it cannot be done permanently, as would be necessary in an orthodox lake, without a great deal of trouble. When topping up is required, only small quantities of water are wanted, and there would be no difficulty in filtering it through a box or pipe filled with gravel. This would ensure the exclusion of undesirable fish at all times.

Finally, either pollution, or excesses of chemical substances, or similar imbalances would have no affect on an offset lake already filled with clean water. Other factors, such as the position of the stream relative to the available land, might render such a solution desirable. These factors could include the proximity to the stream of buildings, a belt of trees, a coppice or a particular meadow, or even because one bank rises too suddenly and too steeply to make excavation a practical proposition. The various features of each selected site must be the deciding factors in determining whether the lake is to engulf the stream or to be positioned adjacent to it.

The illustration of a simple offset lake on page 67 presupposes a situation where the proposed lake could be constructed adjacent to the course of the natural stream. This may not be possible if the stream, running through the site, so divides it that neither bank is sufficiently spacious, or convenient, to accommodate a lake of the required size. In such circumstances, the feeder stream must be diverted along a line close to one boundary of the site. The new course must be on a down gradient, and this can best be achieved by following a suitable contour line clearly defined by a professional surveyor.

The practices and principles applicable to the erection of the

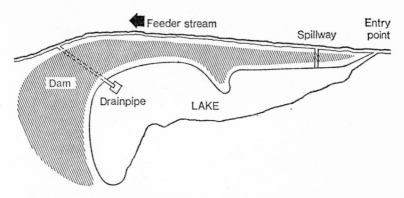

Plan view of Offset Lake. (Courtesy of W. S. R. Malcolm Brown, Esq.)

main dam are similar to those already described. It will be readily seen, however, that although the dam can conceivably meet the rising virgin ground on one side, it cannot do so on the stream side. It must therefore make a sharp turn and interpose itself between the lake and stream, eventually meeting solid ground in the vicinity of the point of water entry, or preferably a little above it. This will necessitate feeding the lake through a pipe or channel which passes below the top of the dam. The reason is as follows.

In extreme spate conditions, when flood water racing down the stream is likely to spill over its banks, it must be kept out of the lake. This is desirable even if a spillway large enough to cope with it is

provided in the structure. Therefore the external wall of the intervening dam must act as a screen and barrier between the lake and
the flood water. It would be an advantage if the embankment, or at
least that section of it likely to be assailed, were built at the same
angle as the inner wall, that is, no steeper than one in four. In extreme
cases, the section should be protected by a shield of concrete or
masonry. With these safeguards, the spillway would be confronted
with the light task of evacuating surface water only, and could be
of moderate proportions.

The space allotted between the feeder stream and the lake for the
intervening dam must be sufficiently generous to permit comfortable
and safe manoeuvring of the earth-shifting machines at a safe
distance from the stream. Tractors and caterpillars can withstand
a fair degree of tilting in the direction of travel, but they cannot
do so laterally; the former, so useful for compacting the soil of the
dam, will be called upon to make many trips up and down the sloping
walls, and if the stream is too close to the area of operations, the
dangers of mishaps are considerably enhanced.

Pipes connecting the stream and the lake, whether for feeding or
emptying, should be as straight as possible. Sharp bends must be
avoided, so that in the event of an obstruction arising, rodding is
possible without the need for manholes or rodding eyes. The feeder
pipe should be fitted with an internally expanding stopper in order
to regulate and control at will the water supply into the lake. If
a feeder channel is preferred to a pipe, a sluice should be included
in it.

The feeder stream should also be equipped, a little below the
tapping-off point, with a sluice, which when in the closed position,
will divert the water through the open feeder pipe or channel.

Alternatively, a pipe with a stopper, running through a build-up
of the stream bed immediately below the tapping-off point will
ensure an uninterrupted flow of water through the feeder pipe or
channel when required.

The feeder pipe may be protected from the incursion of coarse
fish, dead leaves and sundry debris coming down the stream by a
wire mesh screen positioned at an angle to the flow of water in
such a way that the current itself tends to keep it clear and unblocked.

The depth of the lake will be partly dependent upon the same
considerations as have already been described in an earlier chapter,
if a system of draining the lake by gravity is to be built-in. Once

again the limiting factor will be the gradient of the feeder stream over the relevant distance.

The problem of excluding eels from an offset lake is a little more complex than from an orthodox one, for not only must they be denied access through the spillway and over the land adjacent to it, but they must be discouraged from negotiating the full length of the intervening dam lying between the stream and the lake. In addition, passage through the feeder pipe or channel must be closed to them during filling and topping up by screening the flow. Both the spillway and land routes can be made impassable by the methods previously described.

In some cases, no precautions need be taken, for the lower reaches of a number of rivers are so polluted that the elvers refuse to ascend them.

The desirability of incorporating an integral system of gravity drainage in a lake free from coarse fish, as a properly constructed offset lake should be, may validly be questioned. It is true that the benefits of such a system are reduced, but they are certainly not eliminated, for a drained lake facilitates repairs to dams and other works, and if allowed to lie fallow for a period, it rejuvenates itself by exposing the bed to the sun and the elements. Soil lying continuously under water generally decreases in the fertility necessary to nourish the creatures trout feed on, but it can be restored if the water is removed and it is permitted to dry. Mud tends to acidity, is often full of noxious gas, and smells offensively. The air, aided perhaps by a little lime, reduces the acids and encourages the locked-in substances to grow. Indeed, it has been asserted on excellent authority that maximum utilisation of a stillwater requires draining off the water yearly for the duration of the winter, but as this is hardly practical, it should be done every few years. If this is not possible, the water level should be lowered in the winter so that the shallows are exposed, particularly if the weather is fairly dry.

Of course, a small lake without a gravity drainage system can be drained at a reasonable cost by hiring water pumps. The drawback to this method lies in the possibility of the deeper parts of the bottom being below the level of the water table. Should this be so, the pumps would be required to work continuously for the period needed for repairs or for rejuvenation. This could prove quite costly.

[8]

The Trout(1)

meanwhile the calm lake
Grew dark with all the shadows on its breast,
And, now and then, a fish up-leaping snapped
The breathless stillness.   WORDSWORTH

The trout, known to our ancestors as the "truht", probably derived its name from the late Latin progression of words "tructus, tructa, trutta". The origin of the latter is thought to be the Greek "trogein", meaning "to nibble dainty foods", an attribution deservedly conferred on a fish which delights in feeding on insects. Ironically, the fish itself is a dainty food which humans (and other predators) delight to nibble. For this reason, and because of their sporting qualities, they have been introduced into and cultivated in waters all over the world where the physical conditions are suitable. What are these conditions?

Primarily, they are temperature and oxygen content. To some extent, they are inter-dependent, for the ability of water to hold oxygen reduces with its increase in temperature. But irrespective of oxygen content, trout will die very quickly in water at a little over 28° C (82° F) and irrespective of temperature they will die in an oxygen content of only about 5 parts per million. Generally, in a stillwater temperatures above 20° C (68° F) are dangerous if sustained for more than a short spell. In artificial lakes, both these factors can be regulated a little by avoiding too great an area of shallows when excavating, by partly protecting the water with a screen of tall trees from the sun's rays, and by control of the algaeic and plant growths, of which either an excess or a deficiency can be detrimental.

Other factors such as pollution or the influx of sewage can render a stillwater untenable by trout. So indeed can too high a concentration of carbon dioxide, although this can be mitigated by the application of chalk or other forms of calcium. Carbon dioxide is produced by algae and plants at night, by bacteria in the decomposition of decaying substances and by the fish and other aqueous creatures in respiration. This has a tendency to combine with water into carbonic acid. ($CO_2 + H_2O = H_2CO_3$). Waters with a high acidity, unless treated, are not appropriate for trout.

Providing the temperature and the oxygen content are adequate, and the natural acidity not too sharp, trout should flourish in accordance with the quality of the supervision. Of course, the water in which they live will play a large part in determining their growth and their health, but within limits this is subject to amelioration, as has been shown. At Two Lakes, the conductivity of the water (a method of describing the amount of dissolved substances in it) in 1949 was 180, a low figure compared with that regarded as suitable for a trout fishery, which is at least 300. The calcium carbonate figure, or the hardness, was also low compared to what is considered desirable (10 parts per 100,000 as against about 30 parts per 100,000 for a chalk stream). These, and other traditional disadvantages, did not militate against the eventual success of the fishery, a success contrived by the devotion and the determination of the management.

Apart from food, which is perhaps the most important factor in promoting the well-being of the trout, they require protection from predators, and from the feeding competition of rival organisms. These have been dealt with in earlier chapters. Their physical health, and, odd as it may sound, their mental health must be protected as far as possible. The latter is usually referred to as "stress", which is defined generally as any practice or event which influences or changes the behaviour or the internal metabolism of the fish, or even of its progeny, though we are not concerned with this. It can of course be argued that all evolution is the result of stress through environmental deviations occurring very slowly over long periods, during which all organisms adapt themselves or become extinct. The modern studies of stress, however, are concerned with revolutionary changes introduced by man over a very short period.

Although not all environmental changes due to man's interference are harmful to trout, some probably are. In closely controlled waters such as Two Lakes, the practical elimination of predators and the frequent removal of competing coarse fish probably relax some of the strains of aquatic existence. But there is considerable evidence to show that trout react unfavourably to certain practices and conditions that lie within our ability to modify. A recent study conducted by The Pennsylvania State University in conjunction with the United States Bureau of Sports Fisheries and Wildlife is of great interest.

Prior to the opening of the 1969 trout fishing season, all the trout in a 2/3 mile section of a river famous for its wild trout were collected by electroshocking. Almost all were brown trout, and after examination, all fully grown fish, from 2 to 6 year old, were tagged and coded. All the fish were returned to the water, whether tagged or untagged, and when the season opened, they were fished for in the normal way by nearly 300 anglers in the catch-and-release method. Any fish with a tag was reported, and any small ones without a tag were fin-clipped according to an arranged system, and also reported.

The study was ended by July, when it was found that about 50 per cent of the tagged fish had disappeared; about 16 per cent had been captured once, about 7 per cent twice, and about 2 per cent more than twice. Among those caught more than once, not a single one of the older fish was found. A summary of the results, ignoring the question of age, is as follows. The figures are approximate.

Of the 200 fish tagged   50 were caught.
Of the 50 caught   14 were caught twice,
and   4 were caught three times.
At the end of the study period, 100 had disappeared.

The fin-clipped younger fish were caught a little less frequently than the tagged fish. Some of them were recognised as hatchery raised, and it was noticed that a much higher proportion (about double) of these fish were caught more than once. It was presumed that these hatchery trout had migrated into the study area from above or below it.

The trout which disappeared at the end of the study period consisted of about 15 per cent caught fish, and 85 per cent uncaught. But whereas about 50 per cent of all fish had disappeared by July, the proportion of lost hatchery-reared fish was up to 92 per cent.

The study merely confirms what has been suspected for many years, that pricked fish, or hooked fish that get away, are disinclined to rise to an artificial fly, and are therefore a liability to a fishery. This is recognised at Two Lakes and reflected in the regulations. First, no captured fish may be returned to the water. They must be killed, but those under 1 lb (·4 kg) are excluded from the permitted retainable quota. Secondly, shooting head lines are not permitted. The reason for this is that such lines have only one purpose, which is distance casting, and there are grounds for belief that trout which rise to a fly at the extremity of a long line are more liable to be pricked, or insecurely hooked, than otherwise. Thirdly, no wading is permitted, not only because the bed of the lakes near the banks is a popular resort of numerous snails and caddis larvae which would be crushed by trampling boots, but also for its effect on the trout. Nor are boats made available so that trout are not pursued or harried in every nook and cranny of their domain. Finally the fish are rested for a full 6 months every year, and fishing during the season forbidden prior to 9 a m and after dark.

Overstocking can create stresses, in addition to reducing the average amount of nutriment available. So indeed can the insufficiency of open water due to the over-abundance of weed growth. And in water adjacent to airports, research is being conducted into the effects on fish of noise pollution. In the future, it may well be decided in some fisheries to discourage the use of fine leaders and very small flies in order to reduce the number of fish lost after being hooked.

In a commercial fishery, the spectre of disease floats menacingly and unseen over the waters and its inhabitants. Its transfer from place to place is shrouded in mystery. The mischievous agent may be carried by birds or insects, or may travel through the air on breezes or by their own volition. For all we know, their origin might lie in the rain clouds above, or they might be present in small numbers or in an impotent strain in all waters until a synchronism of events produces an atmosphere favourable to their expansion and virulence. Although therefore it can never be prevented entirely, the threat can be minimised by various precautionary measures, some of which have been described.

In natural conditions, the mortality rate of brown trout is enormous, and this probably applies to rainbow trout too in countries where they spawn without interference. Some authorities, after having conducted extensive research, put the survival rate at the end of a single year at a bare $2\frac{1}{2}$ per cent, and of these only about 1 in 5 will be alive to celebrate their second birthday. If these figures are correct, the average number of eggs shed by the female fish and fertilised must be no less than 400 to ensure survival. This figure is about normal on hungry rivers, but on the rich chalk streams it is nearer 1,500. In this case, if population figures remain constant, losses must be far higher. Nor does this take into account the ravages of the angling fraternity. It is likely that the general biological concept of the survival of the fittest ordains that the weaker members of the species are removed from participation in the procreative processes; but in the modern hatcheries where the number of ova are between 2,000 and 3,000 per fish per annum, losses are very small indeed, due chiefly to protection against predators. Therefore the stock will contain many weaker fish whose resistance to the hazards of aquatic life is considerably lower than surviving mature wild fish. More care must be taken therefore to safeguard the health of hatchery fish than would be necessary with wild fish. In an enclosed society such as a stillwater, any contagion can spread rapidly and decimate the population.

Trout, like most living creatures, support a number of parasites, some of them virulent and, if numerous, lethal. These parasites may invade the intestines, the air bladder, the gills, the eyes, the skin or the bile duct. Some attach themselves to the fish and suck its blood, and other interfere with the ordinary metabolic processes. The fish may be attacked directly, or the parasites may be acquired from infected food. Fortunately, none of the organisms that infect trout have any effect on man, particularly if the fish is cooked. In most cases, fish accumulate parasites with age, so that the dangers of serious infection increase as the fish grow older. The remedy for this is to ensure that the older fish are removed and younger fish introduced to replace them. Indeed, the higher the turnover of captured fish, the more healthy the fishery is likely to be. Finally, the less coarse fish in a fishery, the less the chances of an epidemic.

In the main, however, the ever present dangers of disease are best overcome by the ability of the fish to resist the attacks of the infesting organisms, whatever their origin. The stock must be healthy, the environment wholesome, tension avoided, and above all, food must be adequate and nutritious. As in all living creatures, food has a double function; first, to provide energy, and secondly, to renew and add to the bodily tissues. If the supply is insufficient, the energy can be adversely affected, and the growth can be retarded or even diminished. The heavier the fish, as is obvious, the more its food requirement. But this also varies in accordance with the temperature; in very cold water, when the temperature is just above zero, trout almost cease feeding, and in water over 18° C (65° F) their appetites become very much less sharp. In between these extremes, it will generally be found that the higher the temperature, the more food they will consume, the best feeding usually occurring in the warm days of spring. It has been noticed at Two Lakes that irrespective of these general rules, there are occasions, not infrequent, when the growing fish in the rearing ponds do not respond to manual feeding in the normal brisk manner. On the contrary, they all but ignore the food being showered on them. The reason for these lapses is unknown, but it is significant that at such times the fish in the various lakes are almost impossible to bring to the fly. Various theories have been advanced for this phenomenon, but they all appear to be more igenious than convincing. Observation has shown that this disinclination to feed is not dependent on temperature, or on a particular atmospheric condition. It can happen in good weather or in bad, wet days or dry, warm or cold. Generally however the following day brings a change in the weather, and feeding re-starts in rearing pool and in lake. It may be thought that the fish possess some sentient faculty which enables them to predict approaching weather changes, but even if this is true, it's hard to see why this should put them off their food.

Advances in artificial feeding of trout in rearing ponds have been rapid and of revolutionary effect. Until the Second World War, fish had been raised on a diet of horseflesh, usually liver, cut manually and monotonously into small morsels. The scarcity and high cost of labour made fish farms ready to welcome the American post-war introduction of pellets, prepared mostly from white fish meal, yeast, skimmed milk and proteins, the latter amounting to approximately 37 per cent of the bulk. It was soon found that 3 lb of pellets produced 1 lb of trout flesh, whereas the same weight of horseflesh produced only 7 ozs. Unfortunately, the pellets were responsible for the fish contracting skin diseases, due to certain deficiencies in the diet. This was remedied in due course, and the best pellets produce 1 lb of trout flesh for something less than 2 lb of pellets. Smaller fish do even better, converting at something like 1·4–1·75 :1, depending on conditions. A typical modern composition manufactured by a leading nutrition company is as follows:

Marine Fish Meals	45%
Vegetable Protein	5%
Cereal By-products	$33\frac{1}{2}$%
Grass Leaf Meal	$2\frac{1}{2}$%

Fats and Oils	$2\frac{1}{2}\%$
Fermentation By-products	$7\frac{1}{2}\%$
Vitamins and Minerals	$3\frac{3}{4}\%$

The size of the pellets vary according to the size of the fish for which they are intended. The Manufacturers usually give instructions on pellet dispensation relative to fish size and current temperature.

Where pink fleshed trout are required, the pigment Canthaxanthin, which is a specific Carotenoid, can be added to the pellets for a little extra cost. Many anglers, including the writer, have always preferred pink trout for the table, considering it to be gastronomically superior to the white or greyish kind. But until the introduction of Canthaxanthin, the capture of a pink fleshed trout appeared to be quite fortuitous, for the same stretch of a river, or the same stillwater would produce either at apparent random.

Full pigmentation takes at least 6–8 weeks, or more when feeding is at a low intake. If the pigment is withdrawn, the flesh will gradually lose colour, unless plenty of food containing Canthaxanthin is found naturally in the water the trout inhabit. Shrimps and snails fall into this category. The pellet method, and perhaps the pigment additive, has another extremely beneficial boon, in that the mortality rate of young trout has fallen to a figure of less than 1 per cent of the stock; but of course this might be due to the inclusion of various vitamins or antibiotics in the mixture, or to the balance of its ingredients, and not particularly to the pigment. Certainly many fish farmers attribute the low stock loss to the pigment, and some believe it has a special value for reproduction. Whatever the truth, I am sure that the superiority of the eating quality of pink fleshed trout is most marked.

The part played by Mr Alex Behrendt in the introduction of Canthaxanthin, or Carotene as it is known, into Gt Britain should, I think, be recorded. In actual fact, the pigment had been used on the Continent of Europe for some years, mostly experimentally, and Mr Behrendt through his contacts abroad was fully informed of developments. But whereas in Europe synthetic carotene was being incorporated in trout food, if only in experimental doses, in Britain its use had been limited by specialist zoologists to such purposes as maintaining the bright colour of Ibis and other birds, and as a rich source of pro-vitamin A. Mr Behrendt decided to make some experiments himself, and immediately took steps to import a quantity of shrimp meal from Norway. This was incorporated into a quantity of pellets made for him by a local miller, and fed to a number of trout in an isolated stewpond. The result, after many months of waiting for some evidence of change, was negative, probably because the carotene content was far too small. This did not deter Mr Behrendt for the very good reason that the propagation of pink fleshed trout would probably render their acquisition more desirable than ever. He decided to ask the advice of one of the fishermen who had fished Two Lakes for many years, a Mr Alan Dalton. To him one day in conversation Mr Behrendt mentioned the subject of carotene, and spoke of his wish to discuss the matter with a nutrition expert. Mr Dalton pointed out that he consulted such an expert regularly in the course of his work with life-stock, and invited Mr Behrendt to his farm to meet the gentleman on his next visit. The expert, Mr R R Wartret, was interested, although his Company had no experience of fish pellets. After consultation with his Directors, it was decided to import some synthetic carotene, and to formulate 4 cwt of pellets. When made, they were delivered to Two Lakes, and fed to the trout. In 8 weeks, the flesh had turned as pink as a salmon, and in the weeks that followed the fish appeared to be at the peak of conditon.

Mr Behrendt decided to continue using the pellets, but the Company concerned pointed out that the cost of making the initial quantity had been extremely high, and to manufacture them on the same lines would make the price prohibitive. They calculated that the minimum quantity they could entertain would be in the region of 5 tons, a quantity too large for a fishery the size of Two Lakes. Still undeterred, Mr Behrendt approached a few prominent and friendly trout fisheries and cultivators in the southern part of the country, and persuaded them to participate. They agreed, probably, I suspect, because of their respect for Mr Behrendt's ability and acumen. There is little more to add, except to say than now carotene-containing pellets are almost universally used in trout fisheries.

With typical incongruity, however, Mr Behrendt continues to feed his trout with horse liver once a week, and to see them at it brings to mind a horde of children making a dash for the ice-cream at a party.

The fish have for many years been fed by hand, but this is a practice that will shortly be coming to an end. The best results in manual feeding were achieved by frequent, but restricted, meals. By this means, the fish were saved long bouts of boredom, and it was possible for the dispenser to assess nicely their appetite and to cease supplying the food when it was obvious that they were indifferent to it. The disadvantages of this system were that a great deal of time was spent at it which could have been usefully expended elsewhere; the more vigorous fish obtained too great a share of the food; and when they were released into open water their capacity for foraging for themselves was blunted. Influenced chiefly by the first reason, that is the necessity for conserving labour, the Continental fish farmers introduced automatic dispensing. Various methods were tried, each with the same end, namely, to release a pre-determined quantity of pellets at given intervals. This was not altogether satisfactory, for the machine showered the pools with food whether it was wanted or not. In the latter event, it was wasted, and what was worse, left to rot, for sodden pellets are refused by the trout. The method most favoured is one which allows the fish to operate a pendulum themselves, and in doing so, a machine releases a pellet. It is claimed that the fish learn to operate the instrument within a week, but on one of the largest fish farms in southern England, it was found that they mastered it in 3 or 4 hours, much to the delight of the proprietor. The advantages of such a system are outstanding; no food is wasted, and no external power or labour is required. The cost of such machines, at the time of writing, is well below £20.

[9]

The Trout(2)

The trout by Nature mark'd with many a crimson spot,
As though she curious were in him above the rest,
And of fresh-water fish did note him for the best.

Polyolbion. MICHAEL DRAYTON, 1613

Trout propagation, as opposed to trout rearing, is a specialised industry which is gainful only when conducted on a large scale and generally when its supervision is entirely divorced from the management of a rod-letting fishery. At Two Lakes, it is not attempted; all fish are purchased from commercial hatcheries.

At the close of the fishing season, the stew ponds are emptied and thoroughly cleansed. New fish, ranging in size from 20–28 mm (8–11 in) are then introduced, the deliveries from the trout farms being made at various times between November and March. A few fingerling brown trout are inserted directly into the lakes in order to make use of the plankton, upon which they feed, but the survival rate is quite small. The few that mature, however, grow into fine fish, and these are regarded as something for nothing. The main stock in the stews is transferred to the lakes at intervals throughout the fishing season. The species are mixed, with perhaps a larger percentage of Rainbows, except during the years when an epidemic of U D N was prevalent. At such times, although Two Lakes escaped the epidemic, only Rainbows were purchased.

Let us dwell a few moments on the different species of trout recognised by the scientific world. (I do not include the Chars, *Salvelinus spp*, sometimes referred to as Brook or Lake Trout). They are as follows:

European Brown Trout	*Salmo trutta*
Rainbow Trout	*Salmo gairdneri*
Cut-throat Trout	*Salmo clarkii*
Golden Trout	*Salmo aquabonita*

79

The last three are natives of America, but the Rainbow is now cultivated in trout waters all over the world. The Cut-throat, like the other two, originating in States west of Mississipi, has been successfully raised in other parts of America but due to its limited mature weight, it has been passed over by fisheries in favour of the Rainbow. The Golden Trout is confined to the Pacific seaboard, chiefly Kern County, and as far as I can ascertain, it has not survived transplanting elsewhere. Our interest therefore lies exclusively in Browns and Rainbows.

In some quarters, both the Cut-throat and the Golden species are regarded as sub-species of the Rainbow, but because of their anatomical differences, American Zoologists and Taxonomists have classified them as separate species, and as the fish are indigenous to America, this view must prevail.

The Browns include a number of types which anglers and, indeed, scientists formerly regarded as different species. Seatrout, silvery in colour and migratory by nature, are actually the same species as the Brown Trout, as are the rusty coloured monsters of the lake, the darting midgets of the hillside burns and becks, the ferocious looking cannibals of the lochs and loughs, and the pale spotted beauties of the chalk streams. Their size and colour are nothing more than functions of their environment, a change of which will alter their size and appearance, or those of their progeny. A rusty-coloured brown trout will occasionally migrate with a shoal of sea trout, and eventually it or its progeny will acquire the silvery coat of its companions.

If, it may be asked, appearance and habit is no guide to species, why is the Rainbow classified differently to the Brown? If appearance is to be discounted, the two types are almost identical. What, then, separates them? The differences are as follows:

The Brown Trout has 100 scales in the lateral line; the Rainbow has 119–135.
The Brown has 40–66 blind-ended protrusions in the intestine (Pyloric Caecae); the Rainbow has 12.
The Brown has 80 chromosomes; the Rainbow has 60.
The Brown has less than 18 gill-rakers; the Rainbow has 20.

There also differences in the spotting of the tails, and of course, the Rainbow has a pinkish lateral band. The tail of a Brown may be spotless, or it may show a few scattered spots around the dorsal edge, whereas the tail of a Rainbow is heavily spotted.

Apart from anatomical and appearance differences, there are disparities of behaviour, disposition and character. Rainbows can tolerate slightly warmer water conditions than the Browns, but they are not too keen on cold temperatures. Their food intake, and their growth, is much the greater of the two, but their life span is shorter. They are believed to be more susceptible to disease and to the ravages of parasites, particularly in the presence of coarse fish, than the Browns, although the recent epidemic of U D N, which attacked Brown Trout, to a large extent passed them by. However, this belief is not endorsed by Mr Behrendt. They are more ostentatious feeders, rising to the fly boldly and conspicuously, whereas the Brown feeds discreetly and with circumspection. When hooked, the Rainbow fights with a spectacular abandon that hastens fatigue and defeat, but the Brown in similar peril conserves its strength and displays its sagacity in making the maximum use of weed, deep water, currents and submerged obstacles. The Rainbow spawns in very few places in Europe, although at Two Lakes they are seen to go through the motions at the due time, but whether any offspring result is unknown. Finally, in spite of views to the contrary, I doubt if there is any recognisable difference in their culinary values.

It is an odd reflection on proprietor/angler relations that on the very same day two anglers made contradictory complaints to Mr Behrendt. The first, who had caught only Rainbow trout on his last few visits, expressed his disappointment that there were no Browns in the lakes; the second, who had caught a succession of Brown trout only, asked querulously why no Rainbows were being stocked that season.

At Two Lakes the new stock when delivered from the trout farms is accommodated in seven stew ponds, of which five are rectangular concrete lined troughs, fed from the feeder stream, exhausting into the Upper Lake. They are approximately 36 metres, by 2·5 metres wide, (120 ft × 8 ft) sloping down from 1 metre, (3 ft) deep at the inlet to 1½ metres (5 ft) deep at the outfall. The water is controlled by sluices at either end. The flow is moderate but sufficient, and when in a dry summer it fails or reduces to a trickle, water is pumped up from an adjacent lake to reinforce it. No water plants grow in them, but nevertheless hordes of aquatic animals, which can be seen when the ponds are emptied, live and thrive on the algaeic growths that line the side walls, and on the myriads of tiny particles washed in by the current. Among them are to be found snails, shrimps, nymphs and the larvae of alder and black fly (*Simulium*). The latter cling by their tails to the fast water streaming in at the sluices, their whiskery heads oscillating like an insane pendulum as they trap in their filaments the microscopic snippets on which their sustenance is based.

The other two stew ponds are very different. One is a circular earthen pond about 10 metres, (33 ft) diameter and about $1\frac{1}{4}$ metres (4 ft) deep, fed by water pumped from an adjacent stew, and drained back to the Upper Lake. It lies in the shadow of a large beech tree which sheds its leaves into it each autumn. Among these decaying leaves is one of the largest colonies of alder larvae I have seen, side by side with numerous caddis larvae housed in cases made from the leaves cut into small pouches. The leaves also appear to form the staple diet of the caddis, an assumption later proved to be correct in my insectary, where they were seen to feed almost exclusively on them.

The last stew pond is nothing more than a super-large nylon net, 10 metres, (33 ft.) by 10 metres, the mesh being 12 mm ($\frac{1}{2}$ in), situated in the littoral region of a lake and held in position by stakes. The nylon mesh, strong though it is, is specially treated for extra strength. It is escape proof and quite satisfactory.

When the fish are delivered, care must be taken to equalise the temperatures in the stew pond and the delivery tanks. Differences of more than 3° C (5° F) can be lethal to trout. In the event of any disparity, water from the stew pond should be combined slowly and in stages with that in the tanks until uniformity is obtained, or nearly so. I have no doubt that the trout farmer can be relied on to take all necessary precautions to ensure safe delivery, but a knowledge of the dangers involved can occasionally be of some advantage. According to J J Armistead, an early authority on trout culture, the fish might benefit if placed in a saline solution, or into a weak solution of permaganate of potash, and allowed to remain there until they appear sickly or turn on their sides. The solution he recommends is ·45 kg of salt to 70 litres of water (1 lb salt to 15 gal water). I doubt if this advice is followed nowadays, except perhaps in the case of an ailing fish.

In the stew ponds, the trout put on weight rapidly, and, depending upon the length of their stay before being put out into open water,

can be anywhere between ·45 kg and ·9 kg (1 lb and 2 lb) or even a
little more, before they are faced with the freedom and the dangers
that await them in the seven lakes of the fishery. In a stream or river,
the distribution of fresh trout should be fairly widespread and the
localities selected. Some of the stock may quickly move downstream,
or more likely upstream, into other fisheries, and therefore the
middle reaches are favoured. In a stillwater the stocking point can be
the same for the whole operation. Any convenient spot will do,
providing the area is clear and unrestricted by weed growth or
other obstacles. The fish will spread throughout the lake, and find
their own shelter. Nor need any fears be entertained for their safety
when they confront the older and larger inhabitants, for trout
of this size are quite capable of avoiding the nefarious attentions of
their more developed brethren. Indeed, in the stew ponds fish of
28 cms (11 in) in length cohabit peacefully with fish weighing over
$1\frac{1}{4}$ kg (3 lb).

Some authorities advocate starving the trout in the stew ponds
for a day or two prior to transferring them to the open lakes, in the
belief that hunger will compel them to forage more quickly and thus
expedite their integration into the new and more competitive society
which they have joined. This is not practised at Two Lakes.

The fish are transferred from the rearing ponds to open water as
the season progresses in small batches but at frequent intervals.
The occasions are determined by depletions in the stock due to
captures, or by the inactivity of the trout in residence. The first is
known at once because the fishery regulations require immediate
notification of the weight and place of capture of all trout taken.
The second is obvious upon observation and upon the reports,
often caustic, of the anglers. In the latter case, it is quite remarkable
that the introduction of a few strange trout into a lake which is
fishing badly seems to stimulate the remainder into a period of
activity that can last for days or weeks. It is supposed that the
newcomers inspire excitement, or resentment, or fear of losing
their lair, or some other emotion in the existing population that
disturbs the even tenor of the habitat. Certainly it improves the
fishing considerably.

[10]

The Trout's Diet

Summer is come, for every spray now springs:
The buck in brake his winter coat he flings;
The fishes flete with new repaired scale,
The adder all her slough away she slings;
The swift swallow pursueth the flies smale;
The busy bee her honey now she mings;
Winter is worn that was the flowers' bale.
                    EARL OF SURREY, Description of Spring. (16TH CENTURY)

When the fish are transferred from the rearing ponds to open water
and find, after what must seem to them a fearsome upheaval, that
the world has expanded into one of apparent limitless boundaries,
they probably experience a sensation akin to exuberance mingled
with curiosity. Perhaps they spend the first hours exploring the
neighbourhood and finding a permanent retreat. But as the hours
pass, and the food that fell on the water with tidy regularity fails
to appear, perplexity and anxiety probably cloud and confuse
their way of thinking, whether conscious or subliminal. A few
cannot adapt themselves to the new conditions, and after a period
of near-starvation, they either perish or become easy victims of
the fly-fisher's art. Others take a little time to learn how to feed
themselves, and eventually they recover the condition which semi-
starvation had lowered. The majority, actuated by the ancestral
pressures that shape their instincts, learn quickly to pursue and
devour any small creature that exhibits any symptoms of animation,
and eventually, if they survive the menace of the barbed hook, they
are able to discriminate and to select their victims, real or pseudo,
by using a yardstick of which we know little, and about which many
erudite theses have been written. During this learning period, they
are extremely vulnerable to the artificial fly, and many a profound
but specious treatise has been written, by anglers whose prowess

with a pen is far greater than with a rod, extolling a particular artificial fly because of its success against these novices.

It is principally by stomach examination that the diet of trout is ascertained. Obviously, this depends on the water in which they live, and upon the creatures that live in it. To a large extent, the organisms upon which trout feed in any particular stretch of water are acceptable to trout everywhere if they are available. So we are able to list those items which form part of trout's diet with a fair certainty. The list is a formidable one, comprising almost every living creature to be found in an aqueous environment; in fact, the trout is as carnivorous and predatory as the pike although not quite so accomplished. It is also a cannibal, when the opportunity arises; as many as sixty fingerlings having been found in the stomach of a large trout. At Two Lakes, the only coarse fish are tench, and the trout will certainly feed on them when they can. Some authorities recommend stocking with sticklebacks on the grounds that they feed mostly on plankton and thus hardly compete with trout, unless the latter are very young, but form an important item in the mature trout's food supply, if available. Anglers fishing Blagdon are fully aware of this, and at times the use of an artificial fly resembling the stickleback provides excellent sport. As against this, it must be remembered that the incidence of disease in a trout lake is greater if coarse fish are present.

The various aquatic animals which form the diet of trout have been grouped by Macan & Worthington into five different classes. They are;

> Surface forms,
> Stone and weed-dwelling forms,
> Floating forms,
> Swimming forms, and
> Burrowing forms.

Such a classification cannot be sharp, for in many cases they overlap. Many midge larvae, encased in shaggy tubes which are difficult to recognise, spend their time prior to pupation in the bottom debris, but as pupae, particularly in the hours before emerging as adults, they inhabit open water, often very close to the surface. Alder larvae, and to some extent Phantom larvae burrow except when feeding, when they swim in open water quite freely. Sedge larvae may be found on the bed, in the weeds, and on or under stones, and at

Two Lakes, I have discovered many of them buried beneath underwater mounds of fallen beech leaves, enclosed in cases, more like purses, made of the same material. Certainly the bottom mud contains worms, and various microspic creatures; I have no doubt that there are occasions when trout seek their food on the bottom, disturbing the bed to uncover any likely victim. When in the early weeks of spring there is a lack of movement in the lake, I have slowly drawn an artificial fly along the bed, and captured many trout, though most of them were comparatively young. This manoeuvre is not possible later in the year because of weed growth, but it is well known that sometimes fish forage deep and anglers search for them as near the bottom as possible.

The surface dwellers are the easiest to define, perhaps because they are visible to an observer. They are an interesting lot, versatile and varied. Some stand or run on the surface without breaking it, and others are able to suspend themselves from it while remaining completely submerged. A small Gerris can leap from the surface film and alight upon it without getting wet. A Water Boatman swims upside down, and when it chooses to do so, grips the under-surface film with its legs and tail and remains stationary upside down, looking upwards for a falling land-based insect. The Whirligig Beetles spend their adult lives on the surface, whirling around looking for food presumably. From the position and anatomy of their eyes, it is believed that they are able to see up and down simultaneously. To a large extent, these surface dwellers are immune from feeding trout, although I have on occasion found Water Boatmen in captured trout. Nevertheless, at Two Lakes, the surface dwellers appear to pursue their lives without interference from the trout, and I have yet to see a trout rise to one. Feeding mostly on a variety of organisms that fall onto the surface, and apparently unattractive to fish or other aquatic creatures, it is doubtful whether their contribution to the economy of a lake is of material value, and I do not propose to devote any further time discussing them.

The main areas of trout food lie in insect larvae and nymphs, snails, shrimps, worms and water slaters.

Of the Upwing nymphs, only those of the Pond Olive (*Cloeon dipterum*), the Sepia Dun (*Leptophlebia marginata*), and of Caenis, appear with unfailing regularity at Two Lakes. The nymphs of Dragonflies (Anisoptera) and Damselflies (Zygoptera) are discussed in a later chapter.

The nymphs of the Pond Olive, like those of the Sepia Dun, are weed dwellers, though occasionally they may be found on stones. Both species live quiet lives, grazing on the fixed algae, but if disturbed they become very active and nimble in seeking sanctuary, after which they settle down to their peaceful occupation once more. Here amid the dense green growth, virtually impenetrable to fish, they feed, moult and mature if permitted to do so by lesser predators such as dragonflies, beetles, water slaters, and so on. After successfully surviving these dangers, they encounter the greatest hazard of all when the time arrives for them to quit the water they have known all their lives and prepare for brief life in the open air.

At approximately one hour before metamorphosis, the nymph shows signs of agitation, slowly at first but gradually increasing in intensity. It begins to flex its body, and darts continually from side to side and from the weed to the surface and back again to the depths. Occasionally it rests, sometimes lying on its back and sometimes on its side. The body is now sparkling and scintillating as though from a thousand miniature diamonds. Progressively the contortions become more eel-like and it is apparent that the creature is suffering considerable discomfort. After a period varying between 30 and 70 minutes, the nymphs comes to the surface and rests quietly as though exhausted. Then with startling suddenness the outer skin of the upper thorax splits, and through the gap the Dun emerges. The tails emerge last, and to extract them the insect raises its abdomen until the tail reaches its head. The empty case is then cast off, probably by the joint action of it being held firmly by the legs while the tail withdraws. The wings, folded concertina-wise, now inflate, and the insect takes off into the air. Here too it must avoid the swifts, the swallows, the martins, the wagtails and the flycatchers that await it. Upon examining the shuck, it will be found that it still contains a volume of air, or gas, equal to about 30 per cent of its internal cavity. This is the cause of the brilliance of the insect immediately before emergence, and no doubt of its discomfort, as the bulk of the nymph within the case must compress the air considerably. Indeed, it seems to me that the Dun is propelled out of its case by the compressed air or gas. During this hour-long process, the insect is exposed to mortal danger from marauding trout.

The theory has been advanced that the insect comes to the surface and swallows air in order to obtain buoyancy to force the nymph to the surface when the change to the winged form is imminent. This view is manifestly incorrect, for if it can get to the surface in order to get the air, it is obvious that it can get there without it. Further, the cast cases of sedge pupae also contain air in similar quantities, and although I know of none that come to the surface either before or during pupation, but know of many that certainly do *not* come to the surface before or during pupation, the theory is untenable. Other reasons are given for this opinion by the great Moseley, who concluded his argument with these words; "if these observations are... accurate. this appears to dispose, once and for all, of the theory that the nymph is floated up from the bottom by the agency of this air." The insect probably knows instinctively that its mechanism for extracting life-giving oxygen from water is about to become obsolete, and it seeks an aerial medium where its new apparatus for doing so in air will function.

The nymph of the Pond Olive varies in size, of course, in accordance with its age. When mature, that is, when the wing cases are prominent and dark, it can be anywhere between 6·5 mm ($\frac{1}{4}$ in) and 10 mm ($\frac{2}{5}$ in), excluding the tails, and occasionally a little larger. The colour is far from constant, tending generally to a brownish olive, but a number have green olive bodies with brownish or orange patches. The three tails generally have light or dark brown rings, widely spaced, often interspersed with faint orange and/or white rings. It can be distinguished from the Lake Olive (*Cloeon simile*) by the shape of the gills and by other minute details, but as these are recognisable only under magnification, they will not be described here.

The size of the Dun is similar to that of the nymph, with very little difference between the sexes. The colour also varies in the same way as the nymph, with green or orange patches indiscriminately distributed along the body. The wings are greyish with a decided blue tinge. The tails are usually ringed with medium or dark brown bands. The spinner, into which the Dun transforms within 24 hours, is known as the Apricot Spinner. I prefer to describe the colour as a pinkish gold, a little deeper on the upper side. I have seen many with green patches on the last two body segments, and on most I have examined the under body is streaked and blotched with orange. The leading edge of the female wings is generally yellowish or golden. The legs are pale gold, with orange patches. The tails are water white with thick dark brown rings, between which are thin

Beech leaf partly eaten by sedge fly
(*Glyphotaelius pellucidus*)

Post-mortem with a marrow scoop

Broadwing (Caenis sp.)

Alder fly (*Sialis lutaria*)

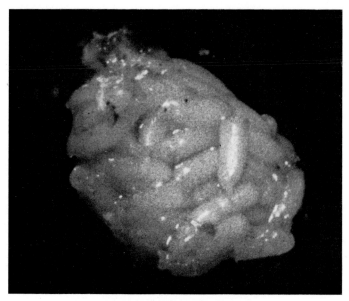

Alder eggs

Alder larva (*Sialis lutaria*)

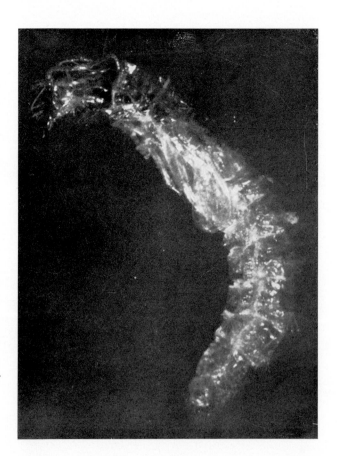

Discarded alder
shuck

orange and white bands. I have also seen green spots on the thorax, and green markings on the last three body segments.

The fly first appears in April, and continues throughout the fisherman's season, although the best months appear to be April and August. This, however, may vary from year to year, depending on the weather.

When trout are rising at or near the surface during the period when Pond Olives are about, a good imitation of either the dun or the spinner can be remarkably effective. The fly should be deposited with the utmost despatch as near the fish as possible, and hardly moved. If it has not been noticed by the fish, or ignored, it may be recovered very slowly indeed. I hesitate however to recommend the use of a close imitation of the nymph, for reasons which I hope to develop later. In this case, the best results I have seen have been obtained by an artificial very much bigger than the natural, but of similar hue and complexion. A typical example, known as Warbey's Green Nymph after its inventor, Major H B Warburton, who is often to be seen at Two Lakes, is dressed as follows:

Hook: No. 12 long shank

Tying silk: Green or Orange

Body: Built up heavily with green floss, and covered with green peacock herls twisted together, ribbed with fine silver wire.

Hackle: Short green (or black) hen at the throat.

For the Dun, almost any medium olive will do. My own favourite is as follows:

Hook: No. 14 or 15

Tying silk: Orange

Body: Olive P V C over condor herl, natural straw colour

Hackle and Tails: Olive cock

Wings: Starling.

For the spinner, I use the following dressing:

> *Hook:* No. 14
> *Tying silk:* Orange
> *Body:* Pink P V C over any light brown herl
> *Hackle and Tails:* Red cock
> *Wings:* Two pair blue/grey hackle tips laid flat.

The artificial nymph described is at its best fished as a wet fly, but will also be taken without demur by fish feeding at the surface.

The Sepia Dun appears in April, although a few early arrivals can be seen in mid-March, and is not seen again until the following year, except for some remnants that persist into the early days of May. In my private insectory, because of the higher indoor temperature, the Duns emerge no later than the end of March. The mature nymphs, averaging about 10–12 mm in length ($\frac{2}{5}$–$\frac{1}{2}$ in), are pretty little things, of a brownish amber colour, with just a hint of maroon. The segments have dark bands at the edges. The head is dark chocolate brown with light brown patches. The tails are long and very whiskery, and the head, thorax and abdomen have many light-coloured hairs when closely examined.

The Duns vary greatly in length. I have recorded females from 7·5 mm ($\frac{1}{3}$ in) to 13·5 mm ($\frac{1}{2}$ in plus), and males from 8 mm to 13 mm ($\frac{1}{3}$–$\frac{1}{2}$ in plus). Generally, however, they are 10–12 mm ($\frac{2}{5}$–$\frac{1}{2}$ in), with the female possibly slightly bigger. The body colour is much the same as the nymph, some with a distinct maroon tinge, and some undiluted brown. The thorax is usually, but not always, brown with light patches, somewhat like tortoiseshell, but in many the darker portion of the thorax is almost black. The wings are usually pale brown with strong grey venation. Often the leading edges are a deep sepia brown. The legs too vary a good deal, sometimes being entirely amber colour, but frequently partly grey and black. The segments of the abdomen have pale edges. The eyes fluctuate between brown and black. The three tails vary in colour from chocolate brown to deep brown, almost black, and are noticeably held wide apart. They are approximately the same length, with the centre one often slightly shorter—and occasionally slightly longer—than the two outside.

The Sepia Spinner varies in length as does the Dun. The wings become transparent, and the fringe hairs of the Dun disappear. The apex of the wing leading edge has a dull grey patch characteristic of the species. The body acquires a deep plum colour, the segments being separated by pale bands. The Thorax is almost black, and the tails much the same. The legs are a deep amber colour.

The following patterns may be found attractive to trout during the Sepia period:

NYMPH
Hook: No. 12 or 13
Tying silk: Maroon or Claret colour
Body: Pheasant tail fibres ribbed fine gold
Whisks: A few pheasant tail fibres spread wide apart
Hackles: Honey or brown, with dark list

DUN
Hook: As above
Tying silk: Maroon or Claret
Body: As the Nymph
Hackle and Whisks: Furnace cock
Wings: Brown Game cock wings, speckled side out, two pair

SPINNER
Hook: As above
Tying silk and body: As Dun, darker if possible
Whisks and Hackle: Furnace cock
Wings: Tips or Rhode Island red cock tied spent, rather large feather.

Both the Pond Olive and the Sepia Dun belong to an Order of insects known as Upwing flies, or Dayflies (*Ephemeroptera*). I prefer the former as being more descriptive, although the latter is closer to the scientific name. But my choice is based on the fact that numerous flies which are not members of this Order live only for a day, whereas I know of no fly that can be described as "upwing" except those of this particular Order. Of the forty-eight species listed by Kimmins I have encountered only five at Two Lakes, including the two mentioned above. The other three are Caenis, sometimes called the White Curse, or the Broadwing, the Iron Blue, and the Pale Watery.

The Pale Watery was a nymph (*Centroptilum luteolum*), captured on August 4th 1965. This insect has lately been named the "Small

Spurwing", because of a minute anatomical feature, which, I presume, came to be known by an angling writer who intended that his erudition should be publicised, even though no angler (or even entomologist) could possibly identify it as such unless he carried a microscope around as part of his fishing equipment. I do not include such exceptions as one well-known writer who unblushingly claimed the ability to identify the species *and sex* of duns emerging at the far bank of a fairly broad river. Unfortunately, the name has been adopted by other angling writers, in spite of its futility, perhaps because of an uneasy fear of being considered not quite "with it". I shall continue to call it a Pale Watery for angling purposes, and a *Centoptilum luteolum* for positive scientific purposes.

Whether or not the specimen referred to was an isolated one, or whether a colony exists, I am unable to say. I have no evidence of any other of the species being found, but as the lakes are spring fed, access to a strange nymph is unlikely from above, and almost impossible from below. I therefore think that a small colony is indigenous to Two Lakes.

On August 11th 1965 I captured an Iron Blue spent fly, lifting it off the water with my plankton net. The fly, known as the Little Claret, was a female of the species *Baetis pumilus*. Once again, this was the only one of its type I have seen at Two Lakes, and I am inclined to believe that it had strayed from some nearby stream.

The last Upwing fly I have encountered, the Caenis, is no doubt resident at Two Lakes in quantities. I understand that the only one positively identified by Mr D Kimmins, is *Caenis robusta*, the largest of the five species making up this genus. His identification was based on an egg-laying female lifted off the water by Mrs Behrendt one late summer afternoon, and on some nymphs collected by Mr Behrendt from one of his lakes (Border Lake), where they were found clinging to the undersides of stones. Mr C F Walker states that all the four stillwater Caenis species have been found at Two Lakes, and although he gives very little detail, this is quite possible, even if some experts claim that *C macrura* and *C rivulorum* are confined to rivers only. If this is so, some confusion arises, for if out of five species, two inhabit rivers only, then only three live in stillwaters.

I personally have witnessed only one heavy fall of Caenis spinners. This occurred in the late afternoon, and because for the last few years my studies at Two Lakes have been confined to Sedges only (except for an intermediate period on Phantom Flies), I collected no specimens. I am informed by Mr Behrendt however, that in early summer mornings, between 4.30 a m and 6 a m, clouds of dancing Caenis duns can be seen, but no rise to spinners occurs until late afternoon. This is in contradiction to the observations of Mr F Sawyer, who tells of witnessing enormous hatches of duns at dawn, and of their transformation into spinners "within a few moments", and then, still at dawn, of their return to the water to lay their eggs. Of course, Mr Sawyer, an outstanding observer, is referring to running water, and the species seen is no doubt different to those at Two Lakes. On the R Test, the prevalent Caenis is *rivulorum*, and this emerges and falls as a spinner at dusk. According to Moseley, *horaria* and *rivulorum* hatch late in the day, and *macrura* in early morning, as also does *moesta*. If the above, all of which I have taken from other sources, is correct, a simple key to species can be constructed for stillwater Caenis.

1. Caenis hatching at dawn   *moesta*
   Caenis hatching late in the day   2

2. Caenis very small, up to 6 mm   *horaria*
   Caenis rather large, approximately 9 mm   *robusta*

I must stress that this key is a rough and ready one for anglers at the waterside. For accurate classification, anatomical examination under magnification is necessary. The only such examination I have personally made was on a nymph captured on July 28th 1965. It was *C. horaria*, and was taken at the base of some milfoil with a sweep of the plankton net. We are told on good authority that the nymphs of all the species are to be found in the bottom silt, but I can only vouch for the single one I have examined.

That trout rise freely to the nymphs, duns and spinners cannot be doubted, and the apparent contradiction that their remains are rarely, if ever, found in autopsies is probably due to the speed with which, on account of their diminutive size, they are rendered unrecognisable by the digestive processes. Many good patterns have been devised, particularly for the spinner, but I hesitate to use or to recommend them on stillwaters, for the reason that the hooks on which the imitations are tied are too small and the leader too fine to justify against large lusty trout. I personally stopped using anything smaller than a No 15 hook after having twice experienced a No 17 hook straightening out. When fish are feeding on small surface flies such as these, I find that the artificial of a larger insect that is *likely to be on the water at the time* is usually an adequate substitute.

[11]

The Alder

HAMLET: *Dost know this water-fly?*
HORATIO: *No, my good lord.*
HAMLET: *Thy state is the more gracious; for 'is a vice to know him.*

HAMLET, V II. 84

To those of us who find relaxation in the bustle of the countryside, the advent of spring brings with it a series of conundrums left over from previous years that increases our impatience for winter's departure. Not least of them is the paradox of the Alder or Orl fly, of which 2 species, both with aquatic larval lives, are found in Britain. They are *Sialis lutaria* and *S fuliginosa*, of the Order MEGA-LOPTERA, Suborder Sialoidae, Family Sialidae. The difference between them, though definitive, are so slight that for all practical purposes they may be ignored except for taxonomic classification. For those interested in systematics, the differences are as follows:

1. *S lutaria* is generally the smaller of the two, and its wings are light brownish. The wings of *S fuliginosa* tend to be blackish.
2. Both have heavily veined wings, but *S lutaria* has 10–11 costal veinlets, and *S fuliginosa* has 12–15.
3. *S lutaria* has 3 gradate cross veins in line. Those of *S fuliginosa* are not in line.
4. *S lutaria* is found in running and still waters. *S fuliginosa* is found only in running water.
5. *S fuliginosa* appears later than *S lutaria*.

It is interesting to note that the males of S fuliginosa, when mating, produce a capsule containing sperm (a spermatophore) which the female devours. The process was fully described by F J Killington in The Entomologist of March 1932, Vol LXV, and it is believed that the same pattern is repeated by *S lutaria* and by certain of the Lacewings, which are closely related. I must confess that my many endeavours to observe the mating act of artificially raised groups of *S lutaria* have come to nought. Nor in many years of search have I captured a single specimen of *S fulinginosa*.

The insect, which is at home equally in fresh or polluted waters is known to inhabit lakes and rivers in Europe, America, Asia Minor, Siberia, Japan and many other countries. I am informed that in America, owing to the natural insect rarely returning to the water in its winged state, and then only by accident, the artificial fly has never been a factor in fly-fishing, although they have an artificial wet fly of the same name which is sometimes used. In Great Britain too there is no apparent reason for the winged fly to return to the water, and because of it, some writers, no doubt taking their cue from Halford, deprecate the use of an imitation. On the other hand, many fly-fishers have found the use of an imitation *during the Alder season* so profitable in terms of captured trout that the logic of Halford and his copiers seems to them to be vulnerable. More of this later.

The life history of both Alder species are believed to be almost identical and therefore they are treated as one and the same fly descriptively, although the following version is based on studies of *S lutaria* only.

The eggs, numbering anywhere between 500 and 3,000, are laid in bundles or clusters on the flat surfaces of plants or stones or spirally on stems of vegetation. They are cylindrical, clinging to the supporting base tightly, and at the free end is a small pointed projection a little paler in colour than the main body of the egg, which is a dirty brown with a hint of orange. It is through an aperture in this projection, called the micropyle, that the male sperm enters. After about 8 or 10 days, the young larvae emerge, and make their way to the water, where they bury themselves in the mud. Hence the name *lutaria*, from the Latin "lutum", meaning "mud". The word *fuliginosa* is from the Latin "fuligo", meaning "soot" or "black paint", often used by Roman ladies of fashion to darken their eyebrows.

It is stated by some authorities that the larval stage lasts nearly two years, but I have found no evidence of it. At no time have I encountered any half-grown larvae that have failed to pupate at the same time, more or less, as the colony in which they lived. It is however apparent that there is a lack of uniformity in the size of the fully grown larvae, differences of nearly 50 per cent being common. The smallest I have recorded was 18 mm (·7 in), and the largest

32 mm (1¼ in), but all have pupated at about the same time. This variation in the size of the larvae might have influenced the belief that the smaller ones were only half-grown, and this leads automatically to the assumption of a two year larval existence.

The colour of the larva is a deep tortoiseshell, clearly marked with pale patches, with a light spot in the centre of each dorsal segment. The thorax is not quite so dark, and the underside, or venter, is a golden amber colour. The width of the head is greater than its length, and is equipped with short simple antennae and a pair of sharp in-curved mandibles which are no doubt formidable weapons of destruction in predatory expeditions. The third section of the thorax is the widest part of the larva, the abdomen tapering down to the 10th segment, which is elongated into a whip tail. Each of the first seven segments of the abdomen carries a pair of feathery gills held backward and half upwards when the creature is at rest; all are fringed with pale olive coloured hairs. The legs are a somewhat darker olive colour. The larvae spend their lives in or near the bottom mud or silt, into which they escape when alarmed, but occasionally, probably when seeking food, they rest on weeds or stones, sitting on their tails with their heads upright, looking very menacing indeed. In captivity they feed almost entirely on caddis grubs.

As the larva approaches maturity, it becomes increasingly evident that the even tenor of its life is in disarray, for it leaves its settled habitat and takes up residence close to the bank. The change is probably triggered off by the temperature, for in captivity the precursory events begin in January, whereas in their natural home at Two Lakes another 10 weeks will elapse before the metastatic urges have an effect on the insect's behaviour. On January 12th, at water temperatures varying according to the time of day between 18° C and 22° C (64–71° F), I observed a larva with its head and thorax protruding out of the water. There was no gill movement whatsoever, and the insect remained thus immobile for 28 minutes, before returning to the water and renewing its gill flapping. Three days later I noticed the tiny tracks of the feet of a larva, or larvae, across the soil which formed a bank to the water in the insectary. On subsequent days, the number of tracks increased, and indeed the sight of a larva, or even of three or four larvae, crawling across the bank became quite common. Occasionally one would lie prostrate on the edge of the soil with its head immersed in the water for some minutes. At other times, they would rest on the dry land. Mostly however, they were in constant motion across the soil, as though revelling in their newly discovered world. On January 18th, I noticed a larva sitting in a hole, and within the next seven days, all the larvae were occupying their individual holes. It was interesting to see them enter the cavity. They did so head first, and almost instantaneously as their tails disappeared, up popped their heads. Obviously they had turned a somersault in the hole, but how they managed it within the close confines I am not sure. Perhaps their bodies are as supple as those of common cats.

An illustration of the pupa of *S lutaria* in a scientific paper published by The Freshwater Biological Association pictures the insect lying horizontally in a closed cell some distance below the surface. This does accord with my own observations. Each of the many I have seen pupate and later emerge adopts a vertical (or almost vertical) posture within an open hole, and at no time has the cavity been closed. It is possible that in exposed soil the action of the wind might cause a drift of particles that would close the hole, but I must stress that this would be incidental to the process and not part of it. After the emergence of the winged fly, the discarded pupal envelope is found within the hole in an upright position.

On January 26th, exactly 14 days after the first pupation commenced, a winged fly was seen at 8.45 a m. It was a female, and in the days that followed emergences increased in number until on February 4th, the last one appeared. All the newcomers arrived a little before or a little after breakfast, that is, soon after dawn. About 5 per cent failed to survive pupation.

I found it curious to observe that the larvae formed two groups for the purposes of pupation, each system of holes being as far distant as possible in a small insectary from the other system. Perhaps this dispersion is a survival rite, in order that the discovery of a colony by a predator will not decimate more than a small proportion of the population. This is merely one of many possible speculations, and I have no doubt that the ingenuity of my readers will prefer others.

The discarded shuck is a pale yellow/brownish colour, and is curiously curved like a banana. Within can be seen the remains of the air or gas, which, as I have said in a previous chapter, probably acts as a propellent to expel the fully matured insect from the shuck when the time comes.

In open water, the emergence of the winged flies occurs in April, May or June, but Killington reports having captured one, *S lutaria*, on July 30th in Hampshire (Entomologist Vol IX, April 1921). It is also reported that the pupae may be found at the roots of rushes and sedges adjacent to the water's edge.

The winged Alder is a medium size fly, with gable shaped wings similar to those of a sedge when at rest. The surface of the wings are, however, hard and shiny, unlike those of a sedge, which are covered in fine hairs. Also, unlike the wavering flight of the sedge, the Alder flies steadily and sedately, and is inclined to rest frequently. Indeed, when endeavouring to escape an enemy, it will often run instead of flying.

The antennae are almost black, the oval eyes brown, the head very dark brown, the thorax mixed light and dark brown, and the abdomen has bands of light and dark brown with a suggestion of purple. The underside of the body is paler in colour, and the legs are dark brown with many golden hairs, as on the body. The wings are very pale watery brown with strong dark venation. There are no ocelli (simple eyes).

According to Halford, in admiration of whose work I am second to none, the winged fly seldom appears on the water surface, and then only by accident or by the compulsion of inclement weather. He admits that trout will rise to an imitation of the Alder, but forcibly expresses the view that they do so in the belief that it is a dark sedge. This has been repeated a number of times by writers who take their cue from Halford. Some go even further. Commander C F Walker states categorically "...I am prepared to say that the winged Alder is never eaten by trout."

On the other hand, Alfred Ronalds wrote of the winged Alder that "it delights to skim the brook", and J J Armistead writes that they "spend much time...bobbing about on the water in swarms". Finally, the late Martin Mosely wrote "in at least two recent cases autopsies have been submitted in which Alder larvae were strongly represented if not pre-dominant".

I too have identified on many occasions the remains of Alder flies in the stomach contents of trout sent to me by Mr Eric Horsfall Turner from the Yorkshire rivers. In almost all instances the body was too eroded by the digestive processes to be identified, but the wings were intact and unmistakable. And on the R Test on a number of occasions I have lifted winged Alder flies from the water on calm days when hardly a leaf stirred. Nevertheless it is apparent that there is no compulsion on the insect to return to the water for any known purpose, and we must therefore apply ourselves to an examination of the life history of the insect in order to establish the circumstances which might lead to its presence on the water in sufficient density to ensure that the trout are aware of it and familiar with it as a desirable tidbit. That it is a desirable tidbit to the trout I am convinced, and I have little hesitation in concurring with the view of Charles Kingsley that, to the trout fisher, it is a "beloved member of the brute creation". During the Alder season, *and only then*, it is one of the fly-fisher's best flies. I personally have had some of my best fish on it, including my biggest of 8 lb 3 oz. And I must make it clear that I have never, at any time, seen any other fly, sedge or otherwise, on or near the water during its airborne days that could possibly, by any stretch of the imagination, be confused with it. It is also a remarkable fact that after the Alder season, the artificial fly is of little use, even when dark sedges are about.

The solution to the paradox might lie in two factors. The first is expressed admirably in a phrase by Macan & Worthington, that "pupation is believed to take place on land, and if this is true, some larvae in Windermere must migrate 200 yards". Such a lengthy journey must expose the larvae to mortal danger from marauding trout and attract the fish to the later winged fly of similar body colour. The second factor lies in the poor flying ability of the Alder. They appear to be overcome by fatigue quite easily, and will alight without hesitation on the hands, neck or face of an individual or any other spot without discrimination. It is not beyond the bounds of possibility that they alight on the water for the same reason from time to time.

In any event, I do not hesitate to recommend most emphatically the use of an artificial Alder either wet or dry at a time the naturals are in season, *but at no other time*. The dressing I recommend is the traditional one.

Tying silk	Crimson
Body	Two or three herls of peacock dyed magenta
Wings	Two pair from the wings of brown game hen, spotted side outside, sloping over the body.
Hackle	Black cock in front of the wings
Hook	10/12 downeyed.

Entomologist. Apr 1921. Vol LIX by F J Killington.
G de Kerville. Bull Soc an Sc Nat Rouen 1930–1 p 363.
Entomologist. Nov 1926. Page 289.
Entomologist. March 1932. Vol LXV by F J Killington.

[12]

The Phantom Fly

Let dreams depart and phantoms fly,
The offspring of the night. ST AMBROSE (4TH CENTURY)

The annals of mythology and the pages of science fiction abound in stories of divine and magical devices endowed with the priceless power of rendering their possessors invisible. This gift of the ability to see while unseen provided a weapon that no odds could overcome and no enemy escape. So fantastic a concept, contrived no doubt originally by the fertile mind of a fabulist is by no means fantastic biologically for in the world of insects there exists a populous group upon which such a blessing has been bestowed. Well might their living prey, could they articulate, complain in words of Shelley, that, "The awful shadow of some unseen Power, Floats though unseen among us."

The insects to which I refer are Phantom Flies, or Midges, called in America Clear Lake Gnats. They are better known in Great Britain, in their immature form, as Phantom Larvae.

Briefly, Phantom Flies are Diptera of the Family Culicidae, genus *Chaoborus;* they may be roughly described as non-biting mosquitoes. The particular species of this history is *Chaoborus flavicans* Meigen. I established its identity by frequent specimen examination of the mandibular teeth of the larvae, of the structure of the pupal anal leaf, and of the distal and paenedistal joints of the male antennae of the imago, in accordance with the specification of Kaj Berg, and confirmed by Edward's key as given in Volume IX, Part 2, of the *Handbook for the Identification of British Insects*, by Coe, Freeman, and Mattingly.

In the summer of 1965, while fishing for trout at Two Lakes in Hampshire, it was suggested that I catalogue the various species of Trichoptera (sedge flies) native to the seven lakes which compose the fishery. Being a Trichopteraphile, I welcomed the suggestion; and, with the assistance of the proprietors, Mr and Mrs Alex Behrendt, I started collecting the winged insects. One cannot, however, assume with safety that a species is indigenous to a water because of the presence of an individual or two of that species (though it may be safely assumed if they are plentiful) as winged insects occasionally "visit" neighbouring waters. I decided therefore to collect the larvae; and, because the exact identification of sedges in their larval state is not entirely reliable, to bring them to maturity in artificial conditions in my own home, when classification can be positive.

In searching the water for sedge larvae, I became increasingly aware of the ubiquity and the vast numbers of Phantom Larvae. Out of curiosity, I made three arm-length sweeps with a small plankton net at different depths, and laboriously counted the captured Phantoms. The number was 872. It seemed to me that even in a group of lakes so heavily stocked with a variety of aquatic insects as Two Lakes, the Phantoms far outnumbered all the other insects put together.

So excessive a preponderance of a particular type posed, upon reflection, a number of questions. Would not the hatches of the winged flies be on a massive scale? What did they look like? What were their habits? When did the larvae pupate, and for how long? What did the usually well-informed fly-fisherman know about them?

The answer to the last question is a short one: practically nothing. In the whole of my extensive library on fly-fishing, there was almost unrelieved silence.

I found some information in three or four British entomological publications which treat of aquatic insects; for the most part, however, it was on the larvae. On the pupa, very little can be found, except in Professor Miall's *Natural History of Aquatic Insects;* but even this is far from complete and not entirely accurate. The winged fly is generally ignored, and, where noticed, the information given is often erroneous. I came across two diagrammatic illustrations of the adult fly, one of them with the wing formation indistinct, and the other with a slight error. Nowhere did I find a visual description sufficiently graphic to enable a field identification to be made.

Fortunately, the United States of America and the Continent of Europe proved more fruitful; but the species concerned were mostly other than *flavicans*, and, even where the species was *flavicans*, there were many differences in the habits of the insects described, and those under observation by me. But again, no account of the appearance in its winged form was sufficiently lucid for quick recognition. I came to the conclusion that in addition to studying the American and European entomological reports, concurrently with constant observation of the insect in is natural state at Two Lakes, it was essential for me to raise small colonies in my own aquarium. This presented little or no difficulty.

The biological success of the Phantom Fly is due largely to its larval transparency, which, for all practical purposes, renders it invisible for the major portion of its life. As our study of the insect progresses, we also learn to admire its adaptation to its surroundings, and its ability to make the maximum use of environmental features for its own advantage, even when, as we shall see, it is confronted with a completely novel situation. Its evolutionary success can be gauged by the extent of its dominance in waters where it has established itself. In Lake Mendota, Wisconsin, out of approximately 15,000 living creatures per square metre of bottom, about 11,000 were Phantoms. Even this pales before Eggleton's estimate of 71,000 per square metre in Third Sister Lake. At this rate, a mere

Eggs of Chaoborus.

10 acres supports a Phantom population of 3,000,000,000, a figure greater than the human population of the world. These incredible numbers are indirectly confirmed by Herms, who relates that around some American lakes the Phantom winged flies are so numerous that the local residents spend large sums of money, to no avail, on suction fans, light traps and electronic and electric appliances to keep the swarms out of their homes; but the dead insects soon clog up the mechanisms and prevent their operation. Nor has any

success been achieved in this direction by the introduction into the lakes of various species of fish which might feed on the larvae.

The resourcefulness of the Phantom starts at the egg stage, for like other highly developed insects, it can produce parthenogenetic eggs; and although I know of no instance where these have matured in artificial conditions, there is every reason to believe they might do so in natural conditions. Normally, the female, after impregnation by the male, returns at dusk to the water and deposits her cigar-shaped eggs enclosed in discs of a mucilaginous substance on the surface close to the banks. When laid, the eggs are white; but they turn brown overnight. In the laboratory, they sink at once into the bottom ooze; and it is believed that eggs laid in the open do the same. Some authorities, however, having failed to find any eggs in the bottom mud after extensive bouts of ovipositing, in spite of careful sifting, are inclined to believe that the eggs hatch on the surface; and that the emergent larvae at once sink and burrow into the mud. Examination at a later stage of the ooze certainly reveals large quantities of the young larvae.

According to Deonier, hatching occurs in about 24 hours; but

Phantom larvae in the bottom mud.

this is open to question. In the laboratory, it takes 2, 3, 6, or even 10 days, according to temperature.

The young hatch in shallow bankside water and grow rapidly. Soon they move to deeper water, where the majority spend the re-mainder of their larval existence. Continental studies have shown that both in the larval and pupal states they retire during daylight hours into the bottom mud, entering free water towards evening. It has also been noticed that for some reason they congregate in shallow ditches in large numbers. The latter is true of Two Lakes, where the narrow channels, joining lake to lake, shelter vast hordes of larvae and pupae. But contrary to Continental experience, they can be found in open water in immense numbers at all times of day from June until September; or October, if the weather continues fine and warm. And throughout the winter, even when the lakes are covered with thin layers of ice, they are not entirely absent, though their numbers are greatly reduced. The largest concentrations are in small exposed bays, in communicating ditches, and where tree roots are densely tangled below the water surface. This may be attributed to the fact that such places are not favoured by prowling trout on the look-out for food. It certainly appears that at Two Lakes the larvae have little to fear from trout, for when I am present at the lakes, I examine the stomach content of almost every fish caught, whether by me or by other anglers, and only rarely is a Phantom larva or pupa present. I doubt if this can be ascribed to their lack of pala-tability, as the flesh of the Phantom larva is highly nutritious, consisting of 67 per cent dry weight protein and 9·5 per cent fat. I fancy that its freedom from serious molestation is a benefit derived from its transparency and its avoiding tactics. I am informed by Mr Behrendt, however, that the larvae are frequently found in young trout; perhaps because their vision is greatly superior to that of older trout.

One of its chief enemies is the eel, which presumably has its own gift of exceptional eyesight, or some other quality, to counteract the near-invisibility of the Phantom; perhaps this is connected with the eel's preference for dark and obscure places. It may well be that the mud-sheltering habit of the Phantom occurs in waters favoured by eels. At Two Lakes, where eels are unknown, there is no evidence of similar concealment.

The species *Chaoborus flavicans* has such powers of adaptation that it has been seriously postulated that it may cover a number of sub-species. It has been conclusively shown that they are indifferent to the oxygen content of water, living in a low oxygen content as comfortably as in water of high oxygen content; indeed, they can live for several weeks in water from which most of the oxygen has been removed. This is probably because their low rate of move-ment involves low metabolism, and this reduces the need for oxygen. They survive in pools formed by the winter inundation of rivers, and which dry out in late summer. It is believed that the eggs sink into the mud and lie dormant until the following spring, after the winter has brought them the floods and the victuals to nourish their lives.

The young larvae grow rapidly, and complete their growth in about three or four weeks, after passing through four instars. When fully grown, they are about 16 mm ($\frac{5}{8}$ in) in length. They lie horizontally in the water, being able to support this position through the agency of four air bladders, two of them in the thorax, and two at the rear end of the abdomen, actually in the seventh segment. These bladders, or sacs, are fairly prominent because they are

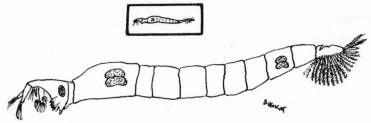

Phantom larvae.

covered with a number of tiny black spots, which, in addition to their black eyes, either mar, or enhance, the invisibility of the rest of the body. The larvae, by expanding or contracting their air sacs by some method not fully understood, can select the depth they wish to occupy, and they are able to maintain their level position even when the anterior part of the body is heavy with recently devoured food.

It is thought by some authorities, that for the first two or three days after emerging from the egg, the young larva does not feed. As it grows, however, it turns its attention to the surrounding plankton, feeding on it until it is somewhat more developed, when its diet consists of live daphnia, copepods, rotifers, the young larvae of mosquitoes and midges, and similar minute creatures. It will refuse dead food; and although it can live for months without food, especially in low temperatures, it will not hesitate under normal conditions to turn cannibal if no other living prey is available.

The antennae of the larvae are of unusual formation, for they are modified into prehensible limbs with which they seize their victims. Nor does this exhaust their special characteristics, for their digestive habits also bear witness to the remarkable degree of evolutionary sophistication reached by a creature destined for numerical ascendancy. More of this presently.

The larva lies motionless in the water with an air of remote indolence until a victim approaches. Then, like Blake's gentle wind, silent and invisible, it moves towards its doomed and wretched prey and impales it on the splines of its raptorial antennae, and transfers it to its mouth. The movement through the water is incredibly swift, and is performed by flexing and straightening the rear end of the abdomen; this is assisted by a tail appendage which consists of a fan-shaped anal fin made up of a row of hairy bristles.

The digestive sequences are interesting. All food is passed from the mouth into a crop-like pharynx, which communicates with the intestine through a bristle-barred gap which permits the passage of liquid only. The food is retained in the pharynx until the digestive processes reduce the greater part to a liquid which passes through to the gut. The solids remain in the pharynx until it is full, when the larva performs a remarkable manœuvre. It turns the pharynx inside-out by projecting it from its mouth, so that it looks as if its tongue is hanging out. The skeletal remains of the food are then washed away by the water; and, the pharynx replaced in position, the larva is able once more to accommodate fresh food in the now empty space.

In the warmth of the summer, and with adequate feeding, the larvae complete their growth in three or four weeks, and very soon begin to show signs of incipient pupation. But with the approach of autumn, growth and the processes of pupation slow down and cease; and the larvae gradually leave the open water and begin to burrow in the mud, where they spend most of the winter, emerging occasionally for food. They again appear in their multitudes the following year when summer warmth dispels the chill of early spring.

During the summer months, the larva, within a day or two of attaining its full growth, occasionally abandons its horizontal position for a brief second, and assumes an upright posture. Almost at once it falls back to the horizontal. These deviations gradually increase in frequency and duration, and after two or three days the thorax bends forward so that the head of the insect appears to be lying on its chest. At the same time a pair of horns, shaped like miniature rugby footballs, but more pointed at the ends, previously lying flat on the thorax of the larva, rise up and stand erect. The tail comb is replaced by a pair of large leaf-like gills plentifully equipped with tracheal tubes, and the thoracic and abdominal air sacs fade and disappear. The thorax and abdomen lose their transparency and become a pale sea-green. The insect is now a pupa, having performed a feat un-fathomable to the human mind.

The pupa is about 8 mm ($\frac{5}{16}$ in) in length, and "stands" upright in the water. In the days that follow, the thorax darkens, until immediately before the emergence of the winged fly it is a light brown colour. In captivity, the pupal stage lasts four days, and during

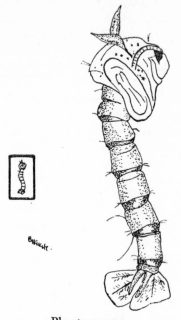

Phantom pupa.

that time, in spite of concentrated observation for long intervals, I did not see one approach the surface. And in the lakes themselves, constant sweeps with a plankton net within an inch or two of the surface failed to capture a single pupa, though many could be taken at depths below 9 in.

The pupa stands immobile, except that every 10 seconds or so it kicks the water with its tail. The frequency of the kick varies with the temperature of the water, being greater as the temperature rises. The water in the tanks of the aquarium varied between 20° C and 26° C (68° F and 78° F), the higher temperature occurring in the late afternoons when the sun shone directly into the room where the aquarium was kept.

Apart from these kicks, which do not alter the position of the pupa, it remains stationary, except for an almost imperceptible drift caused by a small inflow of air at the end of each tank. The depth appears to be arbitrary, but no pupa approaches close to the surface. During this period, the pupa is fully conscious and agile when danger threatens. An attempt to capture one succeeds only after some minutes when it is obviously too exhausted to continue evading its pursuer.

The outer skin of the pupal horns has an irregular cellular pattern. The horns themselves are hollow, with a narrow slit at the apex. It is generally believed that they are breathing tubes, and that the pupa hangs from the surface film and thus has access to the air. As this does not happen, the theory that they are breathing tubes is considerably weakened, although it is possible that they act in this capacity by extracting air from the water by diffusion. However, a simpler and more acceptable theory can be formulated by supposing that breathing is the function of the anal gills and/or the integument, and that the frequent kicks are performed for the purpose of replacing de-aerated water with fresh. The increased frequency of the kicks during elevated temperatures would be consistent with this theory, as the level of oxygen content of water falls as the temperature rises. Also, the general belief that the function of the anal gills is to assist locomotion is untenable, as the pupa rarely moves. As the result of a conversation at the Department of Entomology of the British Museum, I decided to make some experiments.

In approaching the question of the biological function of the pupal horns, I was inclined to the opinion that they were flotation chambers, replacing the four air sacs of the larva. The former are positioned to keep the pupa erect, the latter to keep the larva horizontal. Obviously the horizontal position is desirable in any aquatic insect that must move through the water in search of food, but it is not so obvious why the pupa should have evolved into a vertical creature. It may well be that an erect pupa with two pointed horns at its apex is able to penetrate the surface film of the still water it inhabits with less difficulty than a horizontal one, when the time comes for the winged fly to emerge. If it be objected that the majority of aquatic insects upon the approach of metamorphosis do in fact penetrate the surface film while in a horizontal position, I must reply that many of them do so only after a long struggle, and that the Phantom fly, being one of the most advanced aquatic insects known to man, and one of the most successful, may well have modified its pupal form in order to avoid this struggle.

If the general belief that the horns are breathing tubes is correct, their removal would cause the death of the insect. On the other hand, if they are flotation chambers their removal would not kill it but would be unable to "stand" in free water. It would sink to the bottom.

I divided a number of young pupae into two groups and anaesthetised them. From one group I removed a single horn, and from the other I removed both. Each pupa was then deposited in a small transparent container, one pupa to each container, and the containers, which were cylindrical about 3 in high and 1 in in diameter, three-quarters filled with water. The open tops were covered with "caps" made from a silk stocking, and secured to the container with a rubber band. Approximately 25 per cent of the water was changed each day with aerated lake water from the aquarium.

The removal of a single horn did not appear to affect the development of the pupae; in due course, after the usual interval, the imagines emerged with no sign of mutilation or abnormality. There was one strange exception. Fom one of the pupae two winged flies emerged, one of them a normal live male, the other a dead, stunted female. The incident, however, is irrelevant to our subject.

Each pupa from which both horns had been removed, as soon as it recovered from the anaesthetic, immediately rose to its normal standing position in the water, and immediately sank. Again it rose, only to sink again. Now commenced a continual rise and fall, in some instances with a break for nearly 24 hours, in others for only a few hours. At the end of this varying initial period, the pupae began to rest on the bottom of the container, at first for a minute or two, but later for longer periods, until eventually most of the time was spent in a recumbent position half lying on the bottom and half leaning on the glass wall. Only occasionally would they make attempts, ever more feeble, to rise into open water, but barely could they reach a height of half an inch before the inevitable descent returned them to their starting point. Most of them died on the fourth day, but two survived until the fifth.

A post-mortem examination revealed that all had fully completed the changes to the winged condition. All had split the pupal envelope on the upper thorax, two of them but slightly. With care I was able to extract the imagines from the pupal skin, and, except that the wings were not inflated, each appeared to be normal.

The result of the experiment leads to the assumption that the horns are primarily stabilising bladders with built-in controls for lifting and lowering the pupa at will. This may be done by nervous activation of the walls of the horns, causing them to expand or contract, thus altering the quantity of air or gas within them.

A second assumption that the insects met their death by drowning because of their inability, through exhaustion, to rise to the surface and escape from the pupal skin is attractive but speculative. Perhaps, unseen by me, they had managed to rise to the surface; but, without their pointed horns, had been unable to pierce the surface film, and had fallen back and drowned. Other possible causes of death spring to mind; but the primary conclusion, that the horns are stabilising organs, appears to be unchallengeable.

My next experiment was infinitely more complicated. I removed the anal gills of a young pupa after it had been anaesthetised. But whereas the horns of a pupa stand clear of any obstruction, and are thus comparatively accessible, the gills are in close proximity to the genital lobes, and their removal demands an operation of great delicacy if damage to other parts of the anatomy is to be avoided. The insect died within the hour, but whether this was due to lack of oxygen or to damage inflicted on some vital part is uncertain. If the experiment is to be repeated, it must be done by hands more experienced in dissecting minute organisms than mine.

The darker the colour of the thorax of the pupa, the closer it is to final metamorphosis. This occurred in captivity at the expiry of four days, and, probably because of a phototropic mechanism within the nervous system of the insect, always in darkness. Whether or not the same reluctance on the part of the winged fly to emerge during daylight hours is to be found at Two Lakes, I cannot say; but during the height of the Phantom season I did not once see a single such emergence, though I kept watch while even a vestige of light remained. The countless millions of larvae in the lakes automatically ensure that the emergence of winged flies must be on a massive scale, and an event of this kind, if occurring during daylight, or even twilight, hours, cannot possibly escape notice. Nor do I believe that it occurs at dawn, for on those occasions when I have left my bed in time to witness a possible emergence in my aquarium at sunrise, the newly arrived winged flies were already resting on the fabric cover.

A night-time performance of this perilous operation, which, if

conducted in daylight, would expose the insects while in a particularly
vulnerable condition to the dangers of predation from many sources,
is consistent with the belief that they possess an abnormally high
standard of instinctive self-preservation.

The only description of final metamorphosis I have been able to
find is one recorded by Herms, of the University of California
Experimental Station, who states that when pupation is completed,

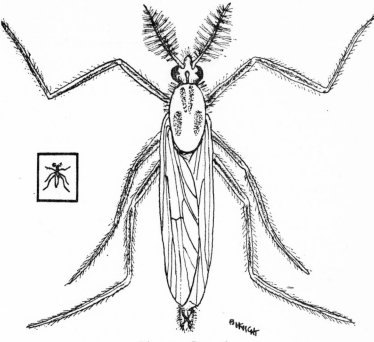

Phantom fly, male.

"the gnats literally pop out of their pupal skins, balance momentarily
on the water, and quickly fly shoreward."

The overall length of the male imago, excluding the antennae,
is approximately 7 mm (about $\frac{9}{32}$ in); the wing length is approximately 4 mm (about $\frac{5}{32}$ in). The female is a little smaller. The
following descriptions are of *flavicans* only, other *Chaoborus* species
differing mainly in colour and markings.

The wings are a pale-grey/olive colour. The thorax has a uniform
pattern of light brown patches on a white background. The eyes

are black, the proboscis and palps a smoky grey; the legs are a uni-colorous pale green with an olive tinge, and the antennae vary from a smoky to a silvery grey. The abdomen is densely covered with long pale hairs.

There are four main differences between the external appearances of the sexes. First, the antennae of the male are grandly plumose; and those of the female are somewhat sparse. Second, the body of the male is slimmer than that of the female, and broadens slightly at the last segment. Third, the body of the male is white on the underside and patchy grey on the upper side, while the fuller body of the female is a pale sea-green. Fourth, from the abdominal extremity of the male there extend two long oval lobes, upon each of which is a very dark brown spur, upturned, crossing the adjacent one to form the well-known crossed swords pattern. The female has two similar lobes, but much smaller, and without spurs.

The Phantom fly is often mistaken for a Chironomid, or Midge; but they can be distinguished by two distinct features. First, the wings of the Phantom, when the insect is at rest, almost cover the whole of the abdomen, in contrast to the Chironomid, whose wings leave the last few segments of the abdomen uncovered when it is at rest. Second, when the insects are at rest, the wings of the Phantom form roughly the shape of an ellipse, and those of the Chironomid form roughly the shape of an isosceles triangle.

In flight, the Phantoms are not easy to see unless they are viewed against a dark background; nor, if seen, can they be identified. But if immediately before nightfall on a fine summer's day a small pale insect is observed close to the lakeshore, the chances are that it is a Phantom fly. If fish are at about the same time rising close to the bank, they are in all likelihood feeding on the ovipositing Phantom females.

Each tank in my aquarium consists of a transparent plastic box, in one wall of which a small hole is cut about an inch from the top to allow the entry of a flexible tube connected to a small air pump. The tank is surmounted with a fine fabric "bonnet," which fits over the sides. The total height of the air space between the water and the cover is about 4 in, so that the fine fabric permits a clear view of any activity within. It also provides a suitable resting place for emerging insects, which, until the introduction of the Phantoms, remained stationary on the fabric until they were transferred to containers for further study. The system had worked well with many species of Ephemeroptera; and with sedges, damsel flies, midges and crane-flies. But the resourceful Phantom, displaying the same sagacity as a winged fly that it had shown as an aquatic creature, crawled down the inner sides of the cover, pushing its way between it and the outer walls of the tank, and found its way to freedom. After the initial losses, the escape route was blocked by a rubber band which secured the sides of the cover tightly against the walls of the tank.

It is recorded by Herms, writing of a Phantom Fly native to America (*Chaoborus lacustris*), that mating occurs in the late afternoon on windless days. He states that the females rest on the leaves of trees while the males fly around, eventually entering the precincts of the trees where mating takes place. He does not say whether it occurs at rest or in flight.

Around Two Lakes, the banks and countryside are densely packed with flowering shrubs and tangled bush between the towering heights of willow, larch and rowan, pine and beech. Among the thick foliage, out of range of the human eye and secure from the attention of devouring birds and voracious dragon flies, the Phantom adults rest until mating time, which probably starts when day begins to fade. Soon, when night begins to overtake the dusk of twilight, clusters of females return to the water, and trout begin to rise close to the banks, feeding greedily on the spent females which now lie exhausted after having accomplished the task which is both the climax and the swan-song of their existence.

Because of the practical difficulties in observing the mating routine in natural conditions, their behaviour in captivity gains an added importance, even though it is recognised that divergencies occur between behaviour in captivity and in the wild state. Yet the nebulous forces of instinct, deep-rooted by time, often make conformity with established generic or species custom inevitable. I did not therefore abandon hope of finding evidence of the natural mating pattern from the activities of the imagines in the aquarium.

Throughout the months of July and August, the long summer evenings, whenever possible, were spent watching the movements of the winged Phantoms of which there were never less than six nor more than twenty-one within the aquarium air extension. Irrespective of numbers, or of the varying proportion of the sexes, each day was a repetition of the first, with the single exception that the activity I am about to describe did not start strictly in accordance with any chronological measurement, but rather with the degree of sunlight. Thus the temporary disappearance of the evening sun behind a heavy cloud would trigger off the display, but its reappearance within a few minutes would halt it. The phototropic mechanism of the pupa was no doubt inherited by the imago.

For most of the day, the insects rest on the inner fabric cover. Movement is minimal, consisting of very infrequent shifting of position that is little more than a stretching of limbs. Occasionally one would fly down to the water, where, it seemed to me, it drank a little water, and returned to its original position. There was no preference shown for any particular location. But with the decline of day, signs of restlessness appeared. First one, then another, would crawl or fly to a different place; this became more frequent as twilight approached, each changing its position many times. When the sun had sunk below the horizon, all the males, easily recognisable by their copious antennae, were stationed in a group on the right of the cover, and all the females on the left. A large space in the middle was unoccupied.

All activity by the males now ceased; but the restlessness of the females continued unabated, no longer, however, aimlessly. Crawling along the fabric, first one then another approached the male group, retreating, approaching and again retreating, apparently indecisively, while the males remained unmoved. Gradually individual females grew bolder and slowly crawled on until their wings touched the wings of a male. The pair would then take flight, but in the limited air space this was but momentary, as almost at once they collided with the fabric, and the flight ended. Each returned to its own group, and the routine continued. The abortive nuptials persisted until darkness put an end to all activity.

The insects died three days after having attained their winged state. Accordingly, each of them would have participated in the mating activity, even though unconsummated, on two or three occasions, and probably in this repetition lies the explanation of the invariable orientation of the sexual grouping. If the first males grouped arbitrarily on the right, and repeated it on the second and third occasions, the pattern would be established for all newcomers to follow.

The inferences drawn from the aquarium routine suggest that copulation probably takes place in flight. This is supported by the design of the male forceps, which appear to be too powerful for use if the mating act occurs at rest. They also suggest that the ritual follows closely that adopted by *C lacustris*, but with the initiative taken by the female, not the male.

To the lake fly-fisher who is dedicated to the use of a large sunken fly of conspicuous design, whether singly or in a team, the history of the Phantom Fly will be of academic interest only. To those of my readers to whom fly-fishing is something more, it will present new possibilities in the art of trout deception; an art that can bring a fish to the net when the more popular methods fail.

The four stages of the Phantom's life when it is exposed to the perils of feeding fish are, (1) as a larva, (2) as a pupa, (3) as an emerging winged fly, and (4) as an egg-laying female.

During the first stage, the larva is nigh invisible, and cannot be imitated.

The second stage, however presents opportunities for the angler particularly on those still summer days when the unruffled waters, heavy with sun-haze, are least responsive.

The third stage, occurring as I think in the hours of darkness, is of no interest.

The fourth stage, when the female returns to deposit her eggs on the surface of the water, can be used by the resourceful fly-fisher for his own advantage.

Dressings for both the artificial pupa and the winged fly are given below; but the methods of presenting them are equally as important as their dressings. The movement of both the artificial pupa and the artificial winged fly should be as imperceptible and as slow as possible within the control of the angler. The pupa fishes best hanging a little below the surface, and this is achieved by greasing the whole of the line and leader with the exception of the last few inches. The winged fly is fished in the traditional style of the dry fly.

The recommended dressings are as follows:

PHANTOM PUPA   *Hook:* No 15 (No 0) downeyed

Tying silk: Black

Body: A thin strip of P V C dyed lightly in picric acid tied tightly over white swan or goose herl, or flat silver. The body must stop at the bend

Thorax: Cinnamon turkey tail, or cinnamon wool or kapok

PHANTOM FLY

Hook: No 16 (No oo) downeyed
Tying silk: Black
Body: As for the pupa, tied very thin
Wings: Pale starling, dipped for a few seconds in picric acid. Tie them short, sloping well back
Hackle: Pale watery
Tails: Pale watery cock fibres, rather short. Although the natural is tail-less, they are included to give improved buoyancy, and to imitate the backward spread of the long hind legs of the natural

[13]

Sedge Flies

"Some to the sun their insect wing unfold,
Waft on the breeze, or sink in clouds of gold".

ALEXANDER POPE. Rape of the Lock

In 1965 I embarked on the task of cataloguing the various species of sedges native to Two Lakes. My visits being restricted to one a week, I asked Mr Behrendt to collect specimens for me and to hand them to me when I arrived, or forward them to me by post. On a number of occasions I collected the insects in their larval form and brought them to maturity in my own insectary, when identification of species could be positive. Owing to the limited time at my disposal, devoting two or three evenings in every week to the task, the maximum number of specimens I was able to examine, was twenty-five per week. On the whole, this quota I set myself could be successfully accommodated, but all too frequently my work rate was retarded by difficult specimens which demanded clearing in boiling caustic potash, an operation which would consume almost the whole of a single session. Of course, there were many weeks in the winter months when no specimens were collected, none being available.

In all, I examined a total of 547 specimens, excluding a quantum of moths and lacewings that my host inadvertently included, and which appeared so interesting that I discarded them with considerable regret. I recorded particulars of each specimen briefly; its sex, dimensions of major anatomical parts, colours of wings, thorax, legs and abdomen, descriptions of antennae, the date (but unfortunately not the time) of capture, and the general appearance. When, under compulsion of competing activities, I put an end to the work, I had identified 56 different species. I am given to understand that Mr D Kimmins and Dr Macan had separately identified specimens from Two Lakes not found by me, but I have omitted them from my lists. They are, for those interested, the following:

> *Limnephilus hirsutus*
> *Oecetis testacea*
> *Plectocnemia geniculata*
> *Psychomyia pusilla.*

I must add that in some instances, where identity was doubtful, either due to damage of critical lineaments, or malformation, or to dessication, I fortunately had recourse to Mr D Kimmins' Assistant at the British Museum, Mr Peter Ward, whose professional experience and access to the microscopic slides, collections and archival resources of the Department of Entomology either confirmed or corrected my tentative identification.

My identifications were based on data supplied in British Caddis Flies, by the late Martin Moseley, augmented by separate papers, illustrations and photographs by Mr D Kimmins, Mr Pelham-Clinton, Herr D Winkler and Monsieur Marlier, besides many papers published in the Proceedings and the Transactions of the Royal Entomological Society of London. I am particularly grateful to Mr D Kimmins for furnishing me with a copy of his as yet unpublished genera key based on the spur formula, and for permitting me to reproduce in my personal copy of British Caddis Flies his corrections of certain texts and illustrations with which his own copy of the book abounds. The errors in the original publication were inherited from the great McLachlan, whose illustrations were drawn as he examined the minute anatomical features of the insects with a low-power hand lens. The wing illustrations, drawn by Mr Kimmins for Mr Moseley, were immaculately accurate.

Of the 56 species I identified, only 42 were true caddis, or case making sedges, although the fashion now is to describe all sedges as caddis flies. Of the remaining 14 species, 10 are free-swimming, the remaining 4 species constructing tunnels, or tubes. The former are net makers, an artifice by which they collect drifting fragments of food. The nets are usually sited close to the inlets or outlets of stillwaters, or occasionally in shallow littoral regions where wave action creates a water flow. More of this later.

From the tables on pages 126-8, it will appear that certain species dominate both numerically and persistently, but this is not necessarily so, as some species, such as *M longicornis* (Grouse Wing) are so readily identifiable on sight, that collecting specimens merely for recording species, is a dispensable luxury. Thus the quantities examined and included in my list are not always related to the density or endurance of any particular species. It is worth recording that on two or three occasions, I collected specimens from a swarm of straw coloured sedges which proved to be *M longicornis*, without the three dark wing bars typical of the species.

It will be noticed that some species are included on the evidence of a single specimen, but many of these were adults raised from larvae removed from the lakes, and thus undoubtedly natives. Also, we know from the original work of Karel Novak and Frantisek Sehnal that many Limnephilid species aestivate, sometimes for months, while their reproductive organs mature. Their appearance in widely separated months of the year will not in such cases signify new emergences, but merely a return to the water from distant hiding places for the purpose of mating and reproducing.

The discovery of the diapause that induced the aestivation of certain sedge species was a result of the examination by Novak and Sehnal of the newly emerged female adults. They found that the ovaries were immature, and therefore conception was impossible. This led to a prolonged study of the growth of the ovaries in a number of Limnephelid species, and the discovery that in such species, the newly emerged adult females are incapable of egg-laying, unlike other species which are capable of mating and egg-laying almost at once. Usually, these resting species are mature by the autumn, irrespective of the time of emergence. Thus females that emerge in June take longer to mature than those emerging in July or August, an admirable example of Nature's mechanisms for ensuring synchronisation of ovipositing.

It is not known whether the diapause is present in males as well as in females. My inquiry to Dr Novak for any information he might have on the subject brought the following reply:

Prague, Dec. 16th 1964

"Dear Mr Jacques,

As far as I have understood your question you would like to know whether the male sex of the Genus Limnephilus suffers the diapause as well as the female. It is very probable but I did not make any research in this direction. Fact is that the males appear in natural conditions together with the females from Spring till late Autumn. But I did not observe the male reproductive organs and therefore I cannot tell you whether the evolution of testes is interfered with during the Summer period in the similar way like the evolution of ovaria of the females. The determination of the stage of maturity of testes is much more difficult than of the ovaria and therefore I cannot assure you whether the copulation takes place in Spring or in Autumn, but I take the second possibility as the more probable.

Yours sincerely, Dr Karel Novak"

The incidence of the diapause poses a number of interesting possibilities. That both sexes emerge from the pupae at roughly the same time is well authenticated, and indeed I have recorded such emergences on many occasions. If Dr Novak's probability is reversed, that is, if the males are sexually mature at emergence, one may conclude that copulation takes place while the female is sexually immature, and that the sperm lies dormant within the body wall of the female until her ovaries are ripe for fertilisation. Similar processes are not unknown in certain insects, and the possibility cannot be dismissed. On the other hand, the presence of the males at the waterside immediately prior to egg-laying, plus the ability of the males to survive in captivity for many months, suggests that both sexes suffer the diapause.

These facts must be considered in the context of a statement by the late Dr Imms, sometime Reader in Entomology at Cambridge University, that "Caddis flies are incapable of taking food requiring mastication, since they have no functional mandibles" (Insect Natural History, page 50), and of a similar statement by Martin Moseley that "The mouth parts of the Caddis fly are modified and partly obsolete so that the insect is unable to feed on solid matter". (British Caddis Flies, page 7). In captivity, life spans up to 26 weeks have been achieved by feeding the insects with a sugar solution, and it seems to me that the sedge flies that survive the summer during the diapause are able to do so by imbibing liquids sufficiently nourishing to sustain them by extracting them from the vegetation that shelters them. The possibility that, like the salmon, they have stored sufficient nutrient reserves to bridge the gap between emergence and mating cannot however be dismissed.

One of the species included in the above group is the well known Cinnamon Sedge, *Limnephilus lunatus*. The colloquial name is not a reflection of the insect's colouring, as it is widely believed, but of its scent. That it possesses a strong scent cannot be denied, but this is not exclusive to the species, but rather to Limnephilids in general; indeed, the odour is so singular that the Genus can be recognised, in close confines, by this feature alone. To me, however, the smell is more akin to that of a geranium than to cinnamon.

Species of the Limnephilus Genus, the most populous at Two Lakes, are for the most part known as Red Sedges. The wings are not particularly hairy, and some specimens, particularly the larger ones, are irregularly marked with brown patches. The wing lengths vary from small/medium to large/medium, the smallest being about 9 mm (*L auricula*) to 16 mm (*L marmoratus*). The colours of the thorax, abdomen and legs are extremely variable, varying from grey to orange to red for the most part, frequently interspersed with green, wholly or partly. In the Cinnamon Sedge (*L lunatus*) the body is almost invariably green.

The next most populous groups are the Polycentropidae (embracing the genera Neureclipsis, Plectrocnemia, Polycentropus, Holocentropus and Cyrnus), and the Psychomyidae (embracing Ecnomus, Tinodes, Lype and Metalype). On the whole, they are small brown/grey or brown in colour, with a few almost completely black. The bodies are generally brown/grey, occasionally varied to a dull green. Of the remainder, there are large pale types, such as *Halesus radiatus* and *Halesus digitatus*, both known as the Caperer, the Large Red Sedge *Phrygania striata*, (more brown than red), the Medium Brown Sedge *Anabolia nervosa*, the pale thin medium size longhorns (Oecetis spp), the medium to large pale Agrypnia spp, the large marbled *Glyphotaelius pellucidus*, the various black Silverhorns, and the rare and most beautiful *Chimarrha marginata*, with black wings edged with a band of bright gold. (My joy on first capturing one of the latter some years ago on the R Test was indescribable.)

Perhaps I should here give warning that the above descriptions, far from being invariable, are subject to change from individual to individual. Brown sedges are sometimes red, and vice versa, as are pale and red, and black and brown. Sizes can vary, like humans and other creatures, by as much as 20 per cent. Bodies, much to the chagrin of the purist fly man, can suddenly change in an entire emergence to dull green, rendering his carefully prepared imitations totally impotent.

I am persuaded that the function of the gable shaped wings, which cloak the body of the insect so effectively when they are at rest, is largely to preserve the fertilised eggs by protecting them from the effects of rain. As is well established, contact with water causes the egg mass to expand to many times its volume, and in the event of this happening while it is still within the insect's vaginal cavity, that is, prior to the egg mass having been extruded sufficiently to permit ovipositing, the abdomen must become distended to a degree that causes the death of the insect, perhaps painfully. Experiments, not however conducted for this purpose, have demonstrated quite clearly that this is true. For this reason, the imagines after their initial flight, remain firmly on terra firma, with wings folded, until the time arrives for oviposting. Until then, they are to be found sheltering in cracks and crevices under bridges, beneath the bark of fallen trees, on the underside of leaves and in sheds close to the waterside. Many of my best specimens were taken in a disused hut situated near the water, most of them resting on the walls, the ceiling and the window, but some, alas, entangled in the numerous spiders' webs that hung in grim anticipation of the harvest to come.

Hanna describes three methods which Caddis flies adopt to deposit their eggs. The first refers to those species that lay their egg masses on the surface of the water; among them he includes *M longicornis* (Grouse Wing) and *O lacustris*. In the second group, which crawl down vegetation to lay their eggs under water, he includes *P striata* (Large Red Sedge). The third group, containing most of the Limnephilids, lay their eggs on vegetation above the water surface, from where, I presume, they fall onto the water. From my own observations, I would certainly include all the Silverhorns, and probably all species of the Oecetis genus in the first category, that is, among those that lay their eggs on the surface.

There is a distinct lack of uniformity in the shape of the egg masses laid by differing species. They range from indiscriminate blobs to spherical, domed, curved cylindrical or almost bifurcated. The material of the masses is a sticky mucilaginous jelly, usually opaque when deposited, but transparent and colourless when expanded after contact with water. The eggs may be scattered randomly throughout the mass or arranged regularly in rings. The masses of *O lacustris*, roughly spherical, are attached to a filament which may be as much as 15 mm (⅗ in) in length. The filament has been seen to twist itself around submerged vegetation, and it is likely that its function is to anchor the egg mass to a rigid support. The colour of the eggs is usually pale green, often so pale as to appear colourless.

The grubs hatch from the eggs between 10 and 22 days after the eggs have been laid. In the species (*Brachycentrus subnubilus*) I have raised myself, the first grubs in each mass appeared consistently 10 days after deposition, and the last after exactly 20 days. Of the hundreds of masses I have examined under the microscope, there was no variation in the periods mentioned. Other observers, working with different species, have recorded initial hatchings after 10, 11, 12, 13, 14, 15 and 18 days, the last named being attributed to certain Limnephilus species.

The hatching itself is a fascinating sight which I have watched on numerous occasions. The egg mass swells rapidly until it reaches a diameter of 6–9 mm ($\frac{1}{4}$–$\frac{3}{8}$ in), when it becomes transparent, with the individual eggs clearly distinguished within the jelly. After three or four days, the green substance of the egg begins to leave the sides of the egg and to concentrate in the centre from one pole to another. The cheeks themselves remain colourless and transparent like the surrounding jelly, but clearly defined. Gradually the green portion assumes the shape of a bean, and begins to shrink. A few days later two dark spots appear in the clear portion of the egg, and within a day or two, the young grub will hatch, the dark spots being the eyes. The green matter can now be seen as a thin streak within the abdomen of the grub. This sudden unrolling of an inanimate egg and immediate transformation into an animate larva exceeds the human imaginings of fable and fiction beyond all measure and beyond all description.

As I have previously stated, not all sedge larvae construct cases, at least until pupation. Indeed, only those species that do so qualify for the descriptive name caddis. According to the O E D, the word "caddis" (cadaz, cadace, caddys) means a fabric used as a padding, and later a pedlar who, to advertise the ribbons and braids he had for sale, pinned his wares to his clothing. The pedlars became known as caddice men, and according to Hickin, the encased grubs, festooned as they were with fragments of material, were designated "caddice worms".

The methods by which the larvae construct their cases was closely studied by Hanna and published by him in 1960. He recognised eight different methods adopted for initiating the process; in most of them the young grubs join small pieces of leaf, or bits of gravel, or mollusc shells (sometimes still tenanted by their owners) into a mat with the aid of a sticky substance they are able to secrete.

PERIODIC FLIGHTS OF SPECIES

		Apr.	May	June	July	Aug.	Sept.	Oct.	Nov.
Phryganea striata (Large Red Sedge, Murragh)	C		*	*					
Agrypnia picta	C						*		
,, pagetana	C					*	*		
Glyphotaelius pellucidus	C						*	*	
Limnephilus subcentralis	C			*					
,, flavicornis	C				*		*		
,, decipiens	C						*	*	
,, marmoratus	C				*	*	*	*	*
,, stigma	C						*		
,, lunatus (Cinnamon Sedge)	C			*	*	*	*	*	*
,, ignavus	C						*	*	
,, centralis	C		*	*	*	*	*	*	
,, vittatus	C	*	*	*	*		*	*	*
,, affinis	C			*					
,, auricula	C			*	*				
,, bipunctatus	C				*				
,, extricatus	C			*			*	*	
,, luridus	C			*					
,, sparsus	C		*	*	*				
Anabolia nervosa (Brown or Dark Sedge)	C					*	*	*	*

Periodic Flights of Species—(Cont'd)

		Apr.	May	June	July	Aug.	Sept.	Oct.	Nov.
Stenophylax sequax	C		*						
Halesus radiatus (Caperer)	C							*	*
Halesus digitatus (Caperer)	C							*	
Crunoecia irrorata	C			*					
Lepidostoma hirtum	C						*		
Athripsodes annulicornis	C			*					
" atterrimus (Black Silverhorn)	C			*	*				
Mystacides nigra (Black Silverhorn)	C			*			*		
" azurea (Black Silverhorn)	C			*					
" longicornis (Grouse Wing)	C		*	*	*		*		
Triaenodes bicolor	C			*		*	*	*	
" conspersa	C					*			
Adicella reducta	C						*		
Oecetis ochracea	C				*				
" furva	C					*			
" lacustris	C				*	*	*		
" notata	C					*			
Leptocerus tineiformis	C			*					
Hydropsyche angustipennis	N						*		

Periodic Flights of Species—(Cont'd)

		Apr.	May	June	July	Aug.	Sept.	Oct.	Nov.
Neureclipsis bimaculata	N					*			
Plectronemia conspersa	N			*					
Polycentropus flavomaculatus	N			*	*	*			
Holocentropus dubius	N		*	*	*	*			
„ picicornis	N			*	*	*			
Cyrnus trimaculatus	N			*	*	*	*		
„ flavidus	N		*			*			
Ecnomus tenellus	T					*	*		
Tinodes waeneri (Little Red Sedge)	T			*			*		
Lype phaeopa	T			*	*	*	*		
Metalype fragilis	T		*	*	*	*			
Chimarrha marginata	T		*						
Rhyacophila dorsalis (Ronald's Sand Fly)	F					*		*	
Agapetus ochripes	C					*			
Agraylea sexmaculata	C		*						
Orthotrichia costalis	C						*		
Oxyethira flavicornis	C							*	

N.B. C = Case Making   T = Tube Making
N = Net Making   F = Entirely Free

Then, stretching themselves on the mat, either dorsally, ventrally or laterally, they drape the mat around the abdomen and thorax. The ends of the mat are drawn together and cemented, either to each other or to other fragments introduced into the gap. The other seven methods vary to some degree, but most of them are similar to the one described. In some instances, the larva constructs a series of "frames", which are slipped over its head, one at a time, the upper one being cemented to the lower one until the tube or case is complete. A curious variation is adopted by some species, which first coat themselves with a glutinous silk, and then, after burrowing head first into the sandy or gravelly bed on the stream or lake, begin to rotate slowly until the thorax and abdomen are covered with a layer of the sediment. This is usually utilised as a a foundation for a stronger, more permanent edifice.

Generally sedge larvae employ material that is readily at hand, and, where a choice exists, habit forming by species is very strong. Often identification of Genus, or even species, is possible from the material and structural shape of the case. Students of this aspect of aquatic entomology are recommended to read Dr Norman Hickin's monumental work Caddis Larvae (Hutchinson). It must however be stressed that identification of the insects based on structural shape and material utilisation is not infallible, for experimental work has shown quite clearly that under certain conditions, such as when the traditional material in unavailable, larvae will have no hesitation in building their cases from almost any alternative constituent. In the laboratory, this has led to cases being built from splintered mica, which, being transparent, provides an admirable expedient for observing the bodily postures and flexures of the insects under induced conditions. Another cause for possible confusion lies in the observed habit of larvae taking over the deserted cases of entirely different species. My own experience of this phenomenon occurred in 1959, when I discovered a larva of the Hydroptilidae Family occupying the otherwise empty case of a Grannom. The new tenant, no doubt preoccupied with the demands of security, was not only within the larger case, approximately 16 mm ($\frac{5}{8}$ in) in length, but also within its own case, shaped like an elongated seed case but with two V cuts, one at either end; the total length of the smaller case was about 5 mm ($\frac{3}{16}$ in). I removed the larva and its case from the larger one, and watched it with some amusement, probably unjustified because the creature was no doubt alarmed at the sudden deterioration in its security arrangements. However, the larva proceeded to thrust its minute head out of each aperture in turn with such lightning rapidity that at first I supposed it was occupied by two larvae. It seemed to me that the little chap had no intention of being caught napping by either a frontal or rear attack which its changed circumstance indicated.

I sent the specimen to Mr D Kimmins at the British Museum for Genus, or even species identification. In reply, I received a letter of which the following is an extract.

'I should think that the small Caddis which you found in the case of a Grannom is one of the Hydroptilidae, possibly an *Orthotrichia*. As a general rule, *it is unwise to attempt to identify Trichoptera from their cases, as some forms vary considerably in the method and material used in construction.*"   (My italics).

In my list, the following are members of the Hydroptilidae: *Agraylea sexmaculata*, *Orthotrichia costalis*, and *Oxyethira flavicornis*. It is interesting to note that this family do not construct cases until the fifth instar, after which they undergo considerable changes in their anatomy and behaviour. This interpolated change in the larval stage is known as a hypermetamorphosis.

The utilisation by caddis larvae of local material for case building, and indeed for feeding, is illustrated by the behaviour of *Glyphotaelius pellucidus* found in large numbers in the circular rearing pond at Two Lakes. The winged fly is seen in September and October. It is a large reddish sedge, often with dark patches on the wings, which are slightly excised. The larva is a large one, and is generally regarded as being omnivorous. It is known to make cases from the entire, or almost entire, faded leaves that accumulate on the beds of stillwaters. At Two Lakes, the circular rearing pond referred to above is overhung by a beech tree, and the bed of the pond is thickly strewn with its fallen leaves, layer upon layer. The *G pellucidus* larvae make their flat, purse-like cases exclusively from these leaves, ignoring all other types. Furthermore, they feed on these leaves, and in captivity refused all other food. Only the soft tissue is consumed, the veins and stems being avoided.

Case-occupying larvae are possessed of a strong pair of hooks at the tip of the abdomen. With them they grip the case and transport it with them on their travels through the water or on the bed. Locomotion is by means of their front legs which project from the top of the case (except when danger threatens) either for crawling or swimming, although occasionally the median legs are exposed to assist propulsion.

The net spinners operate quite differently, and in fact, are generally of a different physical form to the case builders. The former are known as campodeiform larva, and the latter as eruciform. The main differences between the two are that the campodeiform types hold their heads horizontally, while the eruciform hold them more or less vertically. The former have long slender hooks at the tip of the abdomen for gripping their net, whereas the latter have short, thick hooks, obviously more sturdy, for grasping the case. The eruciform types have more cylindrical bodies, the abdomen of which is usually white or pale green, and possess three protuberances, like humps, on the first segment of the abdomen. *Phryganea striata* is a mixture of both types, and is therefore described as suberuciform.

The net spinners operate by spinning silk-line nets into shapes traditional of their species. Some are funnel shaped, the wide end facing the flow of water, the narrow end sealed by a silken mesh. Others are tube like, and are fixed at one end to a weed or stone, the free end floating in the current. A number of species construct nets shaped like an open purse, or nest, and attach them to stones or weeds. Some spin nets under stones, but in almost all instances the larvae live within or close to the nets, and rely for their food on the particles trapped in them.

A third type live in fixed tunnels made of, or lined with silk. The larvae often use fissures in underwater objects as if they were tunnels, and one species excavates a tunnel in a freshwater sponge. The tunnels are often covered with detritus, and are difficult to find.

A fourth type, with only four British species, (*Rhyacophila*) is entirely free living, but constructs a fixed case when about to pupate.

All species of the Hydroptilidae are free living until the fifth instar, when they begin to build cases.

Some species of the Hydropsyche Genus, including the *H angustipennis* are equipped with a stridulatory organ consisting of a file formation of the side of the head and a scraper on the front leg. The scraping sound was recorded by means of a small crystal microphone painted over with a waterproof lacquer and placed 25 mm (1 in) from a larva. The sound was amplified and fed to a recorder and analysed on an oscilloscope. The larva began to stridulate when attacked with a needle, and this was accompanied by bouts of biting and lunging. It is assumed that the organ is an intrument used to repel predators or intruders.

The following information is taken mostly from McLachlan and Hickin:

Case Construction of Caddis Larvae

Phyrganea striata (Large Red Sedge)

Bits of leaves or stems placed side by side so as to form a spiral band, passing many times round the case, which is open at both ends, tapering when small, parallel-sided later.

Agrypnia pagetana

Very large cases made of pieces of leaves arranged longitudinally. Often inhabit empty stems of water plants. Occasionally, spiral but always cylindrical.

Glyphotaelius pellucidus

Case of entire or nearly entire leaves of trees, flattish and irregular.

Limnephilus flavicornis

Various materials, but especially shells of water molluscs.

Limnephilus decipiens

The case is straight, narrowing slightly, generally composed of vegetable material arranged longitudinally often overlapping. Sometimes triangular.

Limnephilus marmoratus

Cases rather large, generally built of stalks of water-plants arranged transversely, but leaves, sand grains and mollusc shells may be included. Sometimes built entirely from seeds of water-plants.

Limnephilus stigma

The case is barrel shaped, and built from vegetable debris fixed tangentially to the long axis.

Limnephilus lunatus

Cases made of pieces of leaves, vegetable debris, grass, sand or broken snail shells. Often with long twigs attached.

Limnephilus ignavus

The case is straight, only slightly conical. Composed of leaf pieces placed longitudinally on either side.

Limnephilus centralis

The case is curved, narrowing and sometimes twisting. Made of rounded sand grains.

Limnephilus vitattus

Curved cylindrical tube of fine sand, wider at the head end.

Limnephilus affinis

The case is practically straight, cylindrical and generally made of large sand grains, but sometimes of small leaf, or wood fragments longitudinally.

Limnephilus auricular

The case is cylindrical, straight and tapered. Made of pieces of dead leaf, with sometimes a few bits of sand.

Limnephilus bipunctatus

The young larvae make cases of vegetation fragments, but when older use large sand grains or small shells.

Limnephilus extricatus

Case of sand grains or other hard matter, only slightly curved.

Limnephilus luridus

Case almost straight and slightly conical. Made of leaf and twig pieces.

Limnephilus sparsus

Case is conical and curved. Made of pieces of vegetable matter.

Anabolia nervosa

In the early stage, the conical case is made of stalk pieces and bits of vegetation, but later made of sand grains. Usually with one or more long sticks attached longitudinally.

Halesus digitatus (Caperer)

Straight or slightly curved, made of small stones, sand grains, leaf pieces and vegetable debris.

Lepidostoma hirtum

The case is of square section, first made of sand grains by the young larvae, and of vegetable debris hardened by secretion when older. Wider at the head end.

Athripsodes spp (Black Silverhorn etc.)

Curved cylindrical case of fine sand, tapered to the base.

Mystacides spp (Silverhorns, Grouse Wings)

The case is made of vegetable pieces or small stones or both. Sometimes fine sand. Usually with one or more long twigs attached.

Triaenodes spp

Similar to *Phryganea striata* but shorter and more tapered.

Adicella reducta

Case of fine sand or mud lined with silk. They are very smooth, and often russet colour with black patches.

Oecetis spp

The case is strongly curved and tapered in *O lacustris*, and slightly curved in *O ochracea*, both made of fine sand grains. It is made of vegetation pieces in *O furva*, when it is usually straight.

Leptocerus tineiformis

The case is a yellowish-brown colour, made mostly of secretion only, slightly curved. Sometimes faintly transparent in front.

Agapetus ochripes

Case of small stones, never tabular

Agraylea sexmaculata, Orthotrichia costalis, Oxythira flavicornis

Cases of silk, either vase or seed shaped, slit at each end. Often attached to foreign bodies, sometimes moored by threads.

Most sedge larvae are mainly phytophagous (plant eaters), and some are exclusively so. Some are omnivorous, and some largely predatory and carnivorous, feeding on nymphs, Diptera larvae, Copepods, Diatoms, Daphnia, small snails and the young of their own kind. They have been recorded as attacking and devouring small fish, and feeding on the carcasses of mammals and birds sometimes found under water. Certain species live entirely on algae, and their feeding organs are naturally adapted to this purpose.

Sedge larvae, being invertebrate, possess soft bodies covered with a thin hard layer which is largely impermeable to water or gases. This covering, or outer skeleton, is advantageous to small creatures in water and in air, where the perils of dessication are very real. Having no organ resembling lungs, they breathe through a system of fine tubes, or tracheae, which distribute the oxygen throughout the various parts of the body. In many aquatic insects, the tracheae terminate at the outer cuticle in valvular openings, or spiracles, which are too fine to allow the entry of water but are able, by means of extremely tenuous filaments, to extract the oxygen from the water. Normally caddis larvae are equipped with simple or compound breathing gills along the abdomen covered with thin hairs. Some doubt exists whether in fact the "gills" perform any other function in breathing than to induce by rapid flapping a flow of fresh water over the abdomen especially when the oxygen content of the water is low. Wingfield showed this to be the case with *Baetis*, *Cloeon*, and *Ephemera vulgata* nymphs as early as 1939. It is certainly thought by some authorities that there are patches of absorptive membrane on the cuticles of caddis larvae through which oxygen diffuses into the tracheae. The larvae also assist respiration by undulating their bodies, causing a flow of water through their cases and over the outer surface of their bodies.

The rigid outer skeleton, which is incapable of expansion, must be shed from time to time, and a larger one grown in its place, if the size of the insect is to increase with age. The periods between each moult are known as instars, the first being the period between emergence from the egg and the first moult. The name given to this process of cuticle casting is ecdysis. Thus the mature larva at its fifth instar has undergone four ecdyses.

It has been observed in artificial conditions that caddis larvae convey particles of food close to their heads, either for feeling, smelling or closely inspecting, before rejecting or devouring them. From this it is assumed that their vision is not particularly good by human standards, but this is a dangerous assumption, verging on the anthropocentric. It has been pointed out, however, that the position of the eyes often indicates the feeding habits of the larva; if they are to the front of the genae, or cheeks, the larvae is carnivorous, and if they are to the rear, it is herbivorous. If they are set about halfway, the larva is omnivorous.

The habit of stridulating among certain sedge larvae strongly suggests that they possess some kind of faculty for hearing, but as far as I know, no part of the anatomy responsible for it has been identified.

As pupation approaches, the larvae block the open ends of their cases with gravel or vegetation (but not so densely as to prevent the inflow of water) and attach it to some stationary underwater object. The non-case makers now construct a case and perform a similar manœuvre. The larva spins a silk cocoon around itself, not as a shapeless bag, but shaped to its contours. Within the cocoon, the transfiguration from a larva into the imago, through the intermediate and constantly changing pupal stages, takes place. Photographs or drawings of pupae illustrate no more than a fleeting phase of its anatomy, which in a continuous state of flux, although some features, such as the extension of the antennae alongside and around the abdomen appear to be uniform throughout pupation.

Pupation periods vary from about 7 to 24 days, the latter in captivity, but one may legitimately question the relationship between behaviour in natural surroundings and that in captivity. The stimulus for action is often thermal or phototropic, and the different light and heat conditions in the two environments might produce entirely different responses.

The pupa is armed with a pair of sharp projections close to its mouth with which it cuts its way out of its case. It then crawls or swims to the surface with the aid of a pair of heavily fringed median legs which act as paddles, and there it splits its pupal envelope dorsally somewhere between its head and thorax, and the perfect insect emerges, dries its wings briefly, and flies away. It is widely believed that certain species, such as the Caperer (Halesus spp) skirt across the water prior to their maiden flight, but my observation leads me to believe that this is more characteristic of individuals than of species, and can be accounted for by the difficulty the insects encounter in obtaining complete release from the pupal shuck. In

Pond Olive nymph (*Cloeon dipterum*)

Pond Olive Dun (*Cloeon dipterum*) fem.

Pond Olive Spinner (*Cloeon dipterum*) fem.

Sepia Dun (*Leptophlebia marginata*) fem.

Sepia nymph (*Leptophlebia marginata*)

Water Beetle larva (*Agabus uliginosus*)

Brown Sedge (*Anabolia nervosa*)

Cinnamon Sedge (*Limnephilus lunatus*)

Caddis larva in case, probably Limnephilus sp.

Chironomus sp. (male)

Chironomid pupa

Damselfly nymph

all probability, the emerging imago is endeavouring to clear itself from the shuck by rubbing it off against the water surface.

The species that are sexually mature at emergence immediately seek refuge within the obscurity of thick vegetation, or beneath the fractured bark of fallen trees, or in the fissures and cracks of timbered structures, or beneath bridges, or in any other obscure sheltered location. In such retreats, the sexes select mating partners according to a formula of which we know little. Darwin suggested that the females choose for mating only those males possessing characteristics which balance their own in order to transmit to the progeny these characteristics to the exclusion of those of the rejected suitors. This suggestion is one with which few, if any, biologists would concur, and in any event, on those occasions when I have witnessed the mating act, the male is almost certainly the selector. Perhaps the exudation of a distinctive individual pheremone (sexual gland odour), the study of which is becoming increasingly popular, may be the attractant. The postulation by me of a romantic solution would no doubt expose me to the criticism that I am attributing anthropomorphous sentiments to insects.

The mating act, which I have witnessed many times proceeds as follows. The male pursues the female of his choice, after ignoring other females he encounters from time to time. While she is in motion, apparently unconcerned at his pursuit, the male climbs onto her back, forcing her wings apart with his head, the parting of the wings being too unruly to suggest a voluntary action of the female. As soon as the male is in the covering position, he turns his back on the female, and the pair, now in a locked position remain motionless tail to tail while the female is impregnated, except for an intense quivering of the antennae which lasts for about a minute. The union continues for another minute or two, after which they continue their different paths.

The species that are sexually immature, as has been explained, disperse to some distance from their native water and remain there until their reproductive organs are properly developed. This may take many weeks, or months, and their activities during this period are hardly known. This is not surprising, as they remain hidden throughout. Even in the laboratory they hide in the corners of the cages or in the cracks of the rushes, and only in the evenings do they become a little livelier. Subsequent to attaining sexual maturity, they return to the vicinity of the water, and mating, which, it is believed, takes place at night, is presumed to concur with the description given above.

In the laboratory, it was shown conclusively that the ovaries of the Limnephilus species under observation did not develop at all when the insects were subjected to 16 hours of light per day, but under shorter light exposures of only 12 hours per day the development is accelerated. This corresponds with the natural postponement of sexual maturity from the long days of summer until the shorter days of autumn; a remarkable illustration of the precision of Nature's phototropic exactitude.

Some species of winged sedge flies form stationary swarms over the surface of the water. Others form mobile swarms, particularly at dusk, occasionally dispersing and later re-forming. These mobile swarms rarely move from the space above the water to that above dry land, and various theories have been advanced to explain it. Hickin thinks it likely that the positioning of the swarm relative to slight air currents carrying the female gland odour accounts for it. Another theory supposes that the purpose of the swarm is to ensure the gathering of the members of the emerging species into a closely knit community, which, when complete, moves in unison, like a flock of birds, to a common destination, where contacts between the sexes for mating purposes are easy to achieve.

A distinction must be made between emerging swarms and egg-laying swarms. The latter are in evidence usually in the late afternoons, the most familiar being the Silverhorns, the Grouse Wings and the Oecetis species. Whereas the emerging swarms are accompanied by trout activity, which feed on the newly hatched imagines as they leave the pupal sheath, the egg-laying swarms elicit little response from the fish, due to the fact that the insects make contact with the water for only a brief second at a time, and, as far as the trout are concerned, are too elusive to waste time and energy in rising to. Very infrequently, a young trout will be seen leaping at a hovering insect, probably out of sheer frustration. Some authorities believe these swarms are mating gatherings, but this presumes that the mating act takes place in flight. My own evidence contradicts this viewpoint, but more evidence is wanted before an unqualified statement can be made.

With the exception of those species mentioned in the previous paragraph, the flight of caddis flies is more noticeable at dusk. Generally, the larger species emerge just before, or just after, nightfall, and the smaller ones during the hours of daylight. Some emerge during the night, the numbers building up until dawn, when they diminish rapidly. Strangely, rainfall does not deter the flights; on the contrary, it is said that it tends to encourage them, but the evidence for this is tenuous.

Neither on river or stillwater have I seen, or heard of, spent caddis flies lying exhausted on the surface of the water after mating or egg-laying. Species are said to lay their eggs on or above the surface, or to crawl down below the surface in order to deposit them on stones, vegetation or other fixed positions. The latter may well perish under water after parturition, but I have at no time seen a winged sedge go down beneath the water or seen one return, although on rivers I have observed them hanging grimly on to vegetation, while presenting their tail to the current in order to wash off their egg sac. What, then, happens to the spent males and females after they have performed their final function in life?

On a day in late April 1965, I spent my usual day fishing for salmon on the Severall Fishery of the Hampshire Avon. It was a bright day, but a cold east wind made the approach of lunch hour more than usually welcome. I retired to a fishing hut situated on the bank, about 30 yards from the river, and spread my coffee and sandwiches on a table by the window so that I could observe a pool just below me and the river winding away to the bottom of my beat. A sedge (grannom) season was just about over, and only a few of them could be seen in the air from time to time. As I sat and ate, I noticed below me on the near bank a huge flock of birds widespread across the meadow, moving across it towards me exceedingly slowly. As they approached, I recognised them as small black headed gulls. Curiouser and curiouser, I sat perfectly still until they were almost level with the hut; I then left the hut, and at the sight of me, the flock crossed the river and began its slow procession upstream as before. On my knees I examined the grass as thoroughly as I could, and found it thick with the dying and dead insects. I then moved downstream to the areas over which the gulls had passed, and failed to find a single insect. Indeed, one could almost draw a line between the area covered by the gulls and the area they had not yet reached.

I am sure that the gulls are only one of the many saphrophytic creatures that dispose of the expiring or expired caddis flies after they have performed their reproductive assignment. As far as I am aware, trout play no part in it.

[14]

The Artificial Sedge

...but they have planned a snare for the fish, and defeat them by their angling art. They tie crimson wool round the hook and on to it fix two feathers which grow beneath the wattles of a cockerel, coloured like wax. The rod is two metres in length, and the line the same. They cast the bait and the fish which is attracted and excited by the colours, rises, with the idea of securing a dainty tidbit; when it opens its jaws, however, it is secured by the hook and enjoys a bitter mouthful, and is caught.

AELIAN. De Animalium Natura. BOOK XV

An examination of my fishing records confirms that by far the majority of outstanding events that fill my store of fishing memories have been associated with the artificial sedge. Included among them are two fresh run salmon that invaded a trout water, each over 10 lb, brought to the bank by a floating sedge imitation on a trout rod and tackle. But first I must emphasise that I refer to the heavily hackled winged fly that sits high and prominent on the water. So succinct a definition is interposed because of the majority custom at Two Lakes, at least among my colleagues, of describing a dry fly as one which is fished with a floating line, even though it swims in the surface film or just below it. Far from criticising this interpretation, I accept it in the context of stillwater fishing, but I must leave this to a later chapter. For the present, my use of the term "dry fly" must be understood as I have defined it.

My river background to dry-fly fishing to a rising fish dominated my early years at Two Lakes so forcibly that I fished no other way, undeterred by my relatively empty baskets and long hours of apparent inactivity, although in reality these were periods of appraisal of the water and its aquatic fauna. Nevertheless, the lesser totals of my inactivity were compensated by the substantial if infrequent solatia of fine fish, for my three largest captures were all beguiled by dry flies, two of which were sedge imitations.

If we accept the ancient proposition that an artificial fly presented to a fish must not only be in accord with the natural insect it is presumed to depict, but also in phase with it, it becomes apparent from my previous chapter that an artificial sedge is at its deadliest at dusk in summer and early autumn. That this is indeed the case is as near a subjective certainty as anything in fly-fishing is likely to be. The sinking of the sun below the horizon is the signal, at the right time of year, for fishing a dry sedge. The temptation to start earlier is very strong if the fish are rising well, and is probably justified if the natural sedges have made their appearance. But I have found that during daylight hours, the larger fish, their instincts sharpened by the menace of line and monofil incessantly thrown at them for the previous three or four months, tend to shy away from the fly after approaching close to it. I believe that this can be remedied, or at least moderated, by keeping the leader submerged while the fly floats, but more of this later.

The most numerous types of sedges at Two Lakes are the medium to large reds, with body structures consisting of reddish wings, and abdomens varying from fawn, to orange, to red, and occasionally to sea-green. They have been imitated by fly fishers from the earliest times, but I doubt whether the traditional Little Red Sedge, in hook sizes 14 and 11, with an alternative green-bodied standby for special occasions, can be improved upon. For the paler types, such as the Caperer, the Pale Sedge, tied on the same size hooks, has served me well; indeed, its value has been attested with unbroken consistency for many years. The second most numerous group, the dark sedges, are well imitated by Halford's Little Dark Sedge, or by my own version, the dressing for which, together with the two preceding types, is given at the end of the chapter.

I have been conscious for a long time of a degree of rivalry between the river fly-fisher and his stillwater counterpart. The former claims, with some justification, that the stealthy approach, choice of fly and its presentation to a river trout requires a standard of knowledge, dexterity and application beyond what is required for mastering the chilling routine cultivated by the stillwater fisher. But I affirm, with equal confidence, that dry-fly fishing to a rising fish on a stillwater is more involved and more complex than on rivers, for on a river, the data necessary for planning the capture of fish is, or can be, formal and precise, whereas on a stillwater it is capricious and cryptic. The differences lie in three areas, all interconnected. They are firstly, Location; secondly, Imitation; and lastly, Presentation. I hope to show that each of these facets of the dry fly are more formidable tasks on a stillwater than on a river.

Location

On a river, the position of a rising fish can be pinpointed with great exactitude, except on rare occasions. Thus the competent angler who knows his business is able to place his fly at a spot from where it can float down without drag into the trout's window and without exposing the line to his quarry. Subject to his pattern being correct, and providing he has not otherwise betrayed his presence, as like as not the fish will be his. But on a stillwater, a feeding fish is almost invariably a cruising fish, and its rise ring is evidence of where it was, not of where it is. If the speed of the fish is 5–6 km (3–4 miles) per hour, it will be travelling at $1\frac{1}{2}$ m ($4\frac{3}{4}$ ft) per second. A lapse of 3 or 4 seconds between the formation of the ring and the arrival of an artificial fly within it will find the fish anything up to 6 m (20 ft) distant. What, then, can the angler do about it? He can do one of two things. He can try and deduce the direction of travel the fish has taken, and put his fly somewhere in its path, or he can drop his fly into the rise ring within a second of its formation.

Both alternatives are unsatisfactory, but of the two I prefer the latter. Its main drawback is the compulsion on the angler to keep his fly in the air, because of the time factor, ready to drop it into a rise ring at the moment of its formation. This should not bother him if the trout are rising well, but if not, he must be prepared to rest the fly on the water when his forearm tires. In my own experience, and in accordance with the natural Law of Perversity, this usually triggers off a magnificent rise well within covering distance, and by the time the fly has been retrieved and cast, the fish has departed to any point of the compass. Too much haste usually puts my fly up a tree or among the hinterland vegetation.

The first alternative, that is, to predict the trout's direction of motion from its rise form and to drop the fly in its path, a method much favoured by anglers, presupposes a capability beyond human capacity. Any such predictions are as much governed by the laws of chance as the spinning of a coin. There are, of course, rare occasions when a fish, or part of its anatomy, can be clearly seen as it speeds through the water, but this is unrelated to its rise form.

Demonstrations by its advocates have shown the unreliability of their predictions, and indeed a direct question put by me to one of the most renowned adherents of this method as to how often his predictions were correct brought the answer "About 50 per cent of the time". Even this more modest claim I take with a large pinch of salt.

I think there can be no doubt from the above that locating a rising fish for the purpose of putting a fly over it is very much more difficult on a stillwater than on a river, where the fish are in a fixed position.

Imitation

In accepting the axiom (as I do) that trout will rise readily to an imitation of a natural fly on the water or likely to be on the water at the time, we must admit the necessity for identifying aquatic insects even approximately. On a river, an angler with or without some grounding in entomology, preferably armed with a simple plankton net, can station himself at a suitable spot on the bank and lift off the water any insects coming down on the current. Naming the insects is unimportant—all he has to do is to match them as near as possible from his fly box. Thus his choice of imitation can be resolved by positive, or near positive, methods. But on a stillwater, this is not possible, because the emergence or fall of insects over so large an area conceals them from an observer on the bank, although it is true that there are times when an odd insect or a discarded shuck comes in view. But this is very rare, and in any case such isolated examples may or may not be representative of the contemporary biogenetic scene.

The riddle of the fly is a real one even to an experienced ento-mologist, for what cannot be seen cannot be identified. In the long run, we must fall back on trial and error, and here some knowledge of insect chronology can speed up the process. Of course, if one is sufficiently fortunate to land a fish, some indication of an acceptable fly might be found among the stomach content. At best, the still-water dry fly fisher can only grope half blindly towards a solution of the fly problem.

Presentation

I have shown that on a gently flowing chalk stream during low water conditions, with every trout visible, the fish will run to weed if covered by a fine leader with no fly attached. Under normal flow conditions, the leader, or that portion of it in the trout's window, at once becomes deformed and evanescent in the swirling water leaving the artificial fly as the focus of the fish's attention. I have shown too on a shallow section of a stillwater, where, during low water conditions, trout can be seen cruising around, the whole section can be cleared in less than a minute by a flyless line and leader cast two or three times across it.

On a stillwater, after the first few delirious weeks of the new season, trout become highly suspicious of line or leader lying on the surface, although the harmful effect is reduced when a ripple disturbs the water or in poor light conditions. It also appears to me that a leader cast into an expanding rise ring loses much of its prominence by the action of the wavelets. This repelling action of the line, or at least of the leader, does not apply to the sunken line, which appears to merge with the water, whereas the floating leader remains alien to it. Of course, the deeper the leader, the less conspicuous it must be.

In fishing the dry sedge, except at dusk, I found this problem of the floating leader responsible for driving away many good trout as soon as they caught a sight of it. While concealed myself, I have seen fish approach my floating sedge from a distance, travelling cautiously, and when within a metre or so accelerate into the shadows with all the evidence of panic a fish can possibly show.

As a result, I sought a means of presenting a dry sedge while the leader to which it was attached was submerged. My first efforts were made with a floating line and a leader which I variously anointed with glycerine, and wetting agents; the fly itself was liberally coated with a solid silicon line grease. This would do the trick for two or three casts, until the glycerine or wetting agent wore off, and then the leader would float or partially float, which was just as bad. To re-anoint the leader after every two or three casts became tedious, and so offered no solution to the problem.

No greater success was obtained with a sinking or sinking-tip line, each of them dragging the fly under the surface within a minute or two. However, by cutting off the whole of the sinking tip of a sinking-tip line with the exception of the last 45 cms (18 in), and by greasing the floating portion to assist floatation, I found a way round the difficulty. The leader itself is kept overnight between two damp pieces of felt, and the fly, as I have explained, lubricated with a heavy covering of solid silicon grease. In action, the fly is aerialised as much as possible, and when cast, is retrieved only a short distance with short, sharp jerks. I usually limit the jerks to three or four at the most, for if the fish to which the fly is cast has not taken it, either it has not been noticed, or, if noticed, is not wanted, and there is no point in over-wetting the fly. Far better remove it and false cast ready for the next rise. With this combination of fly, leader and line, utilised as described, one can fish a floating sedge with a submerged leader for as long as a hatch lasts.

As I have stated, I keep the fly in the air until my arm tires or until a fish rises within casting distance. In the latter event, I lay the fly down without delay into the ring, changing my tactics according to the light intensity at the time. During the day, particularly if the water is calm, I put the fly close to the near circumference of the ring so as to reduce the risk of lining the fish. At dusk, or in ripply water, when the line and leader are less conspicuous, I put it as near the centre of the ring as possible, on the theory that it is better for the fly to be a radius distant from the fish than a diameter. The fly is allowed to remain stationary for about a second, and is then moved sharply a little; this is repeated two or three times, and failing a favourable response, it is then lifted and aerialised before being dropped into the ring of the next rise.

The rise of a trout to a sedge is usually a noisy one, generally called a slash. Its elevation for the purpose of engulfing a large surface fly is greater than to a small pupa, nymph or spinner, as too is the speed of its rise. As a result, the disturbance is more pronounced, and this may give a clue to the presence of hatching sedges when none are to be seen. But during the sedge season, even when the fish are rising to pupae, nymphs, spent flies or other small creatures, an artificial sedge properly presented can, on a summer evening, be as seductive to a lake trout as a Mayfly to a river trout in June. It should certainly be permitted to try its powers, even if it is necessary to change line and leader. My own practice, to which I adhere as firmly as a diplomat to protocol, is to switch to a second rod previously prepared for this purpose.

Without a precise knowledge of the type of sedge emerging naturally, selection of an artificial must be fortuitous, but in such circumstances, my own priorities, for what they are worth, are as follows. First, a Pale Sedge; second, a Red Sedge; third, a Brown Sedge; and lastly, a Red Sedge with a green body.

A large proportion of fish are lost by failure of the hook point to penetrate the dense mass of hackle fibres surrounding the bend. It is therefore self-evident that the hook points of artificial sedges must be sharpened frequently.

Only on a single occasion were my efforts with a dry sedge frustrated by the size of the natural fly. It happened when swarms of Yellow Sedges (*Psychomyia pusilla*), a smallish sedge, clouded the air over the water, to the immense joy of the trout, which steadfastly refused my larger offerings tied on a No 14 hook. Fishing a few yards from me, my companion Struan Malcolm-Brown, whom I had previously scolded for tying his sedges too small, had a field day. Sic derident stultem Parcae.

The best way of exploiting the sedge as a wet fly is, as far as I know, unresolved. Yet the use of caddis larvae as natural baits has been known for centuries, and has enjoyed a reputation second to none. Known as a cod-bait, the naked larva is impaled on a hook in the same fashion as a maggot, and finished in an orthodox coarse fishing manner. Perhaps its virtue lay in its animation. It is certainly true that caddis larvae in their cases are often found in trout autopsies, but never a case-making larva without its case, and very rarely a non case-making larva or a pupa. The latter indeed is invariably totally enclosed in a case until it is ready to emerge, and at that time it possesses the tectonic physique of the winged fly, with its wings uninflated and its antennae wound around its abdomen for a second or two. After leaving its case, the rise of the pupa to the surface and the splitting of the pupal skin is so quick, that the odds of it falling a victim to a trout is heavily in favour of it happening during the comparatively lengthy period while it flutters on the surface drying its wings. I have therefore discounted the use of an imitation pupa, quite apart from the fact that the anatomy of a sedge pupa is a developing one and not static.

I believe the free swimming larvae are more vulnerable to trout, but they too pupate within a case, and at that stage enjoy the comparative safety of their case-making cousins. But I have noticed that during the summer days, when large numbers of natural brown free-swimming sedges are produced at Two Lakes, a brown bodied wet fly fished at a medium depth and at a moderate speed will do very well indeed on occasions when no other fly has any success at all. At such times, I have used impartially flies tied with pheasant tail bodies, or with brown seal or ostrich, brown silk or wool. Hackles have been equally acceptable whether deep red or chocolate brown, and gold ribbing or its omission have made no difference. Moreover, I have seen my colleagues doing equally well, and better, with their own particular brands of brown coloured wet flies. All this may be a coincidence, but I have my doubts.

DRY FLY DRESSINGS

LITTLE RED SEDGE

Hooks: No 14, 11
Tying silk: Hot Orange
Body: Fur from a hare's ear, ribbed with a stiff red hackle, over-ribbed with gold twist
Hackle: Deep red cock in front of the wings
Wings: Landrail (or substitute), bunched and rolled, and tied sloping back over the bend of the hook

PALE SEDGE

Hooks: No 14, 11
Tying silk: Hot orange
Body: Two or three herls from a cinnamon turkey tail, ribbed with a stiff ginger hackle and over-ribbed with gold twist
Hackle: Bright ginger cock in front of the wings
Wings: From the wing feather of a hen pheasant, bunched and rolled, and tied sloping back over the hook bend

BROWN SEDGE

Hook: No 14
Tying silk: Chocolate brown
Body: Any chocolate brown silk, wool, herl or dubbing, ribbed with similar colour hackle and over-ribbed with fine gold twist
Hackle: Cock feather dyed chocolate brown
Wings: Game cock or hen, plain side outside, bunched and rolled, sloping back to the bend

[15]

Two-winged Flies

As when a swarm of gnats at eventide
Out of the fens of Allan do arise,
Their murmuring small trumpets sounden wide;
Whiles in the air, their clustering armies flyes,
That as a cloud doth seem to dim the skyes.

EDMUND SPENSER. Faery Queen BK 2, CANTO 16

The Two-winged flies belong to the Order Diptera, which, according to Kloet & Hinks in their 1945 Check List, consisted of 5,194 different British species, belonging to 1,132 Genera. It is rivalled for size only by the Hymenoptera, an Order of flies with four membraneous wings, comprising ants, wasps, bees, ichneumon and sawflies, of which 6,212 species were recorded in 1945. There is little doubt that the number of new species established since then have added considerably to these figures.

The Order Diptera is fragmented into Sub-orders, then into Superfamilies, Families, Subfamilies, Genera and Subgenera. Each Genus and Subgenus is finally divided into species, and in many cases even the species have varieties. Often identities are ill-defined, and perhaps there has been some overlapping of nomenclature. According to Oldroyd, a leading authority, Diptera in Britain (to say nothing of the rest of the world, where the number of species is estimated to be somewhere between 75,000 and 100,000) are very incompletely known, probably because of the immense variety, and because of the large proportion of very small types that are not easy to capture or to examine.

Therefore there is a tendency by the less expert writers to group a number of species into a single species. A typical example is the midge fly *Chironomus plumosus*, which, with its variants *C ferrugineo-vittatus* and *C prasinatus*, is striped around the abdomen and which, in the male sex, possesses bulbous and luxurious antennae. Because of

148

these characteristics, all midge flies with striped bodies and thick feathery antennae, of which there are many, are classified as *C plumosus*. Such a contrivance, while expedient, is a retrogression to the days of Ronalds, who gave the identical scientific name to eight different insects, although he took care to stop at the Genus in each case.

Although all Diptera, with the exception of a few aberrant species in which the wings are reduced or absent, are two-winged, it does not follow that all two-winged flies are Diptera. The definition by Oldroyd is as good as any, when he states that "Diptera can, therefore, be recognised as insects in which the hind wings are replaced by halteres, and even if the forewings are reduced or absent, the mesothorax (the middle segment of the thorax) is developed at the expense of the other two thoracic segments".

Halteres are small spherical heads supported on thin stems at the base of which and in contact with which are a number of sensory cells which transmit messages to the brain of the insect when any side pressure from the stems is exerted on them. In flight, the halteres vibrate very rapidly, and in doing so, act as gyroscopic organs in that their inertia resist efforts to alter their direction of motion in space. Thus any deviation in the direction of the flight of the insect causes side pressure by the halteres and this is immediately registered by the sensory cells and conveyed to the brain. It has been suggested that the halteres vibrate at speeds corresponding to the wing beats, but this is doubtful, as they continue to vibrate for a brief period after the flight has ended. The principle of the halteres was adopted by the Sperry Corporation for use in the automatic pilot of aircraft.

The modification over the ages of the hindwings into halteres did not detract from the insects' powers of flight, for Diptera are strong fliers. Various methods have been used to determine the rate of wing flaps in insects and in one Dipterid (*Ceratopogonid forcipomyia*) species it was found to be 988–1,047 beats per second, reaching 2,218 frequencies per second when the wings were trimmed and the insect exposed to a high temperature.

The mouth parts of winged Diptera are adapted for sucking, and in many species, for piercing and cutting. The head usually consists of a narrow strip between the eyes, which dominate the head, and which occasionally meet or even merge above or below the antennae. This is more frequent in the male sex, but it occurs often in some

Families in the female sex. Many species have conspicuous hair growth on the eyes, but often the hairs are so small that they can be seen only under high magnification.

The antennae of the adults are made up of segments which are important in type classification. Generally, long antennae are associated with small eyes, and short antennae with large eyes, suggesting that the functions of each may be complimentary. In the Families Culicidae (mosquitoes) and Chironomidae (midges) the second segment is bulbous or globular, and located within them is an organ known as Johnson's organ which is sensitive to the slightest movement of the stem of the antennae. Thus the speed of flight can be determined by the insect by the wind pressure on the antennae. Moreover, the organ is sensitive to the vibrations of sound waves, and may serve as ears. The males appear to recognise the hum emitted by the constant frequencies of the adult females in flight and are attracted to them and to no other species or even to the young sexually immature females of their own species, which have lower wing frequencies. The mating males have been attracted to tuning forks of the correct frequency. The wing beats appear to act as species sex-attractors in some Families, perhaps substituting or augmenting the attraction of chemical secretions of characteristics (odour?) known as pheremones. Other insects are known to have similar "hearing" organs located in their legs, abdomen or thorax.

The wing speeds of some aquatic Diptera, obtained by various methods, are as follows, given in beats per second. Crane flies, 43–73; mosquitoes 150–587; horseflies 96; and in a biting midge (Ceratopogonidae Family, *Forcipomyia* Genus) closely related to the non-biting midges (Chironomidae) speeds have been determined at 988–1,047, increasing to 2,218 if the wings are artificially shortened and the insect exposed to a high temperature. These compare oddly to the wing speeds of large butterflies at 5–9, moths 8–85, dragonflies 20–28, and beetles 46–91.

Some Diptera do not feed in the winged state, their mouth parts having become obsolete. Others have well developed organs for piercing or sucking, generally the juices of plants, but in some cases, the blood of animals or birds. Some possess teeth for use not only in drawing blood, but also for macerating smaller insects whose juices they subsequently devour.

The number of segments in the abdomen is generally seven or eight, but occasionally there may be as few as four, three or two. The genitalia are usually located below the last visible segment, evolved from what are thought to have been in the dim and distant past additional segments. The structure of the genitalia, particularly that of the male, is of great importance in classification, but frequently this is a difficult task unless associated male and female specimens are available, or, where the genitalia do not protrude, as in some instances, unless the insect is dissected. Another important feature in classification of Families, but not of Genera or species, is wing venation, but for more precise identification, the anatomy must be examined and the authoritative keys consulted.

Parthenogenesis (birth without male fertilisation) is not unknown among Diptera. A description by Edwards in the Proceedings of the Royal Entomological Society of London (Vol 38, Pts 10–12, pp 165–170, 31/12/63) describes a small yellow midge (*Lundstroemia parthenogenetica*) which lays its eggs almost immediately after emergence from the pupa. Of 35 generations raised in 3 years, all were females, and indeed no male has ever been recorded.

The aquatic Diptera are probably the main source of insect food for stillwater trout. They consist mainly of the Families Tipulidae (Crane flies or Daddy Longlegs), Culicidae (Mosquitoes), Chironomidae (Midges), Simulidae (Black Flies), Psychodidae (Mothflies), Tabanidae (Horseflies) and Syrphidae (Hoverflies).

Tipulidae. Of the 291 known British species, comparatively few are aquatic. The majority develop on dry land, but others prefer mud at the edges of streams or lakes, or in marshes, and at least one species lives in salt water. Most aquatic types are probably carnivorous, living on small creatures such as worms, but some are known to be plant eaters. The winged flies are believed to be incapable of feeding, but Wigglesworth records the presence in the gut of some Crane Flies of certain species of bacteria capable of fermenting cellulose, and it may be assumed that such species, and perhaps others, feed on vegetable matter. However, little is known on the subject. The group consists of relatively large flies, and may be recognised by their slender bodies and long legs.

Culicidae. Although this Family was described above as mosquitoes, in fact only one of the three subfamilies (Culicinae) included in it is a biting mosquito. The remaining two are the Chaoborinae, already fully described, and the Dixinae, neither of which have mouthparts formed for biting. The Dixinae have only one British Genus, (Dixa), with 13 species. All Dixa are aquatic, but are not very active

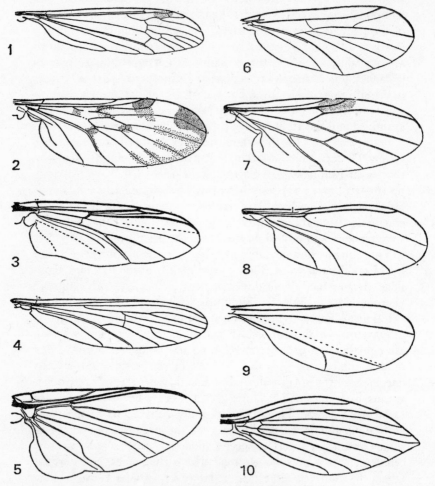

The wings of Diptera (after Oldroyd).

1 Tipulidae, *Limnophila*.   2 Anisopodidae, *Anisopus*.   3 Chironomidae, *Procladius*.
4 Culicidae, *Theobaldia* (scales omitted).   5 Simuliidae, *Simulium*.   6 Mycetophili-
dae, *Symmerus*.   7 Bibionidae, *Dilophus*.   8 Cecidomyiidae, *Lestremia*.   9 Cecidomyiidae, *Mayetiola*.   10 Psychodidae, *Psychoda* (hairs omitted).

swimmers, preferring to cling to underwater vegetation or stones, often bent double in a reversed U-shape, with only head and tail submerged. They live on small organisms carried near the water surface, capturing them by mouth bristles.

The winged fly emerge just before sunset and swarm in small groups. They are small insects, none being larger than the Phantom Fly, varying in wing length between 3 and 6 mm (a little under $\frac{1}{8}$–$\frac{1}{4}$ in). The antennae are small and simple.

The biting mosquito can be recognised by its protruding proboscis. It has received far more attention than the non-biters from students because of its capacity to carry disease among birds, animals and humans. Actually, only the female of the species is the bloodsucker, for without adequate supplies of blood she cannot develop her eggs, although if conditions, or temperature are unsuitable for egg-laying, the bloodmeal will fatten her body considerably. The male is easily distinguishable by its more plumose antennae.

Blood sucking insects carry bacteria from creature to creature, spreading disease widely. Bubonic plague, the Black Death of the 14th Century, believed to have killed over 20,000,000 people out of the 80,000,000 population of Europe, is a result of transference of the disease to humans by mosquitoes after they had killed off most of the rat population by the same method.

The biting mosquitoes consist of 6 Genera and about 30 species. The larvae breathe through pores or tubes (siphons) in the 8th segment of the abdomen, and when feeding or resting they lie with their tails just above the surface film. One type lies horizontally, and the other type at an angle to it, the reason being due to the different position of the breathing apparatus, and of its construction. Water is prevented from entering the apparatus by a waxy film covering it which repels the water. Protection from mosquitoes in some parts of the world is obtained by covering the water in which they breed with a layer of oil or creosole or some other liquid which prevents the larvae from breathing. The mouthparts of the larvae have sets of bristles on each side which are vibrated very rapidly, and the current thus induced brings to them myriads of tiny particles in suspension. These are trapped by the bristles and devoured by the insect. One type of larva (*Anopheles*) actually sweeps the under face of the surface film for any small bits of food that cling to it, and having secured them, convey them to their mouths. When danger threatens, they immediately submerge.

The pupae hang from the water surface, breathing air through trumpet-like organs situated on the thorax. They are similar in shape to the pupae of the Phantom pupa, but with a far greater curvature of the abdomen. Usually, the pupal stage lasts about 4 days, and the winged fly emerges very quickly, and after a minute or two, depending on the weather, takes off to prepare for the final episode of its life span.

Simulidae. These are known in Britain as Black Flies, in some parts of Scotland as Birch Flies, and in America as Buffalo Gnats. Altogether there are 35 British species, all known and described in detail. All females of the species are blood suckers, but together with the males they also suck nectar from flowers. In many parts of the world they are a great nuisance because of their blood sucking habits, occasionally causing fatalities among lifestock on a large scale. Like female mosquitoes, blood is necessary for egg development, but in some countries various species are incapable of biting, as their mouthparts are too reduced. In many cases, including two British species, (*Prosimulium hirtipes* and *Simulium argyreatum*) the females are normally able to develop their eggs without a blood meal. It is thought that this, known as autogeny, is a stage in the evolution towards an eventual non-biting condition. Generally, the British types prefer attacking birds or animals, but they will not hesitate to attack humans if necessary.

Black Flies are also known to be carriers of parasites, transmitting them to their victims, even, in some tropical countries, to humans. Only one (*Simulium ornatum*) British species is known to be capable of transmitting a parasite to cattle.

The larvae are widespread in rivers and streams except where pollution is severe. They cling to stones or vegetation, by means of a suction pad at the base of the abdomen, in fast flowing water, their bodies swinging to and fro in the current like crazy pendulums. Around the jaws are thick brushes acting as filters, and in these they trap the many minute particles suspended in the fast water. This forms the bulk of their nourishment. At Two Lakes, the larvae can be found in large quantities in the fast currents entering and leaving the rearing ponds. They are a dark grey or black colour, and about 13 mm ($\frac{1}{2}$ in) long. The shape of the body can be described as elongated pear-shape, the wider end being closer to the tail than to the head. The larva is a poor swimmer, quite unable to swim against the fast current in which it anchors itself, and it is assumed that it reaches its anchorage from above or from one side. It should be explained that the larva possesses an auxiliary suction organ formed by the fusion of a pair of legs near the head, (actually on the thorax). It can therefore crawl by grasping its anchorage first by the sucker at its tail end and then by the one at the head end, releasing its hold on one as the other grips. If for any reason it is compelled to quit the stone or vegetation to which it clings, it is found to be hanging on to a silken thread, spun by itself, which is attached to its former lodgment, and by means of which it hauls itself back when the reason for its detachment has gone.

Immediately before pupation, the larva forms a conical cocoon and cements it to some rigid object in the stream. The open end of the cone faces downstream, but is closed temporarily until the larval skin has been cast. The incipient pupa then protrudes the respiratory filaments attached to its head through the former open end, and by this means collects oxygen from the fast water. It eventually escapes from the cocoon in an ingenious manner. As maturity approaches, usually after about 10 days or so, the pupa collects a quantity of air within its pupal skin. When eventually the pupal skin splits, the bubble of air rises to the surface, carrying the newly emerged winged fly with it, and as it bursts, the insect runs along the surface to some solid support, and hangs on grimly until its wings are sufficiently dry for it to take flight.

PSYCHODIDAE (MOTHFLIES), TABANIDAE (HORSEFLIES) AND SYRPHIDAE (HOVERFLIES)

The Mothflies are represented in Britain by two subfamilies, the Trichomyiinae and the Psychodinae, the former with 2 Genera, each with a single species, and the latter with 5 Genera and 70 species. (A list by Dr Paul Freeman gives a total of 73 species. My figures are based on Kloet & Hincks, 1945.) The aquatic types are usually found in sewage works or putrid water, and it is doubtful if they are present in the spring waters of Two Lakes. The adult flies are very hairy, and very small, generally with a wing length varying between $1\frac{1}{4}$ and $3\frac{1}{2}$ mm ($\cdot 05$ and $\cdot 14$ in).

The Horseflies, some species of which are also known as Clegs, are inveterate biters, though it is only the female that sucks blood. The bite, whether inflicted on humans or animals, can be very painful, and their absence from Two Lakes, as far as I am aware, is not a cause for regret. They are large, sturdy insects, with broad heads and colourful eyes. They breed in water or in watery habitats, but very little is known of their life history. The Family consists of three subfamilies and 28 species, but some species have differing forms.

The Hoverflies are generally largish, and at first sight may be mistaken for wasps, but of course they possess only two wings. They feed almost entirely on Aphids (green-fly) sucking out the soft interior and leaving only the shrivelled skin. This is probably beneficial, in that they control, together with other insects which feed on Aphids, an insect with an enormous capacity for multiplication. A well-known curiosity of the Family is known as the Rat-tailed Maggot, because of its telescopic tail at the tip of which is found its breathing gill or siphon. The larva lies on the bed of the lake and although only about 2 cms (¾ in) in length, can extend its tail a distance of nearly 20 cms (8 in) so that it protrudes through the surface to the air. I find it just as great a curiosity that all authorities, with one exception, refer to the Rat-tailed Maggot as *Eristalis*. The one exception is the late Dr Imms, who refers to it as *Eristalis tenax*, the common Drone Fly. In fact, there is no Genus Eristalis, although there is one Eristalinus, with one species only, *sepulchralis*. There is, however, a Genus Tubifera, with 10 species, one of which is *tenax*. At one time, this was known as *Eristalis tenax*, and I presume this is the insect referred to by Dr Imms.

Chironomidae (*Midges*). This family is the most widespread of all aquatic Diptera, being found in still or sluggish waters, and in a few cases, in swift rivers. However, not all Chironomids are aquatic, a large number being terrestrial, living in dung, decaying timber or vegetation, moss or grass roots. In some parts of Europe, attempts have been made to classify stillwaters by the Chironomids native to them, but in spite of the amount of research done on them, their life histories are known in only a few cases.

The Chironomidae Family probably provides the most important contribution to trout food in stillwaters, particularly in the pupal stage. The Family consists of six subfamilies (of which the most important to anglers is the Chironominae), 26 Genera (most of them aquatic) and about 400 species. Some of the larvae are white, some yellow, and some (Chironomus—a Genus of the Subfamily Chironominae) red. The latter are well known as Bloodworms. Some live among weeds, some at the surface, and some (mostly the Bloodworms) in the bottom mud or silt, where they usually

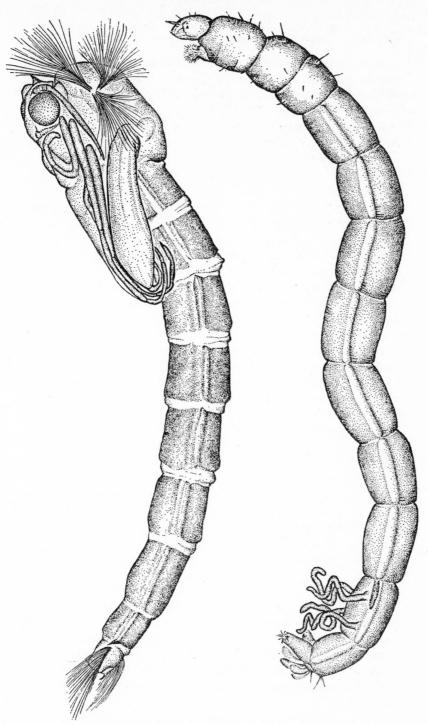

Left : Chironomid pupa. *Right :* Chironomid larva.
Magnification approximately X10.
(After Johannsen)

camouflage themselves by constructing shelters made of the surrounding debris. The red colour is due to the presence in their make-up of haemoglobin, a substance which possesses the property of conserving oxygen, and as the larvae spend their time in the bottom mud, where oxygen is scarce, the haemoglobin, which they replenish with oxygen by occasional trips to the surface, is no doubt a useful attribute.

The females generally return to the water after mating, and lay their eggs on the surface of the water or on projecting vegetation. Sometimes the ovipositing female propels the eggs through the surface film with no little force, and as they absorb water they expand and sink slowly. Three or four days later the larva emerge and burrow into the bottom sediment, hiding very effectively in rough fibrous shelters or tubes, or, depending on species, swelling the mass of zooplankton as they feed on algae.

The Chironomid pupae, like those of other Diptera, are at their most vulnerable to feeding fish during the brief period just before the emergence of the winged fly. In the Genus Chironomus, the pupae lie in the bottom sediment with the head and thorax protruding. Unlike the mosquito pupa, which breathes air through head trumpets, the Chironomus pupa extracts oxygen from the water by means of filament on the first segment of the thorax. These they sway to and from by flexing the thorax. As maturity approaches, the pupal skin fills with air, and the pupa floats to the surface, where the pupal envelope splits and the winged fly emerges, and after a moment or two, flies away.

When trout are feeding on Dipterous pupae, they pose a problem to the angler, a problem of finding an artificial fly, correct in size and colour, to whet the appetite of a trout within eye-shot. To those who are of the opinion that such a fly must resemble some contemporaneous aquatic creature on which the trout have been feeding, particularly in colour and to a lesser extent dimensionally, the problem automatically generates the necessity of finding some evidence of what the trout are feeding on, or likely to be feeding on. This, as I have earlier pointed out, is a task of some difficulty, to be solved only (unless one is very lucky) by trial and error. It seemed to me that some knowledge of the types of Diptera emerging from the larval state during the different months of the fishing season would at least provide some guide as to what might be expected at various times. I stress the word "might", as obviously patterns may change from year to year. But some evidence is better than none, and I therefore decided to raise Diptera in my own home from larvae taken from Two Lakes. Starting in March 1966, I at first entertained the idea of identifying each specimen as it emerged, but the task was a formidable one, and after a few weeks of painful and prolonged research reaching into the small hours of the morning, I decided to record only brief details of the hatched insects, concentrating on size and colour. Where, as often happened, the colour differed in the different parts of the anatomy, the general appearance only, or a brief resumé, is given. The results are as follows:

		Length mm	
March	8 pupae	6·0	Tortoiseshell colour, black bars. *Pentaneura maculipennis.*
	4 winged flies male	6·0	Olive colour, brown rings, pale olive legs. *Pentaneura maculipennis.*
	2 winged flies, female	6·0	Olive colour, brown rings. *Pentaneura eximia.*
	Winged fly	9·5	All black.
	2 winged flies	11·5	Colour grey/black. Thorax green.
	Winged fly	8·0	Deep olive colour, black head. Crane fly. *Genus Limnophila.*
	Winged fly	5·5	All black.
		6·0	Tortoiseshell colour, black rings.
		6·0	Pale olive colour, black thorax.
March	Winged fly	6·5	Olive colour, brown rings.
		9·5	All black.
		6·0	Grey colour, thorax pale green, amber legs.
		·5·0	Black colour, legs grey.
April		5·0	All black.
		10·0	All black.
		9·0	All black.
		1·5	Golden olive colour, black rings.
		9·0	Black colour, cinnamon rings.
		3·5	Olive colour, black rings.
		4·0	Black and olive colour rings alternating.
		3·0	Golden olive and black rings alternating.
		2·0	Olive colour, black eyes.

		Length mm	
April		2·5	Black proboscis, golden thorax, sea-green body fading to orange. Olive legs.
		6·0	Eyes coppery green. Thorax grey Body olive colour with black rings. Olive legs.
		7·0	Apple green colour.
May		7·0	Golden olive colour with black patches and creamy white sides to thorax.
		2·5	Very dark grey colour with olive coloured legs.
June		7·0	Pea green colour, black thorax.
July		4·0	Pea green colour, thorax light brown.
		2·5	Pea green colour, light brown thorax.
July	Winged fly	4·0	Emerald green colour.
		2·5	Deep orange colour.
		5·0	Emerald green colour.
		1·5	Golden yellow colour, light brown thorax.
		7·5	All black with golden hairs.
		6·0	Emerald green colour, light brown thorax.
		5·5	Deep orange colour.
		8·5	Grey colour abdomen dorsally, dark amber colour ventrally, black thorax.
		6·0	Thorax black, body pea green changing to brown at last three segments. Legs orange.
August		8·0	Dark grey colour.
		6·0	Emerald green colour, changing to grey/black at tail. Yellow head, black eyes (captured by John Elliott).

The months of May and June were singularly unproductive, but this is no doubt fortuitous. Early in August I ceased stocking my insectary with fresh larvae in order to concentrate on other activities. Although therefore the list is far from comprehensive, it is fairly representative of the wide variety of Diptera present at Two Lakes, and of the difficulty of fly selection on the imitation presumption. It will also be observed that the early part of the fishing season is highly productive of black Diptera, and this appears to correspond with the success of black artificials. Black is about the only colour that cannot be varied into lighter or darker shades. Black is black, whereas olive can be pale or dark, as can grey, orange, green, or almost any other colour. I have noticed that when a dark brown fly is well received, a light brown one will be ignored, and so on throughout the spectrum. It is also noticeable that after the first few early weeks of the season, black flies are taken by the fish on infrequent occasions only. This again corresponds to the list, in which we find only one all-black specimen after April.

One incident is worthy of the telling. On August 12th 1970, few fish were being caught, and those that were caught, were taken on flies in which the colour green predominated. After lunch, I was hailed by John Elliott, who was fishing 50 yards or so from me, and told that he had captured a green insect. I immediately collected it, and stored it in a small container for later examination. The description recorded that same night in my diary was as follows:

"August 12th 1970. Two Lakes. Captured by John Elliott. Emerald green Dipteron, female. Body length 6 mm. Golden yellow head, very pale green legs, black eyes; body gradually changes to grey/black at tail. Many silvery hairs. Chironomid, perhaps *Chironomus xenolabis*".

[16]

Of Sundry Fauna

...like the fly,
That spreads his motley wings in th'eye of noon,
To sport their season, and be seen no more.

WILLIAM COWPER. The Garden

Of the insects I have found at Two Lakes and not yet mentioned, or only very briefly, there remain, to the best of my knowledge, the Dragonflies (including the Damselflies), the Lacewings, and the Beetles. To what extent they contribute to the diet of trout I cannot say, but certainly Dragonflies and Beetles play crucial roles in the waters they frequent. Of the Lacewings, I have little evidence of their importance at Two Lakes, though their presence has been manifest of many occasions. Alongside the above insects are the Crustaceans, which include the tiny Daphnia, the Water Slater and the freshwater Shrimp; the Molluscs with the valuable Snail population; the Annelids or true worms, the only one of which I know being the Bristle Worm; and the Arachnids, embracing Spiders, (with only a single freshwater species) and Mites.

Dragonflies and Damselflies. These large insects belong to the Order Odonata, of which the main sub-orders are the Anisoptera (Dragonflies) and the Zygoptera (Damselflies). The largest British species is the Emperor Dragonfly (*Anax imperator*) with a wing span of about 10 cms (4 in), and a larval length at maturity of about 58 mm (2¼ in), but this is exceeded in tropical regions by species half as big again. Even these are pigmies compared to their extinct ancestors, which attained a wing length of 60 cms (25 in). The Emperor can be identified by its size and by the blue-green thorax of the male and the grass-green thorax of the female, and the blue abdomen with a dark stripe running down it. It is the spectacular splash of metallic colours that interests anglers in these magnificent ambassadors of summer's majesty as they flit from jutting water plant to bankside vegetation. Their size renders them an excellent group for study, for they need no microscope for identification and are easy to observe and capture during the daylight hours to which their activities are restricted.

Dragonflies are divided into 5 Families with 26 species, and Damselflies into 4 Families with 17 species. They may be distinguished in their winged state by the different postures of the wings when at rest; Dragonflies carry them outstretched at 90° to the body, and Damselflies wholly or partly folded back in line with the body. The nymphs too differ considerably and are easily separated, for the Dragonfly is short, stumpy and pear-shaped, with three abbreviated tails, and the Damselfly is long and slender, with three long tails carrying feathery gills.

The Damselflies and certain of the Dragonflies, when the time for ovipositing arrives, insert their eggs into incisions they make into water plants, the bark of trees or floating weed. The remaining Dragonflies lay their eggs singly on the surface of the water, except in a few instances, where they are laid in masses. The eggs either sink to the bottom or come to rest on an underwater obstruction. It is interesting to note that because of the danger from predating fish to those species which oviposit by inserting their eggs into underwater plants, some types have developed a habit whereby the male grasps the female during the ovipositing and helps her to take off more speedily when danger threatens. Some of the couples descend below the surface enclosed in a film of air that clings to the thoracic hairs and stay for a considerable time while egg laying proceeds. The implantation of the underwater part of the stems is an excellent illustration of Nature's care for the preservation of species, for it safeguards the eggs from dessication should the water level fall during the summer. It is true that some species insert their eggs in water plants above the water level, but they do so only in autumn, a time of year when the water level may be expected to rise during the ensuing weeks. In some tropical countries, the eggs are laid on branches overhanging dried-up ponds immediately before the seasonal rains, and the larvae emerge from the egg and drop into the water at a time coincident with the flooding of the pond.

Very little is known about the duration of egg development in natural conditions, although where it has been observed, emergence of the nymphs occurred after 24 days. In the laboratory the period has varied from species to species, the shortest being about 10 days, and the longest about 38 days. It is known that some species lay eggs that undergo a complete diapause that extends throughout the whole of the winter. With exceptions, this applies to the eggs of those species that oviposit in late summer or autumn.

The nymphs themselves are formidable creatures with some unique characteristics, the best known of which is the "mask", a prehensile growth covering the lower underpart of the head which can be extended forward with lightning rapidity in order to seize any small creature within range. The action is hydrostatically controlled, and is caused by the contraction by a nymph of its abdomen, a manœuvre which forces blood into the region of the mask and operates it. The mask of a recently killed nymph can be extended artificially by squeezing the abdomen of the corpse.

The prey of the nymph must be in motion, must be of the correct dimension, and must be within the maximum striking range for the action of the mask to be triggered off. It has been shown that if the prey becomes stationary, even if of correct size and within striking distance, the nymph ignores it, and indeed appears to lose sight of it, until movement is resumed, when the mask is shot out and the prey acquired.

The nymphs select their abode according to species. Some burrow in the bottom mud, with only the head and tail exposed, the latter for breathing purposes. The gills of Dragonflies are internal, within the rectal passage, and the insects pump water over them through the anus. The gills of Damselflies are borne in the three caudal appendages, but it is believed that they too have supplementary gills within the rectum.

Other nymphs live on the bottom without the necessity of burrowing, while some choose their habitat among the surface water plants. The colour of the nymphs varies a great deal, and on the whole seems to be adapted to the background in which they choose to live. Thus the bottom dwellers tend to brown, whereas the plant dwellers are greenish, yellow or olive, or a mixture of more than one colour, with black or brown mottling. Indeed, the nymphs, in striking contrast to the beautiful winged fly, are drab creatures to look at.

Very little is known about the life duration of the insects, but regular field work has established that some live for no more than a single year, some live for two years, and others for more than two years. It is widely thought that some may survive for as long as five years; stillwater species are believed to be among the shorter lived types.

When the time comes for metamorphosis, the nymphs begin to move towards the surface and towards the shore, and eventually select a plant or other protruding support for their final emergence, sometimes testing it in advance and returning below the surface. A little before the final change into the winged form, the nymph mounts its support, which is usually vertical or almost so, and remains motionless for an hour or more. Eventually the skin of the dorsal thorax splits, and the winged fly makes a partial exit, freeing only the head, the legs and the thorax. The abdomen remains within the nymphal shuck, and the insect, with its head and thorax drooping down, rests motionless for perhaps another hour. The abdomen is then freed, and the insect commences the slow process of extending the length of the body and inflating the wings. Soon afterwards, the nymphal colour is replaced by the splendid colours of the species.

Two Lakes is richly endowed with these ornate insects, particularly the Damselflies, but the only one I have reared was a male of the Large Red Damselfly (*Pyrrhosoma nymphula*), which, with the Common Ischnura (*Ischnura elegans;* black body shading to bright blue towards the tip of the abdomen) are two of the most common Damselflies in Britain. The actual emergence of the winged fly from the nymphal shuck is a sight never to be forgotten, if one is prepared to wait for the expansion of the wings, the elongation of the body, and the change of colour.

The nymphs expose themselves to danger from marauding trout when making their way to the surface or the shore immediately before emergence. The Damselfly swims with an eel-like motion, and the Dragonfly in a progression of short bursts. At such a time, a large olive nymph, not too bright, might attract the fish. A second period of danger, at least to some species, occurs when the female winged fly descends to lay her eggs, and it is noticeable that when species with bright blue colouring are plentiful, sunken lures such as the Camsunary Killer or the Bluefly are at their most effective.

Lacewings. The only specimens I have captured at Two Lakes were terrestial, and all were taken at the height of summer. The species did not vary, for they were all *Sympherobius elegans*, a dark brownish fly frequenting trees, with a preference for beech, oak and hazel. As most Lacewings are active only at dusk, it would not be surprising if other species are present at Two Lakes, but I have no evidence of it from observation of winged flies or from examination of trouts' stomach contents. In fact, only two Families of Lacewings are aquatic (Osmylidae and Sisyridae), and this is strange, because both West and Courtney Williams suggest that trout feed on Lacewings of the Genus Hemerobius, Family Hemerobidae, which are wholly terrestial. Furthermore, as they are crepuscular (dusk fliers), it is impossible to see whether, like the Hawthorne Fly and other terrestial insects, they alight on the water. Nor could this be determined the following morning by a post mortem of a captured fish, for in the intervening hours the insects would be rendered unrecognisable by the digestive juices.

In classifying the Family Osmylidae as aquatic, we are really stretching a point, for they make their homes, not in water, but in the muddy or marshy margins. Only the Sisyridae are truly aquatic, and as during their larval existence they make their homes in freshwater sponges on which they are parasitic, they are well concealed. They must inevitably run the gauntlet of hungry fish they come shore to pupate, like their cousins the Alder Flies, but if this is done during the night, the risk is small. They must also return to the water to lay their eggs, but if, as is believed, they deposit their eggs in small clusters on leaves overhanging the water during the night, and then proceed to cover them with a web of white spun silk, they have nothing to fear from the trout.

The eggs are pale yellow, about ·35 mm (·013 in) in diameter, slightly flattened with a disc-like projection at one end. About 14 days later the larvae hatch out, and drift apparently aimlessly in the water until they feel the faint current produced by a sponge, towards which they struggle, and with difficulty (or by chance), eventually reach. Immediately the larva embeds itself, and begins to feed on the sponge. In the autumn it leaves the sponge, and moves towards dry land where it spins a cocoon around itself and winters within it in a pre-pupal stage. It changes into a true pupa in the spring, and emerges as a winged fly at any time from May to September.

There are only three British species, *Sisyra dalii* (Yellow Lacewing), length about 11–12 mm (almost ½ in), *S terminalis* (Grey Lacewing), and *S fuscata* (Brown Lacewing), both a little larger than the first. Of the Osmylidae, we have but a single British species *Osmylus fulvicephalus*, much larger than the three above, with an orange-brown head, thorax streaked with cream, yellow and black, and transparent watery wings marbled with brown and black spots.

Water Beetles (*Coleoptera*). The Beetles are the third largest Order of insects in Britain, exceeded only by the Hymenoptera and the Diptera. The Order consists (Kloet & Hincks) of 947 Genera, with a total of 3,690 different species. According to Balfour-Browne, 220 of these are aquatic or Water Beetles, all of which he lists. In some cases his nomenclature differs from Kloet & Hincks, owing to different interpretations of the rulings of the International Zoological Congress which governs modifications and changes. Dr Mellanby

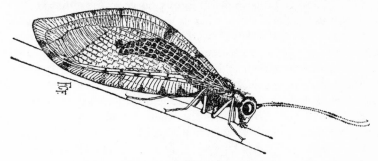

Lacewing (Osmylus fulvicephalus).

confuses the subject a little more. As an example, writing of a certain Water Beetle (Genus Deronectes) she states that the Genus contains five British species, although she mentions only *elegans*. Balfour-Browne gives six, listing them, and showing that *elegans* has been superseded by *depressus*. Kloet & Hincks give the Genus seven species by treating *elegans* and *depressus* as separate species. Further confusion arises by Mellanby's inclusion of a number of aquatic species which Balfour-Browne does not include in his list. Again, Mellanby enumerates various species as aquatic for part of their lives only, and some of them are included in Balfour-Browne's catalogue of aquatic Beetles, but most are excluded. The situation is bedevilled by Miall, who states that some species of the Family Chrysomelidae (Leaf Eaters) lay their eggs at the base of submerged plants, upon which the larvae feed when they hatch from the egg. He mentions in particular the Water Beetle (*Donacia crassipes*) and relates how the female bites holes in the leaves of water plants and lays her eggs around them. The larvae eventually fall through the hole onto the bed and feed on the roots of the plant. Mellanby repeats this almost entirely, and so does Balfour-Browne, but for some reason the latter does not include them, or any other member of the Family or Genus, in his list. Perhaps the answer is given by Clegg, who refers to "true" Water Beetles as opposed to those which spend only part of their lives in water. The objection to this lies in the fact that even the "true" Water Beetles pupate on dry or marshy land, and thus spend one of the four stages of their lives (egg, larva, pupa, winged fly) in a non-aquatic habitat.

Most of our knowledge of Water Beetles is concentrated on a few species that have been reared artificially. Of the majority we know little, and as has been shown, there is no great unanimity among the various authorities on what is known. This is attributed to the large numbers involved, and to the fact that many Beetles, although their general structure is fairly uniform, have adapted themselves to land, water and air, often spending part of their lives in all three. For this reason, I do not propose discussing the life histories of Water Beetles even where they are known, for they have already been published so many times that there would be little point in repeating them here. For those interested in the subject, reference may be made Mellanby, Clegg, Miall, Imms and Balfour-Browne, or for those wishing to specialise still further, to the German naturalist Korschelt, who wrote nearly 2,000 pages on one single species of Water Beetle, the Great Diving Beetle, *Dytiscus marginalis*.

For hundreds of years trout anglers have tied imitations of beetles with unfailing regularity. Courtney Williams lists them as follows: Coch-y-bonddu, Soldier Beetle, Sailor Beetle, Water Cricket, Doctor, Devonshire Doctor, Explorer, Governor, Imp, Green Insect, Little Chap, March Brown, Marlow Buzz, Red-eyed Beetle and Simple Simon. He omitted the Bracken Clock, which is as good as any. Later he illustrated a number of natural beetles, naming them scientifically, and where possible, in lay language. They are *Aphodius aestivalis* (Cowdung), *Phyllopertha horticula* (Coch-y-bonddu), *Chrysomela polita*, *Chrysomela haemoptera*, *Coccinnela 7-punctata* (Ladybird), *Xylodrepa 4-punctata*, *Otiorrhyncus singularis*, *Phyllobius pomaceus*, *Phyllobius maculicornis*, *Cantharis livida* (Sailor), *Cantharis rustica* (Soldier), *Elater balteatus* (Click or Skipjack), *Feronia madida* (Rain) and *Elaphrus cupreus* (Common Earth). Two others that he included, a smaller Soldier and Sailor, I have been unable to trace. I have also brought his nomenclature up to date.

Curiously enough, every single one is terrestial, although some species of the Family Chrysomelidae, Genus Donacia, spend their larval lives in water. It is also known that other terrestial beetles spend some part of their lives in or on water, particularly those that make their homes close to the margins of streams and still-waters.

Apart from the Soldier Beetle (*Cantharis rustica*), an old acquaintance, which in summer is prolific around Two Lakes, I have not identified any beetles in the locality, although they are present in a wide variety, as in most expanses of water. The subject is too vast for amateur or part-time study, and the data too uncertain. In addition, autopsies on captured trout at Two Lakes have revealed quite clearly so far that beetles are not an important constituent of the trout's diet. This is surprising, and perhaps one day I shall eat my words, for in autopsies I have conducted on trout captured in rivers I have found beetle larvae sometimes in overwhelming proportions of the whole. Indeed, the favourite artificial fly of the Yorkshire Derwent, the John Storey, is a very good imitation of a beetle larva native to that river. Probably Terry's Terror, popular on the Kennet plays a similar role there, for the main features of both, a body of bronze peacock herl, and a red hackle are common. This dressing may be varied locally by substituting a green peacock herl for the bronze, and by a furnace or coch-y-bonddu hackle at the head. One of the more modern and successful dressings to imitate the adult insect, invented by Eric Horsfall Turner, called appropriately Eric's Beetle, builds up the body with yellow floss below a bronze peacock herl, finished off with a black head hackle.

The above dressings are basically standard imitations of beetle larvae, and are worth trying on days when "the beetle wheels her droning flight".

Crustacea. No inquiry into the waters of Two Lakes can fail to take account of the incredible numbers in the summer of the tiny transparent creatures known as Water Fleas (Daphnia), though they are unrelated to true fleas. Because their outer covering, or carapace, is transparent, they are informative creatures, for even under low magnification one can see the passage of food through the body, the action of the heart and the circulation of the blood. Certainly they are fundamental props of the food system, converting the phytoplankton into animal tissue and supplying it to larger creatures that feed on them. Their importance cannot be overstressed.

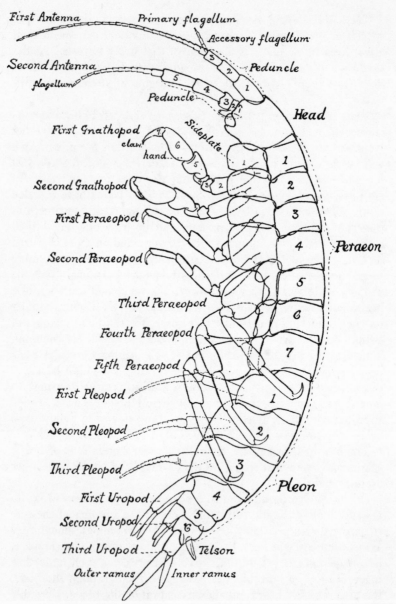

First Antenna
Primary flagellum
Accessory flagellum
Second Antenna
flagellum
Peduncle
Peduncle
Head
First Gnathopod
claw
hand
Sideplate
Second Gnathopod
First Peraeopod
Second Peraeopod
Peraeon
Third Peraeopod
Fourth Peraeopod
Fifth Peraeopod
First Pleopod
Second Pleopod
Third Pleopod
Pleon
First Uropod
Second Uropod
Third Uropod
Telson
Outer ramus
Inner ramus

Diagrammatic drawing of Gammarus (After Sexton).

The colloquial name was acquired because of the jerky movement of the creatures through the water, due to the short vigorous strokes of the antennae which they use as swimming instruments. Their importance in the ecosystem is no doubt a function of their vast numbers, which in turn is a phenomenon generated by their ability to lay parthenogenetic eggs which develop into either male or female, though for the most part the female offspring dominate. However, after the birth of a male mass, the female eggs require fertilisation if they are to hatch out. Before being laid, the eggs, and the young which hatch from them, are stored in a space under the top of the carapace known as the *ephippia*, from the Greek word for "horse", the reference being to the young riding on the back of the female as so many horsemen. A day or so later they are released into the water to fend for themselves.

The countless numbers make it virtually impossible to identify with any degree of certainty the species existing at Two Lakes, and although those I have examined have proved to be *pulex*, the chances of other species being present cannot be dismissed.

In this Class we are chiefly concerned with the Freshwater Shrimp, of the Genus Gammarus, Order Amphipoda. The species most common in the southern regions of Britain is *G pulex*, found in all types of well-oxygenated freshwater, often under stones, on weeds or on the bottom mud. The males are about 2 cms ($\frac{3}{4}$ in) in length, and the females a little less. They have bodies curved into arc-like shapes and compressed laterally, and when disturbed they swim away on the side in a peculiar scurrying manner. The colour is a light brown, with a grey or slightly pink tinge, but this varies from place to place.

The body consists of three sections; the head, the peraeon and the pleon. The head carries two pair of antennae, the eyes, and the mouth with its various appendages. The peraeon consists of seven segments, each with a pair of legs with large expansions of the first joints called sideplates. The first two pair (gnathopods) are used as hands, or grasping organs, and are more developed in the male than in the female. The other five pair are walking legs (peraepods), the first two bent forward at the joints, and the last three bent backwards. The third section, the pleon, carries three pair of legs (pleopods), known as swimming legs, used not only for swimming, but also for creating a current of water over the gills which are situated at the base of the front legs. Behind the swimming legs are a last three pair (uropods) used for jumping.

Although some species of Gammarus are able to produce eggs without having mated, this cannot be done by *pulex*. The fertilised eggs are fairly large and comparatively few, rarely more than 20 in a batch. In summer conditions they hatch out after 16 or 17 days, but remain within the female's pouch for a day or two before being extruded. After about a week, the young begin to moult, but in colder temperatures this period is extended. The adult stage is reached after ten moults, when egg laying becomes possible. The pouch in which the female rears her young consists of a receptacle between the protecting plates of the front legs, known as broodplates.

The male usually carries the female, holding her under the abdomen with his grasping legs, the gnathopods, not, as described by Commander Walker in his excellent book Lake Flies and their Imitations, on his back. This method of transporting the female is not only for mating purposes, but also for affording her assistance during her moults, which, from all accounts, are critical occasions. Frequently the old cuticle is cast piecemeal, and sometimes must be removed forcibly in shreds, not, from appearances, a comfortable experience for the individual concerned and in which the co-operation of her mate might be essential. An observer of one such event noted that during the process, while the female appeared to be in some difficulty, the male kept his head bent over the female so that the antennae of both were in contact, suggesting that they were in communication. It was also noticed that antennae torn during the moulting are regenerated, although other parts of the body are not.

Numerous artificial patterns have been devised to imitate the shrimp, and although trout will undoubtedly feed on the naturals when they can get them, no artificial has established itself at Two Lakes as a reliable and consistent trout catcher, although from time to time a fish is taken on one. The fault with most imitations is that the hackle feathers tied in to suggest the numerous legs fold back along the body against the pull of the line, destroying any resemblance to a natural shrimp. Perhaps one of the better dressings is given by Commander Walker in his book on lake flies, although I think it could be improved by the omission of the hackle feather completely. He suggests that a number 12 hook should be bent a little to produce a slow arc, and a wire base tied in to assist sinking. A light brown dubbing of seal fur, mixed perhaps with a dash of pink should be tied in extending a little way round the bend of the hook, and then ribbed with gold twist. Strands of the fur should then be picked out from between the ribbing, and the fly finished off with a watery olive hackle at the shoulder. To be fished deep, in short jerks.

Water Slater. Of the six different species, two are common and widely distributed. They are *Asellus aquaticus* and *A meridianus*, both very much alike, although the former is the larger and darker of of the two, and, as far as is known, is the only species of Asellus that carries the female under its body. They are flat creatures, usually brownish grey in colour, attaining a length of about 20–25 mm (¾–1 in). Unlike the shrimp, they thrive in stale water, where they feed on algae and waste organic material of all kinds, and thus are converters of vegetable matter into protein. Their usual habitat is among water plants, on which they browse and crop, but they may also be found on the bottom mud. They cannot swim, and trout find them only when scouring the bottom of the lake or indulging in "nymphing", which is browsing on the weeds and the creatures in them. Occasionally they are found in autopsies, but I hesitate to describe them as a constant source of food. An imitation would have to be fished on the bottom very slowly, a tedious business, or dragged slowly through weed beds, an undertaking which might be very costly in squandered flies.

Bristle Worms. The Bristle Worms are members of the Phylum ANNELIDAE or True Worms, of the Order Limicolae (though this is not universally accepted), Class Oligochaeta, Family Naididae, Genus *Stylaria*. My interest in them may be attributed to their nuisance value in my aquaria filled with water from Two Lakes, a nuisance so consuming that I go to extraordinary lengths to eliminate them from the original water loading and from all replenishments. When some years ago I first became aware of them I thought the transparent walls of the aquarium had become crazed into a mosaic, but on closer examination I found the mosaic to be in constant flux, due the unceasing flexures of the worms. The number in the small aquarium must have reached many thousands, and the only thing to do was to abandon the contents and start afresh. The worm population had increased so rapidly and so enormously that I was unaware of their presence until it was too late. The reason lies in their ability to reproduce by budding off female progeny from the tail end of the body without the assistance of male fertilisation, and without the medium of egg laying. This population explosion, if allowed to go unchecked in the wild, would convert the lakes into a semi-solid body of writhing worms, and as this does not happen, it is obvious that they are preyed on by other fauna to a far-reaching extent, and thus they play an important role in the food ladder.

The worms are thin, almost colourless but slightly yellowish, with many stiff bristles projecting from their bodies. In size they vary according to age, but the largest one I have seen is about 18 mm ($\frac{5}{8}$ in) long. They move by doubling their bodies into a U-shape and then straightening out again, but they have an extraordinary habit of "freezing" when danger approaches, and this makes them very difficult to spot. When lying motionless on weed, they are practically invisible among the folds, and the only way to prevent their entry into an indoor system via the weeds is to hold all plant matter in a strong jet of cold water, turning the plant from side to side so that every part is exposed to the jet.

Obviously they are of academic interest only to anglers, but I imagine that they would provide much interest to a curious observer.

Molluscs. The Phyllum MOLLUSCA is made up of soft, un-segmented bodied creatures with no internal skeleton but, in most cases, with an outer protective shell. It includes in its category cockles, mussels, snails, limpets, slugs, squids and octopods. Our interest lies in Snails, of which at least six species are native to Two Lakes. They are a most valuable source of food for trout and their presence should be encouraged wherever trout are fostered and their well being a conscious objective. This is possible only in "hard" waters, where the suspension of calcium is sufficiently high for shell manufacture and for promoting the richer growth of aquatic plants on which the snails feed. Anglers at Two Lakes are gratified in a subliminal sort of way to see the profuse quantities of various types of snails crawling slowly along the beds of the lakes in the shallow regions close to the banks, and as a measure of protection for these valuable creatures, wading is strictly forbidden.

Originally, the only Snail present was *Limnaea* (or *Lymnaea*) *auricula*, The Eared Pond Snail, but the introduction of fresh types bought in modest quantities by Mr Behrendt (often no more than half-a-dozen of each type) eventually resulted in the spread to all parts of *Limnaea stagnalis*, the Great Pond Snail, *Limnaea peregra*, the Wandering Snail, *Planorbis planorbis*, the Ramshorn, and *Planorbis corneus*, the Great Ramshorn. In addition, an apparently spontaneous appearance of *Hydrobia jenkinsi*, Jenkins Spire Shell, now believed to have arrived unseen in a batch of watercress transplanted from the R Test spread rapidly and deployed in expanding numbers over the whole lake system. This latter species, known only in brackish waters until the end of the last century, since when it has adapted itself to fresh waters in many different localities, consists (apparently) entirely of parthenogenetic females, for no male has ever been found. It is a small dark Snail about 7 mm ($\frac{1}{4}$ in) long, rather attenuated and pointed, belonging to the group of Snails known as Operculates, a group which are able to close their shells with a plate (Operculum) attached to their foot and which breathe through gills attached to a body-covering known as the "mantle". They are usually found in well oxygenated waters.

The second group of Snails known as Pulmonates possess neither the Operculum nor gills, but breathe by absorbing oxygen through their tissues or by inhaling air from a store they retain in a cavity between the shell and the mantle, and which they replenish at the surface from time to time. When the cavity is filled, the Snail is more buoyant than usual, and at such times it holds on to some under-water object to counteract a tendency to rise to the surface. Each type is hermaphroditic, and after cross fertilisation, lays its eggs; some species however are self-fertilising.

John Goddard, in his outstanding book "Trout Flies on Still-waters" describes an artificial for use chiefly when the natural snails ascend to the surface during the summer months. The dressing, designed by Clifford Henry, a well-known member of the Piscatorial Society, consists of "a flat-topped pear-shaped section of cork partly split and bound lightly over the shank of the hook with the flat section facing the eye. This is then covered with stripped peacock quill except for the last two turns near the flattened top representing the pad of the snail for which bronze peacock herl should be used". The hook is down-eyed, number 10–14; tying silk, black.

It seems to me that this could be an excellent device if it can be induced to float with the wide end upwards, for the Snail in life grips the underside of the surface film with its pad, and is able to "walk" along it.

Arachnida. There is some division of opinion among taxonomists as to whether this is a sub-phyllum (Clegg) or a Class (Rothschild). As far as we are concerned, our interest lies mainly in the Water Spider *Argyroneta aquatica*, the only true water spider of the many that frequent the waterside, and in the Water Mites, a small group of about 200 species of the Order Acari. At Two Lakes I have encountered only a small red Mite, distinguishable from a spider by the fact that its body is not divided into two distinct segments. My interest in Mites ceased rapidly when I found that they created havoc among the nymphs and other small creatures I was rearing and in which I had a greater interest. I took drastic action to remove them from my insectaria, but with some reluctance, as they are well worth studying. Most of them are red in colour, but some are green, brown or even blue. They range in size from about 1 mm to 8 mm ($\frac{1}{25}$ in to $\frac{1}{3}$ in), and when young are probably parasitic. Later they become predators, attacking and devouring any small creature they are capable of overcoming. I have never found one inside the stomach of a trout.

The Water Spider *Argyroneta aquatica* belongs to the Order *Araneae*, which includes true spiders, all able to extrude silk filaments from one or more spinnerets attached to their abdomens. Not all spiders utilise these filaments for webs or snares to entrap their prey; in fact the majority use them for purposes such as cocoons, lining of burrows, hinges of trap doors and, in the case of the Water Spider, tent making, but more of this later.

Spiders differ from all other living creatures in that the male sperm-producing testes are situated entirely separately from the copulatory organ. They lie at the base of an opening in the abdomen, and prior to copulation, the sperm is ejected from the testes through the opening onto a web previously spun by the male and laid out on the ground like a mat. Projecting from its jaw are a pair of modified palps, known as pedipalps, with bulbous endings, inside which are receptacles for holding the sperm. The male fills the receptacles with sperm from the mat, and then seeks a desirable female which he begins to court. If she favours his advances, copulation is completed by him inserting his sperm-laden pedipalps into the two oviducts of the female genital organ.

According to Crompton, there are at least four species of spiders that have taken to water to secure the food they need to subsist without actually living in it. He describes two of them, *Dolomodes fimbriatus*, the Raft Spider, and *Pirata piratica*, the Pirate Spider.

The Raft Spider selects a leaf, or two or three leaves stuck together, and uses it or them as a boat or raft. It is a fairly large, brown spider, with two broad golden stripes on its body. As the raft drifts over the water, the occupant searches for likely victims, and when spotting one, leaps overboard to secure it and brings it back to the raft to be eaten at leisure. A secondary, or even perhaps a primary advantage of this mode of life is the fact that most of its enemies are land based and cannot reach it when afloat.

The Pirate Spider hunts on the banks and on the water surface, running across it as easily as over land. Being adept at diving, it is able to secure both floating and submerged food with equal facility. Some scientists believe that it spins silken tubes with the opening just above the surface of the water, and lives in it with its two fore-legs resting on the water.

The Water Spider *Argyroneta aquatica* spends its whole life in or under water, but is unable to extract vital oxygen from the water like most aquatic animals. It overcomes its difficulty by carrying its own air with it or storing it in a dwelling it constructs below the surface. It collects the air at the surface, holding it among the hairs of its abdomen and sometimes between its hind legs. It constructs two types of dwelling, the first in the summer months, a little below the surface, and the second in winter in deep water, thus avoiding the gales and rough waters of the colder months.

For the first dwelling, the spider first spins a very dense web in the form of a sheet, and attaches its four corners to water plants. It is thought that when finished it is covered by a glaze, but this is not certain. It is, however, waterproof and invisible when first made. The spider then makes journey after journey to the surface to collect air in the usual manner, and descending, rubs it off immediately under the sheet. Eventually the supply of air stretches and inflates the sheet like a balloon or diving bell. The spider and its brood can exist within this tent for many weeks, and it is supposed that it is self-supporting or almost so, the fresh oxygen coming from the watery floor, and the carbon dioxide dissolving into it.

The deeper shelter is constructed from more rigid material, such as an evacuated shell, or loose tree bark, and filled with air the same way.

At the approach of the mating season, the male builds its dwelling close to that of a female, and constructs a water-tight bridge between the two. When the bridge is completed, he breaks the intervening wall of her dwelling, thus uniting the air of both abodes. The sudden confrontation of the pair is not always amicable; indeed, more often than not it leads to a battle royal. But the male, unique among spiders, is about $1\frac{1}{2}$ times bigger than the female, having a body length of about 16 mm ($\frac{5}{8}$ in) against her 11 mm ($\frac{2}{8}$ in), and is thus able to hold his own. In a day or so, they settle down and repair the damage to the dwelling caused by the fight, and raise their young. The mother, with a highly developed maternal instinct, cares for the brood for some weeks, but when they are mature, they collect a little air from the common stock, and vanish through the floor.

I doubt if we can ever gather enough data applicable to any single expanse of water which would enable a fully comprehensive catalogue of its inhabitants to be compiled, not only because of its complexity, but also because of its instability and transience. I have substantial evidence to suppose that, slowly but surely, colonisation by immigrant groups is constantly occurring, and that behavioural patterns of the existing populations tend to become modified. As an example, readers will remember that in previous pages I stated that I had found few Phantom Larvae when conducting autopsies on trout. On April 19th 1972, during a sharp evening rise on Spring Lake, I killed a fish of 1·65 kg (3 lb 7 oz). Four hours later, in my own home, I emptied out the stomach and found five very large Chironomid (*C tentans*) pupae, the largest exceeding 2·6 cms (1 in). These were the largest by far I had ever seen at Two Lakes, and astonished me, and later, Mr Behrendt. It suggests that the large "buzzers", as they are known to anglers, are beginning to colonise Two Lakes, and if this is the case, the artificial fly patterns of the future will have to change accordingly. Another surprise was the presence of 62 Phantom Larvae, most of them immature, but all alive and active, as indeed was one of the Chironomid pupae.

The above is a practical illustration of the adage that truth is neither absolute nor permanent, but is merely related to a single point of time in the continuum of events. Nevertheless observations must be recorded as at the time they occur in full expectation that the inherent restlessness of Nature may invalidate many of the logical conclusions drawn from them.

[17]

The Fishing

"...and if so be the angler catch no fish, yet... he hath good air, and sweet smels (sic) of fine fresh meadow flowers; he hears the melodious harmony of birds; he sees the swans, herns, ducks, water hens, cootes &c, and many other fowle with their brood....

ROBERT BURTON. Anatomy of Melancholy,
SECOND PARTITION, SECTION 2, MEMBER IV

The ultimate aim of all fly-fishers is to catch fish. The majority, rightly I imagine, regard their fishing as a pleasant diversion to be enjoyed regularly or occasionally in fine weather and in attractive surroundings, with a possible added bonus of a trout or two, if the fish are co-operative. There are others, more serious and single-minded, to whom the secrets of how to catch fish are of paramount importance, and whose leisure time is dominated by the determination to uncover them and to develop their personal techniques to the highest possible peak. Many, by dint of intelligent observation mingled with years of experience succeed in joining the select group of experts who year after year attain results beyond the capacity of the vast majority.

Spread thinly within the ranks of fly-fishers there exists another group, one consisting of individuals characterised by a mentality in which curiosity is a conspicuous ingredient. These few, among which I count myself, are not so much concerned with "how" to catch fish, but with "why" the techniques that succeed do so. The members of the group formulate theories, and discard them or re-formulate them, on evidence gathered slowly and patiently, acutely conscious that it is almost entirely circumstantial, even though at times it appears overwhelming. But however strong the evidence, no theory based on it can be accepted as a scientific fact unless it is able correctly and constantly to foretell behaviour propounded by its propositions. This we certainly cannot do in

179

fly fishing, and as long as trout are able to exercise a measure of free will, I don't suppose we ever shall.

The reason for this is obvious, and we must accept the discipline of its limitations with a good grace. For it is not possible to predict the response of fish, or any other living creature which subsists on a mixed diet, to food offered to it, with absolute accuracy. Of course, the deeper our knowledge of any particular creature, the closer our prediction will be, but the widespread differences in reactions even within the same species ensure that we will be wrong on a number of occasions. We must therefore accept the unpalatable fact that our science is one of probabilities, not of certainties. All we can do is to assess the "likely" reaction to our efforts, and if we are in possession of strong evidence that they consist of methods "likely" to succeed, we are enhancing our chances to the maximum possible.

The difficulties facing this small band of curious fly-fishers should not be underestimated, for not only must they guard against the dangers of attributing to trout the sensitivities or the motivations of human beings, but they must seek their evidence in a medium different to our own, where events are unseen or obscured. Further, trout reactions to stimuli are so varied, so dissimilar and so multi-tudinous that any analysis becomes complicated and most difficult to interpret. Finally, hypotheses which are valid for a year or two, or even more, suddenly become invalid and have to be scrapped. Paradoxically, prediction on the negative side is fairly positive, for if we are uncertain about *attracting* trout to our offerings, we can lay down the law precisely about how to *repel* them. In brief, anything that will alarm a fish, by betraying an angler's presence or by a disturbing phenomenon in the water, will produce an unequivocal refusal on the part of the fish to accept the proffered "food".

Whether we like it or not, therefore, we must reconcile ourselves to the fact that there is no certain way of bringing a trout to the fly, but that it is a matter of chance, which fortunately we can tip in our favour a little or a great deal according to circumstances.

Fundamentally, the problem of fish catching is divided into two parts; choice of fly and method of presenting it.

The former is perhaps the most controversial item of the fly-fishing world, and at Two Lakes, as elsewhere, opinions are widely divergent. Most of the anglers with whom I have talked are frankly puzzled and have no hesitation in saying so, at the apparent lack of uniformity in the response by trout to the artificial flies offered them. In order to gather the views of the regular anglers, many of whom fish the great reservoirs of England and Wales in addition to Two Lakes, I distributed a questionnaire to about 60 of them. About 55 per cent were completed and returned. On the question of artificial flies, I asked for the names of the three most successful flies in order of success, and apart from some indefinite replies such as "nymphs", "whatever the fish are taking" and "don't know", the names of 35 flies were given. Of them, 15 were mentioned once, 8 twice, 3 three times, 3 four times, 2 five times, 2 six times and 2 seven times. Only a single fly, the Brown & Green Nymph, was the first choice every time it was mentioned.

The 15 mentioned once only I shall not name, as they range too widely over the whole galaxy of artificials to convey anything significant to the reader. The list of the remainder, starting at the most popular, is as follows:

Name	Total	1st choice	2nd choice	3rd choice
Green Nymph	7	3	—	4
Peter Ross	7	1	2	4
Invicta	6	3	3	—
Dunkeld	6	1	4	1
Brown and Green Nymph	5	5	—	—
Buzzers (various)	5	1	1	3
Connemara Black	4	3	1	—
Butcher	4	2	2	—
Derby Beetle	4	2	2	—
Black Pennell	3	1	1	1
Brown Nymph	3	1	—	2
Silver March Brown	3	1	1	1
Zulu	2	—	1	1
Grenadier	2	—	2	—
Grey Wulff	2	—	—	2
Alexander	2	—	—	2
Jersey Herd	2	1	1	—
Teal and Silver	2	—	1	1
Bucktail (sic)	2	1	1	—
Sedge (sic)	2	1	—	1

In an endeavour to reduce the above results to some sort of order, I looked for a consistent factor running through the list, but the only factor I found was a glaring inconsistency. However, if we take the general impression of the colour of each fly as registered on the mind by a quick glance, our list is now seen to be dominated by three colours; (a) yellow/olive/green, (b) black, and (c) silver or gold. (I have presumed that the Invicta is the yellow bodied type.) Here I should interpose with the remark that since the questionnaires were received, the Whisky Fly, with a silver body and an orange wing is the latest fly to attain popularity. We are all aware that there are times when the fish will refuse all flies except a grey, or a green, or a brown, or a maroon, or some other odd colour, but I think it will be agreed by most Two Lakes anglers that the three colours mentioned as dominating the list also dominate the fishing. This is my own belief too, at least as far as the Yellow/Green/Olive and Black are concerned. I cannot include Silver, as I never use a silver-bodied fly.

Leaving the question of colour for the time being, what other elements appear to play a critical part in fish catching, not on the basis of theoretical conjecture, however logical it may be, but from the acid test of waterside experience?

First, I have noticed that over the years continuous long casting is less productive than moderate casting, except on the odd occasion, when a distant fish is seen to rise within casting cover. Perhaps this is due to the fact that continuous casting over a limited area creates an awareness of danger among the trout and they tend to avoid it, particularly on bright days. I have in fact seen, when the light and depth of water permit, how three or four casts over a region have sent a number of cruising fish out of the vicinity in unmistakable panic. If this is correct, then the smaller the "danger" area the better, and long casting merely increases it; indeed, it might be advantageous to concentrate for about 10–15 minutes on the area to the left, and to repeat this in the centre and the right in turn, and so on. This leaves a portion of the danger area unfished for approximately 20–30 minutes, and normalises it. Under such circumstances, a long cast now and then is a positive advantage, providing it is not overdone.

If it is true that over-frequent casting creates a danger zone which the trout tend to avoid, it would naturally follow that long casting accompanied by a very slow retrieve of the fly would not only reduce the frequency of casting very considerably, but would as a result reduce the danger zone. But the slower the retrieve, the deeper the fly will sink, especially if it is weighted, and this is not always desirable.

Secondly, success seems to attend more readily the angler who is prepared to change his fly, when it has become apparent after an adequate period that the current one is ineffective. It is well established that trout often approach a fly, or follow it, and make no attempt to take it, implying that they recognise that it (or something about it) is not quite as it should be. When all, or most, trout in the vicinity have presumably seen the proffered fly without being attracted to it, one must assume that it is probably the wrong one, though of course this is not certain, as an artificial fly in a lake, like a needle in a haystack, can conceivably be fished for an hour without crossing the path of a cruising fish. But we must apply the laws of probability, and assume it has been seen and refused, even while admitting we may be wrong.

This question of the right fly and the wrong fly is perhaps the most perplexing one in the whole study of fly fishing, for a fly may be refused by fish after fish, for all we know, and yet find a taker. This seemingly aberrant behaviour is not unusual in all creatures (including human beings) which possess a measure of free will, any more than in a native of Brazil disliking football or an English housepainter refusing a cup of tea. But if we find that most feeding trout in a stillwater refuse a particular fly, we have no option but to try and find one that is acceptable to as many of them as possible. Without any clues to guide us, our sole alternative is to adopt the method of trial and error. More of this later.

In addition to the permutation of fly patterns, different depths must be probed and different speeds and methods of fly recovery introduced.

But from my observations over years, I am persuaded that the most important element of all in fishing stillwaters is dogged persistence. The fly must be at work for as long as possible if it is to achieve optimum success.

These, then, are the apparent criteria, each with its own conflicting divisions and sub-divisions, governing the arts of freshwater fly fishing; (a) diligence, (b) frequent change of flies and tactics, and (c) minimising the danger area within the casting zone.

In any discussion of fly fishing with a sunken fly on stillwaters, we must not lose sight of the fact that unlike dry-fly fishing where we bring the fly to the fish, we must now bring the fish to the fly, a vastly different proposition. Obviously, the criterion for doing this is, above all else, that the fly should be seen by the fish, for if it is not seen (and in the comparatively vast spaces of a stillwater an object as small as an artificial fly can easily be missed. In fact, huge numbers of natural flies are missed, for if not, none would survive, and all aquatic insects would become extinct) it cannot be taken no matter how attractive and lifelike it may appear. Thus there is some justification for the argument that first and foremost the fly must be conspicuous. That this has long been recognised is evident from the use of outstandingly bright materials in the traditional standard dressings of stillwater artificials, not so much in the main parts, but in the lesser embellishments of tails, cheeks, ribs and so on. The bright tails of tippet or ibis, the prominent cheeks of jungle cock or jay, the wing topping of golden pheasant or kingfisher act as cynosures to the sombre bodies of black, brown or olive without marring whatever realistic properties they may possess.

The above reasoning is no doubt sound, but perhaps a little over-valued, and those anglers that tie their own flies may prefer to ease the task by omitting the minor insignia even if it entails the loss of a trout now and again. I am not even sure that on the well stocked stillwaters of the present era the less bright artificials are at a disadvantage, though in the past, on the more sparsely populated lochs and loughs of Scotland and Ireland, and on the large lakes of England, where the traditional patterns were developed, I have no doubt that the additional splendour was a considerable asset. But at Two Lakes it is quite noticeable that when a black fly adorned with lustrous colours such as the Connemara Black is being taken by the trout, my less radiant offering of a completely black fly, with only a gold rib to decorate it, is equally favoured. And this applies to all other flies. Yet I readily concede that on those dour days when feeding fish are few, the Connemara is more likely to be seen than mine.

On rivers, particularly where the dry fly or upstream nymph are mandatory, the argument for and against imitation has raged for many years. Its relevance on stillwaters is debatable, but the subject is of too great an interest to be summarily dismissed, and I propose to devote some space to it.

On a chalk stream, when fish are rising to the fly, the most likely artificial to be taken is one that closely imitates the natural fly on the water, or likely to be on the water at the time, with the former by far the best bet. That this is so cannot be doubted by any experienced chalk stream angler, and I do not think that the fact that it is equally true on stillwaters when the fish are busily occupied in feeding on large single-species concentrations of nymphs, larvae, pupae or surface flies can seriously be challenged. At such times, the artificial fly most likely to succeed is one that imitates the fly on the water, with all others nowhere, although the odd fish, especially the young or the newcomers from the rearing stews might be tempted to take hold of some totally unrepresentative pattern. The latter usually happens as the artificial hits the water, suggesting that the fish was too impetuous to wait and examine it, as the more experienced ones do. This has been corroborated in actual fact hundreds of times within my own knowledge, when, after a heavy rise to pupae or surface fly, the only artificial flies that were taken closely resemble the colour of the natural insects found by autopsies in the stomachs of the captured trout.

In the failing light of a June evening, in 1972, I was present at an extraordinary rise in Spring Lake. In the central portion of the lake, fish were rising in a density and with a frequency rarely seen, and with an aplomb that played havoc with an angler's sang-froid. It lasted about 30 minutes, finishing when the moon was bright in a darkened sky. I tried every colour of fly I possessed, the later ones being tied onto the leader by the artificial light of a hand torch. All failed, though each was cast time and again into the thick of the rising fish, but when the last fly had been thoroughly tried and refused, and my morale was at a low ebb, it was taken as it hit the water, and, with difficulty because the light had gone, I landed the fish and killed it. Two hours later, at the kitchen sink of my home, I emptied the stomach contents into a dish, and found they consisted almost entirely of large numbers of transparent Phantom larvae, which are impossible to imitate, in all stages of maturity. Not another fish was caught in Spring Lake during the rise, a fact which I mention for two reasons. First, it tends to confirm the remarks of my last paragraph, and secondly it contradicted absolutely my previous belief that Phantom larvae were on the whole immune to the depredations of trout because of their near-invisibility.

One or two qualifications must be made. When trout are feeding on surface fly, whether on a river or a stillwater, the size and contour of the artificial, and not only the colouring, must resemble that of the natural. When the fly is sunken, the size and contour, providing they are not too far out, will hardly matter at all. Colour, and colour only, appears to be the primary feature, but this can be nullified by incorrect manipulation. I imagine that this will be disputed only by anglers whose familiarity with natural aquatic fauna is limited.

It must be clearly understood that little of what has been discussed applies to those occasions, more numerous than any other, when fly is sparse, absent, or varied on a small scale. At these times, fish are taken on such widely different flies that no arrangement of response can be formulated. These are the occasions when the second of my criteria, that flies should be changed frequently, appears to justify its counsel. Nevertheless, even on such occasions, when fish may be taken on different artificials, there is often a colour similarity dominating the majority of the successful patterns. From our observation point outside the trout's environment, the reason for one colour being preferred is difficult, and perhaps impossible, to determine, and for centuries anglers have searched for clues that will lead to a solution of the problem. The solution has been sought in the state of the light, the temperature, the tides of the ocean, astrological calculations, and, believe it or not, in the religious faith of the fisherman. Not a single one, even when taken seriously, has stood up to inquiry for a moment. Yet it cannot be denied that a consensus on "food" selection among the trout of a stillwater cannot be accidental or coincidental day after day, week after week, year after year. This consensus of selection must be the result of some external influence, and the only available evidence, often extremely strong, which has been gathered over centuries suggests that the selection is based on the colour or colours of the creatures on which they are feeding, or have recently been feeding.

At this point, the reader may well ask what proof exists of the truth of this statement, and, if proved, what we can do about it. First, any proof can be only circumstantial, and this can never be wholly and invariably satisfactory. In addition, it is known that often a "wrong" fly will take a fish when a "correct" one fails. But we must remember that we are concerned with probabilities, not certainties, and if the imitative fly catches 10 trout to 9 of the arbitrary, the belief in colour imitation is justified. After all, the "correct" fly may be fished badly, or in an area where there are no fish, or may not be seen by a single trout, which would explain its occasional inadequacy. But over lengthy periods, on those occasions when the fly on the water can be determined, the proof that an imitation of the same colour will attract trout more than any other artificial is, in my opinion and in the opinion of many observers, overwhelming. This book could be filled with instances where recognition of the current insects have prompted a change of fly to the colour of the prevalent naturals with comparatively speedy results where previously there had been none. Hundreds of autopsies have shown that the fish had been feeding on natural insects similar in colour to the successful fly. Where they are dissimilar, the angler has probably had to work hard and long for his fish.

To counter the proposition often advanced, that a fish taking an imitation of the fly on the water would probably have taken any other fly, properly presented, I embarked on a course of what I call negative proof. As most anglers who fish contemporaneously with me well know, I invariably ask the colour of the fly being used when it is taken by a trout. When I have established that artificials of a particular colour are being taken, I avoid that colour like the plague, changing as usual from fly to fly providing it is dissimilar to the one being used by those catching fish. Very rarely on these occasions do I catch anything, and indeed on the eleven occasions I have tried, only once have I done so, when a fish took the fly as it touched down.

What can we do about it, if the above is true, which this seems to suggest? Very little, unless we keep our eyes open for flies in the air or on the surface, and match the colour of the body of the natural to that of our artificial fly. The examination of one or two natural flies can sometimes be misleading, for they can be isolated examples of unrepresentative types. Nevertheless, a little evidence is better than no evidence, and artificials of the same colour should be tried. My own practice, immediately after I have set up my rod, is to make for a sheltered bay in one of the lakes where flotsam is wont to gather, and to scan the surface for insects or shucks, and to use the type or types found there as colour bases for the artificials to be used.

August 23rd, 1972 was a brilliant summer's day. The sun beat down with a bright hard light, and on my arrival few fish, if any had been caught. I took up a place on the sandy peninsular on the south bank of Lower Lake, and in view of what I had seen on the sheltered bay I had just visited, I tied on an Olive nymph. After flogging away for 30 minutes without a touch, I changed to a Grey Goose nymph for the sole reason that it had been presented to me by Professor Raymond the previous day. Nevertheless within the next few minutes I landed a fish which, at 2 lb 6 oz (1 kg plus), I suspect was a newly released one. Continuing with the same fly proved unavailing, and I considered changing it when with startling suddenness the sky above the middle of the lake was streaked by a large flock of swerving, screaming martins. I stopped fishing, and carefully perused the water to find, if possible, what was coming off. I noticed two or three small black fly, and immediately changed to a black bodied fly, ribbed with gold twist, and at my first cast got into a fair sized fish, which, I regret to say, got away after a ten minute play when inches from my net. Fishing close by, on the isthmus, Alan Dalton asked me if I could recognise the fly the birds were taking, and I answered that I thought it was a small black midge. This was immediately before I was taken by the fish just described. Mr Dalton changed to a black fly, and soon had two fish. The birds departed after a few minutes, and I wandered back to my car for lunch.

Referring back to the second of my criteria that govern the art of freshwater fly fishing, where, from observation of the more habitually effective anglers, I advocate a frequent change of fly, it is clear that I do so because of the extraordinarily difficult task of finding natural fly on the water or the surrounding vegetation. Nevertheless, there are times when, as I have just related, the tedium of trial and error necessary for determining the right fly can be reduced by searching for current natural insects, usually on the water surface; for in the air they are not easy to capture, or even to see, and in vegetation they tend to settle in remote places where they rest prior to mating.

I stated earlier that whereas artificial fly size and contour (in addition to colour) are critical when fishing for trout rising to surface fly, it is not so when below the surface, providing one does not go to absurd lengths. The reason for this apparent contradiction is like enough because hatching or ovipositing flies on the surface are fully grown, and therefore practically uniform in size, contour and colour within the same species. The trout are aware of this, and are inclined to ignore any "food", real or counterfeit, that fails to conform to what they regard as satisfying provender. Below the surface, however, the aquatic creatures on which they feed exist in a wide variety of sizes, colours and contours, and a small olive nymph is just as edible as a large one, even though size and contour may differ. Therefore, when trout are feeding below the surface on insects of a certain colour, because they are available in fair quantities, only the colour is important, not the size or contour, providing they are within reason.

A little before noon on August 2nd, 1972, I made my way to the sheltered bay I have described and found a number of Chironomids, male and female, all exactly alike except for sexual differences which are not perceptible at a quick glance. I collected a few in a phial, and on my way to the Upper Lake, found a colleague (Mrs Henny Arnold) and her guest close by. Mrs Arnold, after many changes of fly, had just caught her first fish, and when I showed the captured insects to her, she showed me the successful artificial. I was interested to notice that it was a first class imitation of the naturals in my phial, though half as big again. I too tied on one of my own artificials, a good imitation of the natural, with a yellow body and a black rib, again much larger than the naturals, and so did her guest. Within the next few minutes we both had fish. I scooped out the the stomach contents of the dead fish, and found only yellow pupae with a black rib.

Among the anglers who fish regularly at Two Lakes are a number whose skill and experience on stillwaters and rivers, for trout, sea trout and salmon justifies describing them as masters of their craft. Among them is Lt Col A ("Rags") Locke, and I propose quoting extracts from his letter to me soon after the questionnaires were distributed.

"I prefer... to catch fish on the dry fly, but only about 10 per cent are normally taken by this method, because (I think) the fish are driven down by persistent flogging.... The Ivens Brown & Green Nymph (modified) accounts for at least 75 per cent of my fish.... Very few fish are now caught on traditional flies; imitations, however approximate or caricature-like, do the damage.... Flies which are most successful one season are a complete flop the next; this is something which puzzles me...."
(I shall quote again later from the same letter.)

Artificial flies and their presentation, though closely allied, are separate and dissimilar subjects of study; the latter is not so much concerned with casting as with other factors, for from what I have seen many times, fish can be caught by the most atrocious casting. This anomaly presumes that the captured trout was out of distance when the cast was made, but swam into the subsequent path of the fly while it was being retrieved. On the whole, however, good casting is more productive than indifferent casting by far, providing all else connected with the fishing is of the same standard.

The presentation of a fly refers in the main to the depth at which it is fished and to the speed of its recovery. Depth can be defined roughly (but sufficiently accurately for our purposes) as just below the surface, between the surface and midwater, and between midwater and the bottom. I omit dry fly presentation, which has already been discussed.

When fish are rising to hatching midge pupae, which lie close to the surface, fishing an imitation pupa is most effective, particularly at dusk. This method is indicated by the many rings of rising fish which do not break the surface.

Fishing the fly between the surface and midwater is the majority custom, and is routine when fish are seen to rise occasionally.

Fishing between midwater and the bottom is favoured on dour days when hardly a fish is seen moving. Fishing too near the bottom can cause heavy fly losses due to weed growth, except in the first few weeks of the season.

Depth is a function of two things—the fly and the line, or a combination of both. Each can be constructed to float or to sink, or even, with the use of line grease in the case of the latter and oils or chemicals in the case of the former, to do either. To a minor degree, speed of fly recovery will influence the depth at which a fly fishes, and to a lesser extent, so will the angle at which the rod is held during line recovery.

Fishing the pupa is practised with a floating line, or with a silk line greased to ensure floating, with a long fine leader (except at dusk), usually 3·5 m (12 ft) long, greased the whole length except for the last few inches at the point. The fly is lightly weighted to obtain quick entry into the water, but not sufficiently to sink and to drag the leader down with it. The fly is either retrieved extremely slowly, or left to dangle as in coarse fishing. Some anglers tie the pupa to the leader so that, in theory at least, it hangs down perpendicularly in the water, as does the natural. In addition, they contrive to concentrate the weight near the bend of the hook when tying the fly, so as to achieve the same result. However, neither of the above expedients achieve their objective when tried in the bathroom, due to the resistance of the water, and I doubt very much whether they have any value whatsoever. Fishing the pupa in this manner, even without the latter expedients, has one great virtue and one great fault. First, the line and leader being at all times on the surface, are under maximum control, and in the event of a take, the strike can be meticulously timed and regulated. The method of fishing the pupa by one of the members illustrated this admirably. He greases the tapered leader, which is attached to a floating line, from the strong butt right down to the last knot, leaving only a fine point ungreased. The artificial pupa is tied on a heavy iron, with no supplementary weighting, and when cast out both fly and point sink as far as the knot, which remains on the surface. A knotless leader would slowly slide into the water. With his attention rivetted on the knot, he strikes immediately it submerges. This is timing at its most immaculate, and is best performed with a floating line and leader. Unfortunately this requires good vision, especially when the water is wind-blown and choppy. The fault lies in the prominence of the leader to the fish, a factor I have found to be of great importance, except at dusk. To succeed during daylight requires extremely fine monofilament in the point, and this militates against a successful conclusion if the fly is taken by a big fish.

When fish are feeding below the surface but sufficiently close to it for the rise-forms to be seen, the established method of dropping a weighted fly just within the ring circle as quickly as possible and activating it moderately is, on the whole, as likely to be successful as any manœuvre in stillwater fly fishing, providing the fly is not too alien in terms of size and colour. Frequently the fish will have departed the scene by the time the fly alights, or will be moving in a direction away from it, but if the presentation is speedy and accurate and the results persistently negative, a change of pattern is indicated. The fly need not be tied in the outline of a pupa, or nymph, though on stillwaters any feathered concoction that is not a dry fly, a multi-coloured lure or shaped like a small fish or a pupa is generally called a nymph, even if it bears no resemblance whatsoever to a natural nymph. (My flies for underwater fishing are all dressed with plain unshaped bodies of either dyed seal, silk, wool, or herl, without embellishment save for a rib of gold twist or black thread, completed with a stiff head hackle to suit the body colour.) The main difficulty —too formidable to be treated lightly—of this type of fishing lies in recognising when the fly has been taken; for although there are times when it is grabbed so forcibly that there can be no mistake about it, too often it is so daintily mouthed that detection is not easy. It is believed that many good trout are lost to anglers before their faculties are conditioned to the necessary degree of sensitivity for recognising the minute change of line tension, the trivial water disturbance or the faint distant contact which often betray the take of a stillwater trout.

The natural pupa is varied in length according to its species; the largest I have seen at Two Lakes was a little over 2·5 cms (1 in). The smallest can be very small indeed, but I doubt if the trout are interested in anything less than about 6 mm ($\frac{1}{4}$ in). The colour can be almost anything, often ringed with black. Indeed, as far as I am concerned, only the main colour matters, and unless one can find a clue to it, the solution can be found only by trial and error. My own succession of choice, purely arbitrary, and as likely to be wrong as any other choice, is (1) Olive/Yellow, (2) Black, (3) Emerald, (4) Brown, (5) Hot Orange, (6) Plum colour or Maroon. In most cases, the hook size is 10, 11, or 12.

My own method of fishing, common at Two Lakes, when trout are rising freely to pupae during the day, is to drop my fly at the nearside edge of the ring as soon as possible, and to activate it immediately it penetrates the surface. At dusk the fly is deposited nearer the ring centre. The movement is steady but not continuous or vigorous, and a take can be registered by a distinct pull, or by a draw of the leader, sometimes very slight, or by a correctly sited rise. If the fly is refused by a few fish, I change it, and keep on changing it until I find the correct one. The fly is weighted, and is not tied to resemble the shape of a nymph or pupa. The hook size is No 14, 12 or 10, and the body material either silk, seal's fur or herl, dyed or natural, with a gold twist or black silk rib as appropriate. All have stiff shoulder hackles to match. I rarely incorporate tails in my flies, the exceptions being the Sepia and Damselfly nymphs, and Phantom flies. Nor do I at any time tie in butts, toppings, cheeks or other minor adornments.

The next depth, probably the most popular, is the region between the surface and midwater. In practice, this is usually about 30–60 cms (12–24 in), but it varies according to individuals and their manipulations. In any case, few anglers if any can state with any sort of accuracy the depth at which their sunken fly is fishing, and the figures given by me are based on the apparent position of fish seen to approach, and sometimes to take, the fly.

There are various methods of fishing at this depth. One may use a floating line and a well weighted fly, assisted by frequent coatings of a sinking agent on the leader. The sinking agent can be glycerine (not very effective), or Fullers Earth mixed into a paste with a detergent. I personally use talcum powder made into a paste with a wetting agent, such as Tepol, because it is more pleasant to handle than Fullers Earth. However, this method limits considerably the depth to which the fly can sink, and coating the leader every few minutes is a bit of a nuisance.

Another method to achieve our purpose, one commonly used, is to use a sinking tip line. This ingenious device consists of a floating line with a sinking tip of about 3 m (10 ft). The fly need not carry much weight, the line carrying it down. This is quite effective, and widely used. Its drawback lies in the difficulty of keeping the fly well up in the water when the line is thoroughly saturated. My own method is a modification of the above. I trim the sinking tip from the original 3 m (10 ft) to about $\frac{1}{2}$ m (20 in), and grease the floating portion above it to ensure that it will continue floating all day, even if a scum forms on the surface during the hot summer days. The tip of the line will now sink, taking the fly and the leader (or part of it) under water, the amount depending on the weight built into the fly. Thus I can control the depth of the fly from 15 cms (6 in) to about $\frac{1}{2}$ m (20 in).

However, before the leader and line are thoroughly wetted, there is a tendency for most of the former to float on the surface, and this I believe, keeps the fish at a distance, even when the water is choppy, except in conditions of poor light. In order to accelerate the wetting, the leader may be kept overnight between pads soaked in a detergent or in Tepol, or coated with a sinking agent as previously described. Usually, the first fly I tie on is a heavy one to encourage quick sinking, and if later, as sometimes happens, the leader begins to float, I either re-coat it with a sinking agent, or change the fly again to a heavy one.

Apart from the advantage of depth control, the line, being on the surface for almost all its length, permits excellent sensitive control. In addition, one does not have to rely on touch when a fish takes the fly. The tip of the line, if watched carefully, will often indicate a take by a slight draw, and indeed many fish caught by this method have been hooked without the angler feeling anything at all. Alternatively, when the fly is being fished high in the water, an underwater rise in the vicinity of the fly warrants a quick strike even if nothing is detected by touch.

The weight of the fly is regulated by the hook iron and by an underlayer of wire tied in under the dressing, although 25 years ago we achieved the same result by rolling strips of silver paper (tinfoil or aluminium foil) into short lengths and twisting them round the hook before forming the body of the fly. The introduction by Mr Frank Sawyer of copper wire windings was a great improvement, though I find 5-amp fuse wire quite satisfactory and easier to obtain. All my wet flies incorporate either one or two wire layers wound onto the bed of tying silk before they are dressed, thus providing a stock either lightly or heavily weighted. At the waterside, I am able to recognise each type on sight, but others usually segregate them, or use differently coloured tying silk as a means of identification.

While on the subject of fly dressing, some mention should be made of the traditional and current usage of hackle feathers. In the past, stiff cock hackles were used for floating flies (the stiffer the better), and soft hen hackles for wet flies. This was extremely sound for the periods and conditions in which they were employed, and of course, stiff cock hackles cannot be bettered for dry fly use even today. The best capes for dry-fly hackles are taken from cockerels of at least two years of age, killed by methods which do not stain or mar the feathers. In the ordinary way, cockerels are killed and marketed long before they reach that age, and only those used for breeding are retained. Therefore the economics of raising stock merely for anglers' hackles would price them out of the market. Before the Second World War, the main source of supply was China, but this ceased for political reasons until recently, when the position showed some signs of recovery.

For wet-fly fishing, stiff hackles possessed the disadvantage of poor entry into the water, and were discarded in favour of the soft hen hackles that offered no resistance to penetration of the surface film. Moreover, hen hackles had a tremendous advantage in rivers and lakes, when the soft fibres of the hackle were pressed back by the current or by the act of retrieving the fly so that they lay along the hook, imparting a nymph-like appearance far superior, in my opinion, to any other artificial configuration. For the upstream nymph, where the current or retrieve plays no part, the trick doesn't work, and Skues and others developed alternative forms that did not depend on any exterior force.

The use of weighted flies, now almost universal on stillwaters, has made the question of the fly's entry into the water redundant. However stiff the hackle, the weight submerges the fly instantly. And as only a minor proportion of the food of stillwater trout consists of nymphs, as opposed to rivers, the nymph-like form of artificial flies loses much of its attraction. For pupae no hackle is necessary, as the natural has no visible legs. For all other flies, the hackle I use is a stiff one, for when it is retrieved in a series of short jerks or pulls, the fibres will activate, and animate the fly as the fibres retract during the pull, and advance during the pause. And although it is claimed that trout can be caught by a static fly, if we are prepared to sit on a stool and wait, it must be agreed that animation, in the form of movement, gives reality to the deception by which we catch our fish.

But the custom of using soft hen hackles remains with us even though it is inapplicable to modern stillwater fishing, merely because nobody questions its origins or its derivations. Far better to use the stiff feathers of a cockerel for a hackle on stillwater flies, unless one intends to imitate a nymph.

Fishing the fly between midwater and the bottom is the last resort of a dour and difficult day, and, in the opinion of many anglers, represents the least enjoyable type of fly fishing. Whether this is due to the style of fishing or to the fact that the day is dour and difficult I do not know. But enjoyable or not, if fish are our objective and if they can be found only near the bottom, whether because that is where they are feeding or because the temperature in the lower water is more aggreeable to them, we have no choice but to fish deep. This can be accomplished in a number of ways, the most popular perhaps being by using a sinking line which will lower the fly almost to any practical depth irrespective of whether it is weighted or not. Usually, large bright flies are used in the justifiable belief that they will be more readily seen in the gloom of deep water. There is one outstanding advantage attached to this type of fishing, namely that the line is well concealed in the subaqueous twilight and contributes little to the creation of a danger zone. Long casting, and a fairly slow retrieve, added to the immediate disappearance of the line when it hits the water prevents the casting area acquiring the temporary reputation of being a risk area. Trout will therefore not avoid it.

The weak point of this method of fishing lies in the difficulty of striking efficiently when we feel the take of a fish, for the weight of water counteracts the pull of the line generated by the sharp lift of the rod top which drives the hook into its target. We are therefore obliged to impart a violent pull to the sunken line to overcome the blanketting effect of the mass of water, and if what we suppose is the take of a fish proves to be some bottom weed or obstruction snatching our fly, the ungentle heave of the line disturbs the water in a manner peculiarly its own.

Some relief from these annoyances can be found in speeding up the retrieve of the fly and in holding the rod upright at the steepest possible angle. These have the effect of raising the fly from the bottom, if the manipulation of rod and line is nicely controlled, without it losing contact with the lowest water levels.

There are variations on this theme. One angler at Two Lakes fastens a lead shot to his leader as a permanent feature of his fishing. This has the advantage of varying the weight (and consequently the sinkability) on the leader in accordance with the size of the shot. Certainly it is quite effective, and where used is associated with consistently good results. I have heard this method criticised on the grounds that it makes the act of casting difficult; I have not found this to be so, but I have not been able to secure the shot onto the leader easily, as they slip from my fingers while trying to engage the monofil into the slit of the shot. Nor can I prevent them from whipping off during the casting act, unless they are pinched on so securely with pliers that I find it quite impossible to remove them when I wish to do so. Another method is to tie a heavy fly, with the bend removed, onto the leader as a dropper. (Multiple flies are not permitted at Two Lakes). This too is quite effective, but all too often fish pull at the inoffensive dropper as though aware of its harmless character. This behaviour can be interpreted in a number of ways, but I don't propose to pursue the subject here.

Other methods are in use, either for keeping the fly or flies (where permitted) down, or for keeping the line on the surface while the fly fishes deep. One such, employed by a nationally known angler, consists of the addition of a transparent spherical float to the line end of the leader, supporting the whole of the line while the leader itself is sunken by the weight of the fly alone or with other re-inforcement. It did the job it was intended to do quite well, but my objection to it is based on the disturbance to the surface by the "float" when the fly is retrieved.

The number of ways in which the fly can be retrieved are many, and the permutations almost infinite. Only in the case of the artificial pupa is it established that movement of the fly should be minimal. On all other occasions, the speed of the retrieve is moderate, fast-moderate or slow-moderate, or a mixture of all three. I have seen little, if any, fast stripping of lures or of flies tied to imitate small fish such as are in popular use on many reservoirs. In any event, at Two Lakes flies on hooks larger than No 8 (old), and fish imitations, are not permitted, not entirely on ethical grounds, but more in the interests of the health of the fishery as a whole.

The function of the retrieve is twofold; first to achieve animation, and secondly to influence the desired depth. (I exclude the artificial pupa from this brief survey.)

To secure animation, movement of the artificial is essential, but the movement must be related to events in nature. This has given rise to a method known as sink and draw, where by lifting the rod top and then lowering it and retrieving line, the angler claims to be imitating some aquatic creature rising and sinking from and to the bottom. I do not know of any aquatic creature which normally behaves in this odd way, nor have I yet seen the method to be superior—or even as good as—any other orthodox method. Most creatures on which trout feed move about as little as possible under normal conditions, and any burst of activity is momentary. There are times when insects must rise to the surface to fulfil their natural life cycle, and this they do without seeming to hurry, by our standards, though their bodily contortions may be fairly complex. Certainly the anglers at Two Lakes know from their own experience that the moderate-slow to moderate-fast retrieve covers all occasions quite adequately, and I suspect that fluctuations between the two extremes, if deliberate, are due more to reaching or maintaining the fly at a particular depth than to an endeavour to present an alluring loco-motion. This is certainly true in my own case. I also change the angle at which I hold the rod to supplement the speed of fly retrieve in achieving depth; the higher I want the fly to swim, the nearer the vertical I hold the rod.

The difference in the reactions by trout to unchanging stimuli, including apparent animation, illustrates the individuality to which I have referred many times and which accounts for the impossibility of forecasting their responses in most situations. There are days when the heat and drought of summer reduce the water level in the lakes and expose the fish to our view. They can be seen following our fly, and with bated breath we await either the take or the swim-away —too often the latter. On one such occasion, desperate for a fish, I twitched the fly sharply two or three times, and was rewarded by the the beautiful sight of the fish grabbing the fly as a cat would an escaping mouse. I have repeated this seemingly infallible manœuvre many times since, always with one of two results; either the trout grabs the fly, or it flees the scene in panic. I am never sure which it will be, and on this Sisyphean note I close my chapter.

[18]

Stillwater Fly Presentation

By Eric Horsfall Turner

Hark! to the music of the reel,
We listen with devotion;
There's something in that circling wheel
That wakes the heart's emotion.

THOMAS TOD STEWART. Art of Angling. 1835

A somewhat unfortunate feature of angling is that the experienced performer regards himself as a good caster; and, in a sense, he probably is. Despite this, his knowledge of the complex technique of casting is usually very limited. The problem faced by the casting technician making a commentary on the craft appears to be in two forms. First, he must explain casting technique precisely as it should be for the novice; second, he must be prepared to reply logically to the opinions expressed by the experienced angler who assumes (as many of us did in our earlier days) that good casting is no problem to achieve, and that any advice which is not in accordance with his views, is incorrect. The only possible reply to such an exponent is a question, "Have you taken part in competitive casting?" If the answer is negative, it is unlikely that the critic will have any understanding of the *reasons* on which advice is based. If he is not prepared to accept this situation, he may be well advised to omit the reading of this Chapter; but he might be even better advised that if he reads it, the comments may raise a number of queries on the casting competence he has, and induce a measure of practical experiment to analyse the reliability of his conclusions. Casting of the fly, no matter whether imitative of the natural insect of the water or a lure, is the most difficult for the angler to raise to the best possible standards as they are known.

Towards the end of the last Century, Lord Grey of Fallodon made a clear three-way analysis of angling in one of the best books ever written on the subject. His analysis, strangely enough, has no direct reference to angling. It was based on human interest in the private garden. The owner either maintains it to ensure fine colour; or finds greater satisfaction in perfect lay-out and maintenance; or puts intensive study and practice into developing the plants, year after year, in the hope of obtaining standards beyond those ever known. The inference of the analysis is that the last approach has advantageous influence on the quality of the first two fancies in garden maintenance; but, naturally, the occupation is a diversion. It is a matter of preference for the performer to decide which approach, however limited in ultimates, is the one which gives him the greatest pleasure in life.

If the reader is interested in angling for pure enjoyment of scenery (the scenery of Two Lakes is remarkable, of course, as great landscape artists have shown), climatic conditions and the catching of trout when it happens, rather than when his tactics succeed, a reasonable rod matched to a suitable line will give him all he requires after a period of handling the equipment into the habitual. The widely publicised trout-fly distance cast of recent times, originally devised in the United States at the end of the last century and brought into use in this country during the early 1930s by a limited few who wanted the widest possible tactical means to catch trout, is of little value on the eight lakes in the Two Lakes system unless the angler is interested in the extremes of tactics I have mentioned. At this stage, therefore, let us leave it for further consideration; and confine requirements to the angler who has the preference mentioned.

His requirements are a rod of about 9 ft in length (but no longer) of either split-bamboo (commonly called split-cane) or fibre-glass, weighing no more than $5\frac{1}{2}$ oz; and 25 ft of fly-line which a tackle dealer could identify by "No 3 silk," "HCH plastic floating" or "HDH plastic sinking". Reel design has only two requirements; the lightest possible, and smooth working. The suggestion that the reel weight should be selected to balance the rod, has no merit whatever. Persistent practical fishing will catch the angler plenty of the great Two Lakes trout if the specified equipment is completed with the leader and fly described elsewhere as the most effective on these waters.

When we turn to the equivalent of perfect garden lay-out we are brought to fundamentals in tackle selection and achievement of the habituals. A great many fly-fishers have met these requirements in full. A particularly good example during recent years was the late Oliver Kite. He had never studied or practised casting technique in the full sense; but he became a perfectly competent fly-caster with the split-cane rod and reasonably matched line. My own fly-casting was assessed by one of the best British competitive casters, in 1940, as "perfectly adequate for fly-fishing." It had caught me several thousands of trout with fly from about 1914 to that year; but, of course, my knowledge of casting technique, at that time, was little better than the historical knowledge of an elementary school teacher when compared with the historical knowledge of a specialist university professor.

This brings us to the third gardening fancy; the development of the extremes in plant development. Before going further into the merit of this extreme, it may be well to consider the divisions of fly fishing from the practical standpoint. First, there is the general requirement of water-sense. This covers a rough estimate of trout habits, moods and inclinations; the best tactics for keeping out of sight of the trout to avoid alarming it; and many other strategic requirements of similar type, covered elsewhere in the assessment of the fishing of Two Lakes. Second, though only if the angler feels so inclined, learning the technique (essentially a craft and not an art) of fly dressing. The disinclination merely requires the purchase of professionally made artificial flies. Third, there is the scientific approach to water entomology as a means of influencing the fly-fishers selection of the artificial creation, a caricature at best, which is most likely to induce the trout to take it. Lastly, we come to the requirement of good casting; that is, presentation of the fly to the trout. This, to most of us, has the vital importance in that incompetent performance will be of great detriment to the effectiveness of the first three requirements in catching trout; for the simple reason that indifferent presentation may lay the fly too far from the trout to attract its attention, or may lay the line, fly, or both, in such a manner as to scare the fish.

In 1940, as I have observed, a good competitive caster gave me reason for disregard of competitive casting; and, indeed, there is no ground for a suggestion that he was wrong. Reasonable casting will catch trout; and it can well be that top grade in competitive casting would not enable the angler to catch appreciably more. The technical ability of the latter, however, is comparable with that between a skilled car driver with mechanical knowledge and the average driver. If the car behaves in some inexplicable way, the former soon knows why, and either restores the operation or takes no risks; whereas the latter can neither restore operation nor assess the risks.

Three casting instructional courses are open to the reader. The first is insistence on the reasonable, based on a measure of practice with the specified rod and line. Further reading of this dissertation will be a waste of time to the reader so inclined. The second requires reasonable concentration on fly selection, whether personally made or not; study of water entomology; and both study and practice of casting technique. In the last requirement the findings of competitive casters must be examined in detail, even if there is no inclination to practise them to top quality performance. Finally, the third course is the extreme in learning tackle selection, and practice of a very persistent type to achieve the best performances in all types of cast. In this case, we are only concerned with the fly-casting techniques on still waters; and not any still waters, but the somewhat individual waters, which are not numerous, of the Two Lakes type.

There are two main types of cast on still waters. The first is much the same as the fly-cast on trout rivers and streams, though greater distance is required with considerable consistency. The second is the trout-fly distance cast. Let us consider first, then, the former type.

The need for 20 yds distance on trout rivers and streams is a variable; and certainly not frequent, particularly on broken water. It has its disadvantage in that it increases the difficulty in hooking the taking fish; but the contention that it makes hooking impossible, or even unlikely, it quite wrong if the angler learns his manipulation correctly. In the early 1930s the Belgian, John Godart, was catching large numbers of river trout for hotel purchase with consistent casts of 35 yds.

The 20 yds stillwater cast requirement, however, is definite; and for this reason a 9 ft rod, with medium-fast or full-fast action, is preferable to the rod with medium-slow action required for trout rivers and streams. Excess of 9 ft is unlikely to have merit. The longer the rod, the greater the required wrist strength of the caster to ensure the fastest possible delivery with the forecast, and therefore correct line turn-over. Few anglers have the muscular strength (certainly in full trout-fly distance casting up to the 45 yds distance) to obtain maximum rod tip speed with a rod exceeding 9 ft in length. The weight of the rod is another influencing factor in the speed of line discharge in the forecast; and a rod of over 5 oz to $5\frac{1}{2}$ oz should not be used if avoidable, whether split-cane or fibre-glass.

The nature of the line is entirely dependent on the action of the rod and the average distance required. It must be borne in mind that in competitive trout-fly accuracy tests, a good caster nearly always makes a faultless turn-over with line length outside the rod tip (excluding leader length) of anything from 2 yds to 15 yds. In ultimates of manipulation, the weight of the line outside the tip is not materially influential on the accuracy or turn-over of the cast; but however good the fly caster, he should select the best length/ weight of line, regulated against the rod action, for the main average length of cast required on the water to be fished.

The effect of the line on rod action is entirely dependent on its weight, with trifling difference between diameter thicknesses on air resistance. At the present time certain lines are in course of design which all have the same diameter but are variable in weight. Hitherto, however, weights have varied with the diameter. The best cast, no matter what distance, is mainly dependent on the speed of discharge in the finality of the forecast. The slow-action rod only performs well with a light line; a fast-action rod, with a heavy line in comparison. The reason is that as the rod is driven into the final forecast, the greater the line weight behind the tip, the greater the flex put into the bend of the rod—and, the material point, the faster the speed of the flex recovery to the inert as it discharges the line. A slow-action rod, if equipped with a heavy line, would not have the power to recover flex against the weight; and the fast-action rod would not be flexed appreciably by a light line. This should make the rod/line balance situation quite clear; and its very material importance to the angler in assuring a balanced rod and line to remove many of the serious problems with the unbalanced combination.

The simple line-weight assessment used by the competitive caster is to curl up the line and weigh it on a delicate grain balance-scale, regardless of trade specification. He can then fit the line to the rod and gradually let it out beyond the tip until he is satisfied, on practical feel, what length gives the best discharge and turn-over.

If this length is longer or shorter than that required for the most frequent distance he is likely to want to cast, the alternatives are to obtain a line which combines the best length-weight combination; or to exchange the rod for one with action which reacts well to the right length of the tested line. One point to be borne in mind is that the heavier the line, the greater its impact on the surface as it lays down; in other words the greater the splash, which may alarm nearby trout. This is influenced to some extent by the length of the leader, which may be any length from 7 ft to 12 ft. Even with a fairly light line in use, it has become a general impression that leader length should not be less than 10 ft on any normal chalk stream; and this may well be on the short side for windless conditions on a still water. In windy conditions, with a rough surface, neither the line weight nor the leader length have such importance to the satisfactory fly presentation; and the heavier line, with shorter leader, is better to control in the conditions.

This completes the tackle selection analysis (excluding leader design, which will be covered later) for the normal fly-cast on Two Lakes. It can be summed up briefly:

(1) The rod length should be a maximum of 9 ft. The rod should weigh $5\frac{1}{2}$ oz, or, preferably, less. The rod action should be medium, to medium-fast.

(2) The fly-line length should be about 45 ft, attached to 100 yds of 18 lb test monofil backing. The weight of the 45 ft should be from $\frac{1}{2}$ oz to $\frac{3}{4}$ oz; and the line should be tapered. The line termed "forward taper" can be used; but is not desirable in certain complex respects. The best way to deal with the line requirement is purchase of a double-taper line (90 ft normal length), cut in half, and one half used. The other half can be properly stored for future years.

(3) The reel should be the lightest available, with smooth function. This does not mean it should have no check mechanism, which is desirable on any fly-reel. The reel should have no circular ring through which the line intake is made; but a hardened metal strip on the cross-support of the reel, over which the line is pulled for the pay-out, is desirable.

The next state to be considered is the method of stillwater fly-casting with the specified tackle.

A great deal has been written, over the years, about the correct method of casting. The inference has been that if the reader makes careful study of the advice, he will soon achieve his objective. A simple exposure of the unreliable in this inference is comparison with casting and the riding of a bicycle. If the novice has never attempted to ride a bicycle, reading will not take him far with initial upright balance; but, as with casting, practice ultimately (and often with unexpected rapidity after a good deal of practice) brings performance into the instinctive and habitual. In the case of the fly-cast, practical instruction on the water (not over grass if possible since the line behaviour is entirely different when drawn off water or grass and casting action tends to develop in bad ways if consistently practised off grass) is far more effective than the reading of instruction. It must be remembered, of course, that many instructors in casting have neither established qualification nor experience of the instructional findings drilled in by competitive casting.

In the early day of the London School of Casting, founded and managed over many years by the late Capt T L Edwards, there was the opinion that the best way to start the pupil on the single-handed fly-cast action, was to attach the butt of the rod to the caster's rod-arm wrist. The objective was to prevent the nearly universal excessive bend of the wrist in initial fly-rod handling. It was not long, however, before Capt Edwards realised that the influence of this method tended to eliminate the *essential* wrist influence on handling of the rod. His ingenious butt-tying kit was thrown into the dust-bin some 30 years ago. The reason for his discard of this system (often advised by the inexperienced instructor today) was that practice into an incorrect method, no matter how trifling, gives the pupil a serious problem in its discard and development of the correct.

The fundamental requirement of the single-handed fly-cast is correct use of the rod forearm in lifting the rod, and driving the line outside the tip both back and fore without appreciable variation from a parallel line with the ground behind and the water in front. Once the forearm has begun to hinge to a considerable extent at the elbow, the second requirement is what may appear to be trifling wrist action, but what is in fact extremely important action to ensure proper line discharge on both backcast and forecast.

The most simple way of assessing these two requirements, from the readers standpoint, is to attempt a few casts with the rod and line; then to sit on a box or chair, lay the rod-arm elbow on the knee and keep it firmly there during continued practice casts. Initial attempts with the poorly timed waving will no doubt cause a few tangles; but these will reduce as practice continues, particularly if the wrist begins to come into correct action. This wrist action can be kept in mind very effectively by comparison with similar action in use at times by nearly all the public: the hammering of a nail into a piece of wood. In hammer action, the initial twist forward ends with a powerful flick to reach the fastest move of the hammer head (and therefore the violence of the hit) caused by wrist action. Basically, this is precisely the action the angler requires in the back-cast and forecast if the respective discharges of the line are to be correct. In other words, he should imagine he is driving a nail into a high wall behind him in the backcast; then, as the rod moves forward, there is another nail to be driven in towards the end of the forecast. It may be the impression that the behaviour of the line in the backcast is not so important as its behaviour in the forecast. It is a fact that the nature of the forecast is almost entirely dependent on the line move in the backcast. A curl towards the end of the back-cast makes directly straight discharge into the forecast virtually impossible. In passing, a curl in the forecast can have merit for certain occasional reasons on rivers in order to delay the drag of the drifting fly by line movement caused by the current; but in stillwater fishing this rarely, if ever, becomes a requirement.

If the pupil watches a really good caster in action, he will notice that the line is lifted slowly from the water at the start; then speed of lift increases steadily until the butt half of the bent rod is nearing the perpendicular. The tip half of the rod will have a measure of flex showing. Then the caster will bring wrist into action and the rod flex will increase considerably until, slightly behind the per-pendicular, it straightens firmly into the inert and the line curls into the straight behind the caster. There is then something near an imperceptible pause as the line gets towards final straightening, before the rod begins to move forward and shows the reverse flex. It is common casting advice that the line must straighten out com-pletely before the forecast comes into action. This is incorrect. As the observer of the good caster will see, the forecast starts when the point end of the line and leader is still in a measure of curl before straightening. The simple reason is that the forecast must start when the weight of the line, and its drag, in the backcast makes the caster feel that it has come to extremes; and if the forecast is not brought into action instantly, the line will fall below the parallel to the ground. The rod flex will then increase slowly as the forecast gathers speed. When the butt section of the rod is reaching about 45 degrees beyond the perpendicular, the wrist will come into firm action again. The flex will increase sharply until its fast recovery to the inert as the line goes upon its way. The only final point to be made is that in the forecast, the line is best discharged to straighten on a parallel about 3 ft above the water; from which point it will lose the weight of its fall on the surface and decrease the likelihood of detrimental splash.

The method of rod use can now be summed up briefly:

(1) Sit on a chair or box with rod and line in hand; the line outside the tip being a reasonable length to ensure rod flex. It is well to attach about 7 or 8 ft of 12 lb test monofilament to the point of the line, with a bit of yellow wool of about $\frac{3}{4}$ in diameter tied to the monofilament point and teased out with a needle.

(2) Keep the elbow of the rod-arm firmly on the knee.

(3) Imagine a nail to be struck behind, and another in front; and use the wrist firmly towards the end of the slow-starting but increasingly fast move of the rod in both backcast and forecast.

Once the pupil has achieved what he considers to be the habitual from this position, he can rise to his feet and continue the casts; but if they vary, he should return to the seated position and continue with the elbow-rest until he is satisfied that he can stand up and make casts with identical action despite lack of elbow support and control.

The initial practice should be made with the line (near the reel) trapped under the forefinger of the rod hand. Once the habitual has been achieved, the next move is towards mastery of the line control with the off-rod hand. In the normal fly-cast, this control appears to be slight as one watches the competent caster; but it is in fact quite material in its influence on the rod flex. The line is held in the finger and thumb of the off-rod hand, directly into the butt ring from the grip. As the rod moves into the lift of the line, a slight drag is made by the off-rod hand; and as the rod moves into the forecast, the slight drag is repeated until the instant of final line discharge. The grip is then released to allow the short length of slackened line to be dragged into the forecast through the rings of the rod.

This operation has three influences on the cast. First, the slight drag either way increases rod flex and speed of recovery to the inert. Second, it causes (for reasons better guessed than known) a slightly lighter lay-down of the line on the surface. Third, it is an important influence on the distance of the normal cast. The last point requires analysis.

If the angler wants a steady 20 yds cast, he will find it difficult (and usually impossible) to aerialise 41 ft of line. This length is based on the leader length of 10 ft and the rod length of 9 ft. A competent caster can aerialise about 30 ft of line very consistently; and in some cases, dependent on line weight, up to 35 ft. The addition of 19 ft to this to cover the rod and leader lengths brings the distance of the cast to 54 ft only. The means of adding to this distance is simply by drawing additional line from the reel, which the weight of the 30 ft to 35 ft of the discharged line will draw after it into the forecast, on release by the off-rod hand.

The comments on the off-rod hand action have been based on the normal cast as far as this stage. This was the reason for the comment that it is difficult to aerialise 41 ft of line in that type of cast. It must be borne in mind, however, that the capable competitive caster can aerialise 60 ft of line consistently so long as it is balanced to the right rod with the right weight for that purpose. This type of cast is known as the "trout-fly distance cast"; and has received a great deal of publicity, claims of origination and advice on the correct method for the angler since it showed its practical merit for the fishing of Chew and Grafham. I observed earlier that I do not regard it as having any particular merit for Two Lakes fly fishing. On rare occasions, and in a very limited number of bank positions, it might find the angler a fish that would avoid being caught with the normal cast; and I make this comment with full knowledge of this cast, and a number of sessions of fishing all parts of Two Lakes. Nevertheless, if the reader in interested in extremes in still-water tactics, he could do worse for his own satisfaction than omit the reasonable ability necessary to turn to the trout-fly distance cast for experimental purposes. In the circumstances, it will be specified in sufficient detail to give him a lead to its performance. A major point is that no matter how habitually competent a normal caster he is, he will find the initial action problem of this cast to be similar to that of the normal cast to the novice in handling a rod.

The origin of the trout-fly distance cast took place in the United

States during the close of the last century; and in 1902, using a 5 oz rod, W D Mansfield broke the American competitive record with a cast of 43 yds 4 in. In the early 1930s the cast became known and practised in Britain and the Continent. One of the longest British casters of those days was Capt Edwards. He used an 8 ft 9 in split-cane rod weighing about 5 oz for both stillwater angling and competitive casting; and cast consistently from 35 yd to 40 yd with that equipment. In those days, of course, the line in use was braided throughout; and did not give the caster the facilities of today with the line cut to the best length (termed the "casting head") and backed to small diameter and very smooth monofilament, which slides through the rod rings with far less friction than braided line. Latter day casting of this type has advanced in distance. The right rod and line makes the 50 yd cast possible for a number of competitive casters; but for angling purposes, the convenient length of casting-head line is limited to about 35 ft, against the 45 ft or more necessary to reach 50 yd. The rod has also to be adjusted in action to react correctly to the shorter (and lighter) length of line.

The best practical tackle for this cast is a medium-fast, to fast, action rod of 9 ft, or slightly less, weighing $5\frac{1}{2}$ oz, or less. Modern fibre-glass has a slight advantage, for minor reasons, over split cane, for this type of casting. The casting-head, irrespective of length, must weigh about $\frac{5}{8}$ oz; and, to avoid the risk of backing tangles with thinner line, the monofilament must be of about the 18 lb test. Before attempting the cast the backing must be rubbed and pulled to get rid of any curls which it has developed while wound to the reel drum for any length of time.

The method of the cast is straightforward in description.

The first move is to draw off from 20 yd to 30 yd of the backing, from the reel; or, possibly, draw off this length and straighten out the curls while doing so. The best course is to draw off the line; then straighten and in doing so, lay the curls in reverse on the ground so that when the casting-head is discharged, it draws the loose backing after it from top to bottom rather than the reverse if the backing is laid as drawn off from the reel.

The caster, keeping clear of the backing which lies beside him, must then begin his casting across the water until he gets out a comfortable length for aerialisation. Once the aerialisation is operating smoothly, he must continue to pay out the line and backing, with hand manipulation, until the casting head and 6 ft of backing are outside the rod tip. He will not find this maintenance of aerialisation easy with any length of line, within reason, in the first attempts. It is not unlike the attempt to keep upright on a bicycle for the first time; and may take some hours of practice to move into the sound habitual. The solution, with respect to those whose practical knowledge of the cast is so trivial that they suggest a start with a much shorter line than the 35 ft, is to concentrate on practice with knowledge that in due course the action and timing will *ensure* the habitual aerialisation of the 35 ft casting-head and the 6 ft of

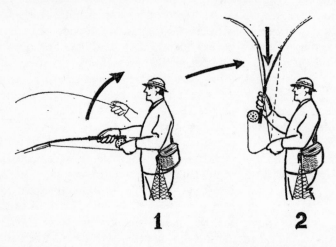

1   **2**

The normal short distance fly cast of the experienced angler is an effortless action, covering the water within about 15 yd of his stance. He can also add another 5 yd by taking back the rod hand slightly from the position shown in 2. The following is a brief analysis of the action.

1. The rod is raised slowly into the cast, ensuring that the line is on the water surface before final lifting into 2.

2. The rod-hand wrist has bent slightly back from the upper position in 1 in the hammer-hit strike of the line into the back cast. The rod hand remains stationary at the point indicated and the weight of the line flexes the rod from forward to backward.

3. The line has straightened substantially in the back cast and the caster moves the hand forward into the wrist hammer-hit action of the fore cast. His off-rod hand pulls the line down from the butt ring to increase the flex of the rod, and its consequential increase of power in

backing, outside the rod tip; and, indeed, will make a much greater length of casting-head manipulative if the caster so desires.

The method of this aerialisation is entirely dependent on extreme exaggeration of the off-rod hand draw, described when dealing with the normal cast. Moreover, there must be extremely accurate timing in the draws of both the backcast and forecast. It is this requirement which causes the delay in acquiring the habitual in manipulation.

Let us now consider how the cast operates. Once the casting-head

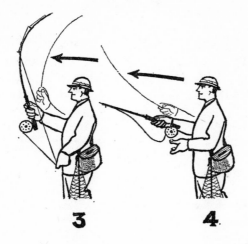

3   **4.**

recovery to inert, to give the forward movement of the line the maximum speed.

4. The hammer-hit of the wrist has cleared after discharge of the line. The line has been aimed to straighten to finality in a parallel to the water surface, about two feet above, so that it drops gently. Addition to this action of the line has been made by the release of the line from the off-rod hand.

The only other points for reference are the faint difference in the body angle of the caster to the perpendicular. The slight back-and-fore sway is a common feature of this type of casting. The legs are also close together, since their position has little influence on the gentle action of the upper part of the caster's body. In learning the system of the cast, there is some merit in keeping the right leg forward to control the action of the rod-arm shoulder of the caster.

is being aerialised steadily with long pulls of the line with the off-rod hand, the gradual intensification can come into manipulation. As the rod moves into the backcast, the off-rod hand should drag the line back from the butt-ring until the arms are spread wide apart; and instead of moving the rod slightly past the perpendicular, as in the normal cast, it should be moved back to straighten into the inert at an angle of about 45 degrees; and as the recovery to inert, greatly increased in power by the drag of the line by the off-rod hand, straightens the rod, the off-rod hand should be allowed to take the pull of the line as a drag to itself towards the butt ring. The objective is to create the longest possible drag as the rod moves into the forecast.

Once the line has mainly straightened into the backcast, with a fractional delay in moving the rod forward, the forecast begins. In a sense, the two hands move forward together; but they are likely to be from 1 to 2 ft apart. As the rod moves into its position ahead of the perpendicular, with the moderate flex created by the drive of the rod forearm and wrist, the off-rod hand is brought downwards with action which could be described as violent. The objective is to increase the rod flex to the absolute maximum, to increase its speed of recovery to the inert and consequential increase in the forward discharge speed of the casting-head. Once the casting head straightens into its fast flight, the off-rod hand releases its hold on the backing; the casting-head pulls forward through the rings a number of yards of the coiled backing lying alongside the caster. The actual distance of the cast is dependent on the speed of the casting head as sent on its way; and the completely smooth pay-out of the loose lying backing.

An interesting and simple description of this trout-fly distance cast appeared under the Editor's initials in *The Fishing Gazette* of 11th August, 1934.

"As far as fly fishing is concerned, the secret of the distance cast can be summed up in a few words—perfect balance between rod and line and perfect timing; quick recovery from the water as the line is being worked out, and stopping the rod on the backcast ten or fifteen degrees beyond the vertical. This, combined with 'shooting the line' at the right moment, is the whole secret of long-distance casting."

This does not make reference to the drag of the off-rod hand; but a photograph of a fly distance caster in action, in the same issue, shows the drag action. The importance of the drag has increased in the experience of later years.

It might appear from the foregoing analysis of the trout-fly distance cast that it means a great deal of manipulation, while practical fishing. This is not the case. After the cast out of from 35 yd to 40 yd, the competent caster will either hand-gather the line in; or give it lengthy pulls through the butt ring if faster fly movement is regarded as likely to induce trout takes. As the line comes to the convenient lifting length outside the tip, he will lift it into the back-cast, and allow the casting head to pull out its entire length and 6 ft or so of backing beyond the tip ring. He will then move straight into the forecast and release the line. The only reasons for more than one backcast, and forecast to follow, are that the line may have been drawn in so close that the lifted weight is not enough to cause it to pull out the right length for the full distance of the forecast; or that the wind conditions have a similar effect and require one or two aerialised actions to get the length out.

Summed up briefly, the following are the requirements for the distance cast:

(1) the rod should be a maximum length of 9 ft and minimum of of 8 ft.

(2) the casting-head should be about 35 ft, weighing about $\frac{5}{8}$ oz. It must be borne in mind that a really good competitive caster can hold up, aerialised, no less than 60 ft of line with similar diameter and the rod action of the fast type; but for practical angling the background trees or shrubs make the 35 ft a much more practical length. It also relieves the angler from the need to reach the extreme distance casting standards; and adds the merit of a slightly slower action requirement in the rod, to ease its handling.

(3) the backing line should be about 18 lb test monofil.

(4) the leader should be from 7 ft to 10 ft in length; but must be tapered if the best turn-over is to operate. The ideal taper should be from $\frac{2}{3}$ diameter against the point of the casting-head, at the top end where attached; with three or four knotted lengths of reduced strength/diameter to the point length.

Practice of this method of casting requires a few hours of persistent action to achieve the habitual; and the novice may well find it easier, initially, to try out the method with about 20 ft of fairly heavy line as casting head. Once he has learned to operate this weight, he can experiment into the longer head.

A point to be remembered is that the shorter the casting head, the more heavily it falls (if the required weight) on the water surface; so that there is good reason for achieving ability to handle a line of reasonable length.

Finally, one other type of cast needs mention: the roll-cast. This is sometimes referred to as the "switch-cast", presumably on the ground that the line can be raised off the water surface before throwing into the forecast; but the action in both casts is precisely the same.

The line is surfaced forward to a reasonable length for handling. The rod tip is then lifted slowly to a point slightly behind the perpendicular, the speed and manipulation being so made as to ensure a consistent hanging curve in the line. Once the line has reached the extreme of the raise, the rod is moved forward with gradually increasing speed until about the angle of 45 degrees, with the moderate flex showing. The wrist is then brought into action with a fast increase to maximum power into the circular curl-over of the line. The curl gradually works out from the rod tip to the extreme point of the leader; and the cast is complete.

This cast meets two requirements. First, it enables the angler to cast out the fly without the line or fly moving to any appreciable distance behind his body; and thereby enables fly presentation when the overhead cast, whether normal or distance, would catch in background vegetation. Second, the line will not lift correctly from the water if sunk below the surface. This applies to any form of cast; and the problem of surfacing before fast raising into the backcast is solved by one or two quickly executed roll-casts.

That concludes the commentary on stillwater fly-casting as it is likely to be required by the angler of the eight fine waters of Two Lakes. May I repeat, once again, that instructional print on the angler's cast is by no means as satisfactory a lead to good casting as practical instruction by a reasonably competent caster. He can watch the beginner in action, and indeed many an old hand at angling, and pick the errors which show; errors which, without question, add to the problems of fly presentation to the trout. One merit of writing on the cast by those of us who have studied the technical problems, is that it gives the learner evidence on which he can question the reliability of the advice by many of the instructors who appear to

assume that casting technique is simple; or that their limited knowledge of the technique is extremely advanced.

A number of hours of fishing on Two Lakes have convinced me
that mastery of the trout-fly distance cast has very limited advantage
when compared with the requirements of still waters like Chew
and Grafham—and, of course, the considerable number of anglers
in action on those waters from time to time. The full distance of
20 yd, or slightly more as the angler learns the technique of the
normal cast, is only needed on occasion; and usually if the angler
is using the sunk fly. Nevertheless, the full knowledge of all available
fly presentation techniques, and ability to practise if necessary to
the fancy of the angler, can be a very satisfying factor when facing
the great variables in location, weather conditions, and fish movements
and moods.

[19]

The Questionnaire

Sage benign!
Whose pen, the mysteries of rod and line
Unfolding, did not fruitlessly exhort
To reverend watching of each still report
That Nature utters from her rural shrine.   WORDSWORTH

We learn from the questionnaire that split cane rods are preferred to fibreglass in the ratio of 6 to 4, but there is a widespread belief that split cane will inevitably be phased out in the years to come, if only because of cost. Length of rods vary a good deal, from $7\frac{1}{2}$ ft (2·3 m) to 10 ft (3·05 m) for split cane, and from 8 ft 3 in (2·5 m) to 9 ft 6 in (2·9 m) for fibreglass. Of the split cane users, over 90 per cent prefer a length within 6 in ($15\frac{1}{4}$ cms) of 9 ft (2·75 m), and of the fibreglass users about 50 per cent prefer the 9 ft (2·75 m) length. A few use both cane and fibreglass, the former for dry fly and the latter for the sunken fly.

With only two exceptions, all members fish an orthodox centre-pin reel, but no information was given on whether it was geared or direct drive. Of the exceptions, one confessed to occasional use only of an automatic, but the other, in the formidable person of Barrie Welham, is so convinced of its superiority that he uses no other. The diameter of the centre-pin reels varies between 3 in (7·6 cms) and 4 in (10·1 cms).

Nearly half the members are equipped with a floating line and a sinking line, employing whichever is thought to be more appropriate to the prevailing conditions. More than a third use floaters only; one member in eight uses a sinker only, and one in ten a silk Kingfisher and a floater.

Leaders (casts) are almost exactly divided between level and tapered, the latter mostly made up. They vary in length from $6\frac{1}{2}$ ft (2 m) to 10 ft (3·05 m) for level, and from $7\frac{1}{2}$ ft (2·3 m) to 12 ft

216

(3·6 m) for tapered. Breaking strains are from 3½ lb (1·6 kg) to 7 lb (3·2 kg).

Individual largest fish averaged just over 5¼ lb (2½ kg), but in this average are included 1 fish weighing over 9 lb (4¼ kg), 4 weighing over 8 lb (3¾ kg), and a few over 7 lb (3¼ kg). About half answering the question were in the 4 lb plus (2 kg plus) category at the time, but no doubt a number of them have since improved their personal best.

I give below an extract from the comments of a long-standing member, Col T A (Terence) Arnold, whose personal best is 7 lb 3 oz (3¼ kg), captured a few minutes after his wife, Mrs H (Henny) Arnold secured her own personal best of 8 lb 1 oz (3·7 kg), surely a world record for two fish caught by a husband and wife within minutes of each other.

Col Arnold. "Mistrust bloodknots! Now seldom use less than 7½ lb (28/100ths mm) having frequently been broken on a light leader. Experience indicates that fish not frightened by heavier leader when fishing medium depth. Use 5½ lb (21/100th mm) breaking strain when fishing dry, but with some trepidation.

Nearly all my nymphs slightly leaded, more to sink to required depth quickly than to go very deep. Probably 60 per cent of fishing done between 1 ft and 4 ft (30 cms and 1·2 m) deep. Brassy sunny days 'bottom dredging' often best results. A surprisingly large number of fish taken almost under one's bank at the end of quite a long run... always worth fishing-out one's fly. Very little success ever with fast-worked flies or lures.

Each day seems to have its favourite basic colour—e.g., black, red, yellow, etc. This, as much as pattern, appears to have a bearing on success. Have taken far more fish on fairly small rather than on larger flies and nymphs."

Col Arnold modestly refrains from stating that he is a most tenacious, industrious fisherman, and that this contributes a great deal to his ability continually to secure his limit of fish.

Col Locke, from whose letters I have previously quoted, comments as follows.

"To fish the full range of nymphs from No 11 downwards one needs to vary one's leader from about 9 ft (2¾ m) early season to

18 ft (5½ m) in the summer. Leader design is largely personal preference, but I use the top end of an old fully tapered salmon cast as a butt and taper down from there by stages to 4 lb (1·8 kg) or 3¾ lb (1·7 kg), usually the latter. Very deep fishing with heavily leaded nymphs produces fish when all else fails during very hot days.

I 'fish the knot', i.e., grease the top part of the cast and strike when this draws away. Midge pupa fishing often means greasing down to within 6 in (15¼ cms) of the fly.... I regard my detergent pads and grease as two of my most important parts of equipment; they enable me to control my fishing depth to a nicety. Sometimes a few inches up or down will make all the difference. How would one of the old traditional loch fishers react if he could see us using 16 ft (5 m) casts greased down to the last 4 in (10 cms)? He'd probably think us mad!"

A final word about my own fishing. I use split cane rods only, Hardy's and Ogden Smiths, both 9 ft (2·7 m) in length. My reels are centre pin, with a preference for geared types, about 3½ in (9 cms) in diameter. I possess a Mitchell automatic, and readily admit its virtues, but after so many years of using the centre pin I am too accustomed to its humours to adjust to another medium even if it is superior. My lines are of three different types, floater, sinking tip, and sinker, but the sinking tip is employed for at least 90 per cent of my fishing, although in a somewhat amended form. This amendment refers to the removal of all the sinking tip with the exception of about 18 in (0·5 m). My leader, 10 to 12 ft (3 to 3½ m) in length, is tapered from 21 lb (9·5 kg) at the butt to 4 lb (1·8 kg) at the point. With this outfit, I fish either on top of the water, just below it, or at any depth down to about 4 ft (1¼ m), depending on the weight of the fly and my manipulation of it. My objective is twofold; first, to keep my leader, or most of it, below the surface except when the light has faded, even when fishing the dry fly, and second, to keep my line afloat.

I do not differentiate between nymph and pupa in method of presentation, although the fashion for fishing the midge pupa requires almost all the leader to be on the surface. That this is probably the most efficaceous method of fishing the pupa I don't dispute, but it requires keener eyesight than I possess, and to sit and watch the minute knot of an almost stationery line for any length of time, as in coarse fishing, but with much greater concentration than is needed for watching a float, tempers the joys of fly fishing without compensating the angler for loss of the pleasures of reflecting on the passing scene. I find that when fish are taking the natural pupa, they will take my imitation readily if fished in my normal fashion.

My wet flies are all simple, mostly without tails or wings, and tied on hooks varying from No 14 to No 10. I use light irons, and give them weight, either lightly or heavily, with windings of fuse wire. All my flies, even pupa imitations, have short stiff hackles, in order to impart by their vibrations the suggestions of animation. Bodies, always ribbed with gold twist or black silk, are dressed with various materials, with baby seal and sewing silk dyed in various colours, predominating.

My most rewarding manœuvre is to drop my fly (nymph, pupa or dry fly) without delay as near as possible to the centre of the ring of a rising fish, so that the line proper is kept at a respectable distance from it, and to impart an immediate and distinct (but not too sharp) motion to the fly. When few fish are rising, I must perforce cast and retrieve repeatedly, changing my fly and varying the depth and the retrieve as already described in an earlier chapter, if I want fish.

Both my concentration and energy leave much to be desired. Rarely do I flog away hour after hour in search of fish, and providing the weather is not unsuitable, I share the day between stillwater and river fishing. Yet I believe that my yield of fish, taken as an hourly rate, is comparable to that of some of the best and most energetic anglers. My greatest failure, for which I am my own severest critic, is neglect of leader checking for wind knots during high winds, or for weaknesses in the monofil after hitting sharp obstacles in the backcast. Because of these factors, my losses due to breakages at the take are far too high. But because I do not pretend that the methods I employ are superior to all others, I have endeavoured to present a picture of successful fishing at Two Lakes by a cross-section of the methods employed by anglers whose techniques I admire.

[20]

The Members

If Patience be a Vertue, then,
How happy are we Fishermen?
For all do know that those that fish,
Have Patience more than Heart can wish.
  Prudens qui Patiens.
Yea, Antidotus vitae patientia est,
Patience is the Preservative of Life.

RICHARD HOWLETT. Anglers Sure Guide. 1706

I use the word "members" for the enrolled anglers at Two Lakes, although it is neither a club nor an association, but a sporting fishery run by an individual proprietor for profit; in other words, to provide a livelihood for himself and his family. In certain politico-economic circles profit is a dirty word, but we cannot ignore the fact that great enterprises, benefiting all mankind have sprung from the minds of men primarily for gain, that is, for profit. So within their own lesser plane of achievement, the Behrendts have paved the way to the creation in this country of small first-class trout fisheries out of sterile marshland, providing excellent sport and recreation in addition to a supplementary crop of 7 tons of highly prized food per annum.

The very fact that their bread and butter depends upon the continued prosperity of the fishery is the best assurance that the proprietors' commitment to it is total and comprehensive. In my years of acquaintance with Alex Behrendt, I have never known him spend a night away from his beloved lakes and their trout. He has resisted all temptations to attend the annual gatherings of the most famous angling clubs and societies, and I doubt if he has since the establishment of Two Lakes fishery taken a holiday, however brief.

This devotion to the fishery automatically demands that the members shall have an attachment of a similar kind, if not of the same magnitude, and for this reason rods are let only on a contractual basis of at least one day a week for a minimum period of one year, with a preference for those who renew their membership from season to season. No permits therefore are granted for transient fishing whether daily, weekly or monthly. For the same reason the regulations are generally lenient, and where restrictive, designed to protect the health of the fishery and the amenities of the members.

No wading is permitted in order to protect the snails, caddis larvae and other small creatures that abound on the beds at the shallow edges of the various lakes. No boats are provided in order to ensure, where possible, that sanctuaries are available to the hunted fish. Multiple flies are not permitted, nor are flies with double hooks, nor single hooks greater in length than 2 cms (0·787 in) from the front of the eye to the furthest point of the bend. Children are not allowed to fish. Each member may have a limited number of guest tickets, and when these are exhausted, rod sharing with a guest is permitted if only one rod is in use, providing the host member is present. Each member, and his guest (if not sharing the rod) may kill 5 fish over 1 lb (0·45 kg) per day, and all fish caught must be killed. Those under 1 lb are not included in the permitted limit.

An easy relationship exists between the members and the proprietor, and in many cases this has developed into a solid friendship. The members themselves form, on their own particular day, a close fraternity, but in almost every instance those fishing on one day of the week are utter strangers to those fishing on the other days. It is related that two anglers completely unknown to each other, met one year in a remote Highland hotel where they had gone for the salmon fishing. After becoming acquainted, they discovered that each fished Two Lakes on consecutives days and had done so for many years.

Newcomers are accepted into the camaraderie of the day of their choosing, but it usually takes a season or two before the final barriers of polite distance are surmounted. Obviously, some fit in better than others, and apart from the odd one or two who, either from shyness or traditional reserve maintain a degree of aloofness for a long time, all members eventually settle down to an agreeable relationship which includes the exchange of flies and fly-tying materials, the occasional participation in a bottle of wine (or even something stronger) over the luncheon table, the distribution of home grown produce, and the general interchange of the civilities common to a well-mannered company. Thus the fishing context becomes inter-fused with a social accretion, which sometimes results in life-long friendships between members and families. Occasionally the publicity afforded to heavy fish captures by individual members, parti-cularly in widely distributed journals like "The Field", has been responsible for the renewal of old friendships that have been inter-rupted by the exigencies of professional life.

I must now confess that, contrary to the propaganda generated for hundreds of years by scores of anglers, including myself, not all fishermen are paragons of virtue. The head keeper of a famous fishery swore a deadly oath in support of a story of a member whom he found playing a fish in the rearing pool, and who explained the situation by declaring that his fly accidentally touched the surface of the rearing pool on the backcast, and was immediately seized by a fish. This parallels the story of the gentleman who, when discovered hiding in a wardrobe by an irate husband who returned home unexpectedly, explained that he was waiting for a bus.

Mr Behrendt tells of the time when he took the 8-year old daughter of a member, an important official, to see a coot's nest. The child spoke with admiration of her father's prowess as a fisher-man, and in proof of it informed Mr Behrendt that he had brought home from Two Lakes the previous week "eleven lovely trout". The father, when confronted later in the day by Mr Behrendt, admitted the offence, but excused it by pleading that the trout "wouldn't stop coming for his fly", and offered to pay for the excess quantity. He did—but with the immediate cancellation of his membership. Another member weighed in five fish when he was clearly seen to have netted six, and when questioned, he claimed that one of the five he had killed "slipped into the water and swam off", and therefore he had assumed the right to kill a sixth. Thus we learn for the first time that trout share with cats the mythical attribute of multiple lives.

It is a closely guarded secret that all fishery owners and managers believe implicity that it is ordained by Heaven that one black sheep in every club is as inevitable as a ball in cricket, and that neither can survive without the other. When I enquired what human charac-teristics or their absence constituted a black sheep, Mr Behrendt replied that such a one was an inveterate grumbler. Nothing pleased him; on the contrary, his complaints about the fishery, its manage-ment, its fish and its members were never-ending. I must admit that my mind, which had been oppressed by thoughts of murder, arson, long term fraud and pick-pocketing, was immensely relieved. Mr Behrendt (who has a sense of humour second to none) went on to tell me of two separate complaints he received in a single day. The first was from a member who in the previous week or two had caught his limit of rainbow trout, but no brownies. He chided Mr Behrendt for his failure to include any brownies in his re-stocking program that year. The second one, who had five brownies in his bag, complained bitterly that no rainbows had been stocked that year.

Owners and Managers are of the opinion that "black sheep" must be tolerated, and that on no account should their membership be cancelled, because, as it was decreed by Fate that they must have one, better the devil they knew than the devil who would certainly replace him. It is also an axiom that quarrelling members (*rarae aves*) should not be allowed to involve the management in their quarrel, or to succeed in a demand that the other party forfeit his membership. Such a penalty should be imposed only for an offence that warrants it, and not because it is demanded by the friction of a quarrel. If the demand is accompanied by a threat of resignation if refused, it must still be resisted to the limit.

Contrasts between the attitudes of the members on successful and unsuccessful days would, I think, delight psychologists and their like enormously. There are those who, on bad days, when all are catching fish and they for the life of them can't touch one, would certainly break their rods into little pieces if it were not for the high cost. They glower from under beetled brows and speak, but only when they can't avoid it, from between set lips that hardly open. They depart in high dudgeon with never a goodnight. Yet ordinarily they are the kindest and most complacent of mortals.

Most reactions are less pronounced, even though vexation of spirit is apparent beneath the outward indifference, and I, for one, having been in the same situation, can heartily sympathise with those anglers, who, when all around are catching fish, can do nothing right. Very few, if any, have escaped the ignominy (if such it is) of being the only angler singled out by misfortune on a day of plenty, and a growl at destiny, astral influences or some other metaphysical doctrine of necessity is no doubt a prophylactic against something worse. Few can emulate that sublime angler, a complete stranger, whom I asked at the close of a June day if he had done any good, and who replied that he had enjoyed a wonderful day. He had raised two fish to his fly, and pricked another. I saluted him then, and I salute him now, assured that when his time arrives to quit this world of ours, he will pass with angelic acclaim through divine portals into the pavilions reserved for the favoured of the Powers on high.

Members, when asked, give a variety of reasons for their attachment to fly fishing, none of them satisfying. One states that he is attracted to the peace and to the relaxed routine, another to the stimulation of the physical exercise, a third to the escape from the turmoil of urban existence. But the relaxation, and the physical exercise, and the escapism can all be found in many other fields, and the question must be asked again; why fishing? One member contents himself (but not me) by answering with an all-embracing platitude that it is a way of life, but he gives no reason why. A few state quite bluntly that they fish for trout because its palatability is unsurpassed, but they turn a deaf ear to my suggestion that it would be much easier, and cheaper, to buy them. For myself, if asked, I would reply that I am fascinated by the art of deluding trout with a man-made fly, but in my heart of hearts I am certain that if fly fishing were forbidden, or impossible, I would not reduce my angling hours by one minute, even if I were compelled to revert to the twig, cotton reel, bent pin and worm of my youth.

The virility of the fishing fever in human beings is well illustrated by a true story told by Mr Behrendt, of an ageing member, his son and daughter-in-law. The latter, a handsome young woman with an infatuation for fishing a fly, arrived at Two Lakes in her own car, the father and son arriving in a separate car. The member and his son left at dusk but the young woman stayed on to continue hostilities against a rising trout that had defied her for some time. Night fell, and Mr Behrendt forgot all about her, and retired to his bed. He was awakened at 11 pm by high-pitched shouting followed by the scream of a reel and the splash of a fish. Dressing hurriedly, he followed the noise to the Upper Lake, where he arrived in time to help the young lady net a goodly fish by the light of his torch. She had continued fishing, all alone in the darkness, unbothered by the strange noises, or the solitude, or the possible anxiety of her family, driven by a relentless urge that only a dedicated fisherman will understand.

In the same vein, though more sombre, Mr Behrendt tells of a distinguished surgeon who accidentally lodged his fly in the lobe of his wife's ear. Without delay, he cut the leader holding the fly, tied on another one, and as he started to cast, advised his wife to ask Mr Behrendt kindly to remove the fly from her ear. This matches the well-known apocryphal story of the fanatical golfer who hurriedly approached a foursome ahead with a request that he be allowed to play through, as he had just received a telephone call that his wife was dangerously ill.

The cohesion of the members probably owes something to the dissimilarity of their various backgrounds. The armed forces, agriculture, the law, medicine, industry, commerce, banking, publishing and many other callings are represented. Many are in retirement, or about to retire. The feminine sex is well in evidence, and at least they hold their own in the quality of their fishing and in their good companionship. Few reside locally, and it is a tribute to the fishing, its management and its members that a high percentage travel in the region of 100 miles each way for their day's fishing even though other fisheries are within comparative stone-throws from their homes.

I am inclined to agree with Colonel Crow, who for many years has managed the Somerley salmon fishing of the Hampshire Avon, that if pollution in our rivers continues, they will be unfishable in 20 years or so, and the only fishing worth having will be in carefully protected fisheries such as Two Lakes. It is sincerely to be hoped that the industrial and chemical destruction of our rivers will evoke an outcry sufficiently strong to stop it before the damage is irreparable. But if not, Two Lakes and its contemporary fisheries will provide sanctuaries for those of our future generations who seek the same peace and happiness as their forebears in the pure unsullied waters of whatever portion or our green countryside remains untouched by future industrial and residential expansion.

Bibliography

J J ARMISTEAD: *Angler's Paradise*. Angler Press.
W H ARMISTEAD: *Trout Waters*. Black.
F BALFOUR-BROWNE: *Water Beetles*. Blacklock Farries.
H BASTIN: *Insect Life*. Hutchinson.
H BAUMANN: *Land of Ur*. Oxford University Press.
R CARRINGTON: *Guide to Earth History*. Chatto & Windus.
RACHEL L CARSON: *The Sea Around Us*. Staples Press.
RACHEL L CARSON: *Under the Sea Wind*. Staples Press.
JOHN CLEGG: *Freshwater Life of British Isles*. Warne.
JOHN CLEGG: *Pond Life*. Warne.
L J M COLUMELLA: *Re Rustica*. Heinemann.
CORBET, LONGFIELD: *Dragon Flies*. Collins.
JOHN CROMPTON: *The Spider*. Collins.
SIR J FRAZER: *The Golden Bough*. Macmillan.
FROST AND BROWN: *The Trout*. Collins.
JOHN GODDARD: *Trout Fly Recognition*. Black.
JOHN GODDARD: *Trout Flies on Stillwaters*. Black.
SIR EDWARD GREY: *Fly Fishing*. Dent.
F M HALFORD: *Floating Flies*. Sampson Law.
F M HALFORD: *Dry Fly Fishing*. Vinton.
F M HALFORD: *Dry Fly Entomology*. Vinton.
F M HALFORD: *Making a Fishery*. Cox.
F M HALFORD: *Dry Fly Man's Handbook*. Routledge.
F M HALFORD: *Modern Development of the Dry Fly*. Routledge.
J R HARRIS: *Angler's Entomology*. Collins.
NORMAN E HICKIN: *Caddis*. Methuen.
NORMAN E HICKIN: *Caddis Larvae*. Hutchinson.
A D IMMS: *Insect Natural History*. Collins.
D JACQUES: *Fisherman's Fly*. Black.
R JENNEL: *Introduction to Entomology*. Hutchinson.
O A JOHANNSEN: *Aquatic Diptera*. California.
F J KILLINGTON: *British Neuroptera*. Ray Society.
KLOET AND HINCKS: *Check List of British Insects*. Private.
R H LOWE-MCCONNELL: *Man-made Lakes*. Academic Press.
T T MACAN: *Biological Studies of English Lakes*. Longman.
MACAN AND WORTHINGTON: *Life in Lakes and Rivers*. Collins.
J J MANLEY: *Literature of Sea and River Fishing*. Clowes.
HELEN MELLANBY: *Animal Life in Fresh Water*. Methuen.

L C MIALL: *Natural History of Aquatic Animals*. Macmillan.

RUTH MOORE: *Man, Time and Fossils*. Jonathan Cape.

MARTIN E MOSELEY: *Dry Fly Fisherman's Entomology*. Routledge.

MARTIN E MOSELEY: *British Caddis Flies*. Routledge.

NEEDHAM AND NEEDHAM: *Fresh-Water Biology*. Constable.

L R PEART: *Trout and Trout Waters*. Allen & Unwin.

RABINOWITZ: *Midrash* Vol viii. Soncino Press.

WM RADCLIFFE: *Fishing from Earliest Times*. John Murray.

G RAWLINSON: *History of Herodotus*. New York.

P ROBINSON: *Fishes of Fancy*. Clowes.

A RONALDS: *Fly Fishers Entomology*. Longman.

LORD ROTHSCHILD: *Classification of Living Animals*. Longman.

SAVORY: *World of Small Animals*. University of London.

JOHN VENIARD: *Fly Dressers Guide*. Black.

JOHN VENIARD: *Further Guide to Fly Dressing*. Black.

C F WALKER: *Lake Flies and their Imitation*. Jenkins.

IZAAK WALTON: *Compleat Angler*. John Major Edition.

LEONARD WEST: *Natural Trout Fly*. Potter.

JESSIE L WESTON: *From Ritual to Romance*. Doubleday.

T H WHITE: *Book of Beasts*. Jonathan Cape.

V B WIGGLESWORTH: *Life of Insects*. Weidenfeld.

V B WIGGLESWORTH: *Principles of Insect Physiology*. Methuen.

A COURTNEY WILLIAMS: *Dictionary of Trout Flies*. Black.

Publications, Papers etc.

K BERG: Biology of Corethra (Chaoborus), Levin & Munksgaard.

D BRYCE: Studies of Larvae of British Chironomidae, *Trans. Soc. Br. Ent.* Vol. 14, pt. 2, May 1960.

COE, FREEMAN and MATTINGLEY: Diptera. Nematocera, *R.E.S.L. Handbook*, Vol. IX, pt. 2, May 1950.

LEWIS DAVIES: Taxonomy of British Simulidae, *Trans. R.E.S.L.*, Vol. 118, pt. 14, pp. 413–511.

D H D EDWARDS: Biology of Parthenogenetic Lundstroemia (Diptera), *Proc. R.E.S.L.*, Vol. 38, pts. 10–12, pp. 165–170.

F W EDWARDS: British Chaoborinae, *Ent. monthly*, Ser. 3, Vol. 6, Dec. 1920.

F W EDWARDS: British Chaoborinae, *Ent. monthly*, Ser. 3, Vol. 46, April 1930.

F W EDWARDS: Notes on Chaoborinae, *An. and Mag. Nat. Hist.*, Ser. 10, Vol. 6, p. 527, Oct. 1930.

J M ELLIOT: Diel Activity Patterns of caddis Larvae, *J. Zool. Lon.*, 1970, 160, pp. 279–290.

F C FRASER: Handbook for identification of Mecoptera, Megaloptera and Neuroptera, *R.E.S.L.*, Vol. 1, pts. 12/13, Oct. 1959.

A M GOWER: Study of Limnephilus lunatus in Watercress beds, *Trans. R.E.S.L.*, Vol. 119, pt. 10, pp. 283–302.

H M HANNA: Egg Laying and Case Building of caddis flies, *Proc. R.E.S.L.*, Vol. 36, pts. 4/6, pp. 57–62.

H M HANNA: Selection of materials for case building by larvae of caddis flies, *Proc. R.E.S.L.*, Vol. 36, pts. 1–3, pp. 37–47.

B HEPHER: Effect of Fertilisation on Fish Yields, *Barmidgeh (Israel)*, 14(2):29–38.

JAMES and SMITH: Observation on Chaoborus, *Mosquito News*, Vol. 18, No. 3, Sept. 1958 (Manitoba).

Two Lakes Course Report 1970, Janssen Services.

Two Lakes Course Report 1971, Janssen Services.

G W JOHNSTONE: Stridulation by larvae of Hydropsychidae, *Proc. R.E.S.L.*, Vol. 39, pts. 10–12, p. 146.

D E KIMMINS: Keys to aquatic Megaloptera and Neuroptera, Sci. pub. 8, Freshwater Biol. Ass.

D E KIMMINS: Species of Caenis new to Britain, *Entomologist*, Vol. LXXVI, June 1943.

LEWIS and TAYLOR: Diurnal periodicity of flight by insects, *Trans. R.E.S.L.*, Vol. 116, pt. 15, pp. 393–479.

T T MACAN: Caenidae. Key to British Nymphs, *Ent. Gazette*, Vol. 6.

T T MACAN: Caenis moesta, *The Entomologist*, Vol. LXXVI, Oct. 1943.

T T MACAN: Revised key to British water bugs, Scient. Pub. No. 16. Fresh. Biol. Ass. 1956.

H P MOON: Growth of Caenis horaria, Leptophlebia vespertina and L. marginata, *Proc. Zool. Soc. Lon.*, Ser. A, Vol. 108, pt. 4, Feb. 1939.

M NUN: Breeding fish in days of our ancestors, *Fisherman's Bull. Israel*, 3(6):12–16.

M NUN: From the past, *Fisheries and Fish Breeding (Israel)*, 1(1):46–49.

H OLDROYD: Diptera. Introduction and Key to Families, *R.E.S.L.*, Vol. 9, pt. 1, April 1954. Handbook.

E W SEXTON: Moulting and Growth stages of Gammarus, *Journ. Marine Biol. Ass.*, Vol. XIII, No. 2, Apr. 1924.

M SHILO: Use of copper sulphate against harmful algae blooms in fish ponds, *Barmidgeh (Israel)*, 4(3/4), 29–38.

P H WARD: Collections in a light trap, *Entomologists Gazette*, Vol. 16.

P H WARD: Contribution to knowledge of Osmylus fulvicephalus, *Entomologists Gazette*, Vol. 16.

C A WINGFIELD: Function of Gills of Mayfly Nymphs, *University of Birmingham*, Zoology Dept.

Index